D0506961

100 LANDMARKS OF THE WORLD

First published by Parragon in 2011

Parragon
Queen Street House
4 Queen Street
Bath BA1 1HE, UK

Created and produced by Jollands Editions

ISBN 978-1-4454-3779-8

Printed in Indonesia

100 LANDMARKS OF THE WORLD

A JOURNEY TO THE MOST FASCINATING LANDMARKS AROUND THE GLOBE

BEVERLEY JOLLANDS

PAUL FISHER

Bath • New York • Singapore • Hong Kong • Cologne • Delhi
Melbourne • Amsterdam • Johannesburg • Auckland • Shenzhen

Contents

Introduction

A mountain is one kind of landmark—the oldest kind. Large, changeless, visible from afar, it is a landform that travelers, seafarers, and mapmakers can use as a reference point to establish where they are in the world. A few mountains appear in this book, but they have been chosen not for their position on the earth but for what they have become in the human imagination. This is because landmarks have long been more than physical objects: they are not just a matter of geography, but of cultural identity.

The earliest human societies invested the outstanding features of their surroundings with spiritual importance. Mountains were the homes of gods, rivers ran from this world to the next, forest trees grew in sacred groves. Such landmarks anchored the lives of ancient peoples, and even where the old spirits no longer seem so present, this cultural attachment to local natural landmarks is one that we have not altogether lost. Table Mountain, for example, is the emblem on the flag of Cape Town, and Japanese pilgrims still climb Mount Fuji respectfully dressed in white robes.

Most of the landmarks described on the following pages are not natural features, however, because for several thousand years humanity has been stamping its own marks on the world.

The urge to build, to leave behind lasting monuments, has dotted the earth with remarkable structures. Some spectacular relics of the most ancient civilizations, such as the Great Sphinx of Giza or the enigmatic figures of Easter Island, we have yet to fully understand, while others, such as the Parthenon or the Colosseum, help us to see more clearly into the lives of our distant ancestors.

These great ruins are not only symbols of the ancient cultures that created them, but of the places where they still stand. The Colosseum still says "Rome" and the Parthenon still says "Athens." Every country, every city, has acquired its icons over the centuries, and the choice has not always been predictable. Some were initially trivial or unpopular—such as the Hollywood Sign or Eros in Piccadilly—but have become world famous simply by winning local public affection. Others are so outstandingly beautiful, original, or clever that the world beats a path to see and admire them. Cathedrals and temples, elegant bridges, giant statues, historic clocks, modern skyscrapers, and structures of many other kinds have established themselves as unique landmarks, defining their locations but also helping to define the societies that live around them. Here are their stories.

Many of North America's great landmarks enjoy official recognition and protection, at state, national, or international level. But there are various routes to landmark status: portentous events, disasters, or triumphs, spiritual significance, public affection, or just being the oldest, newest, tallest, or strangest. Across a huge continent, iconic buildings, monuments, and artifacts pinpoint moments of history and enhance people's sense of place, community, and belonging.

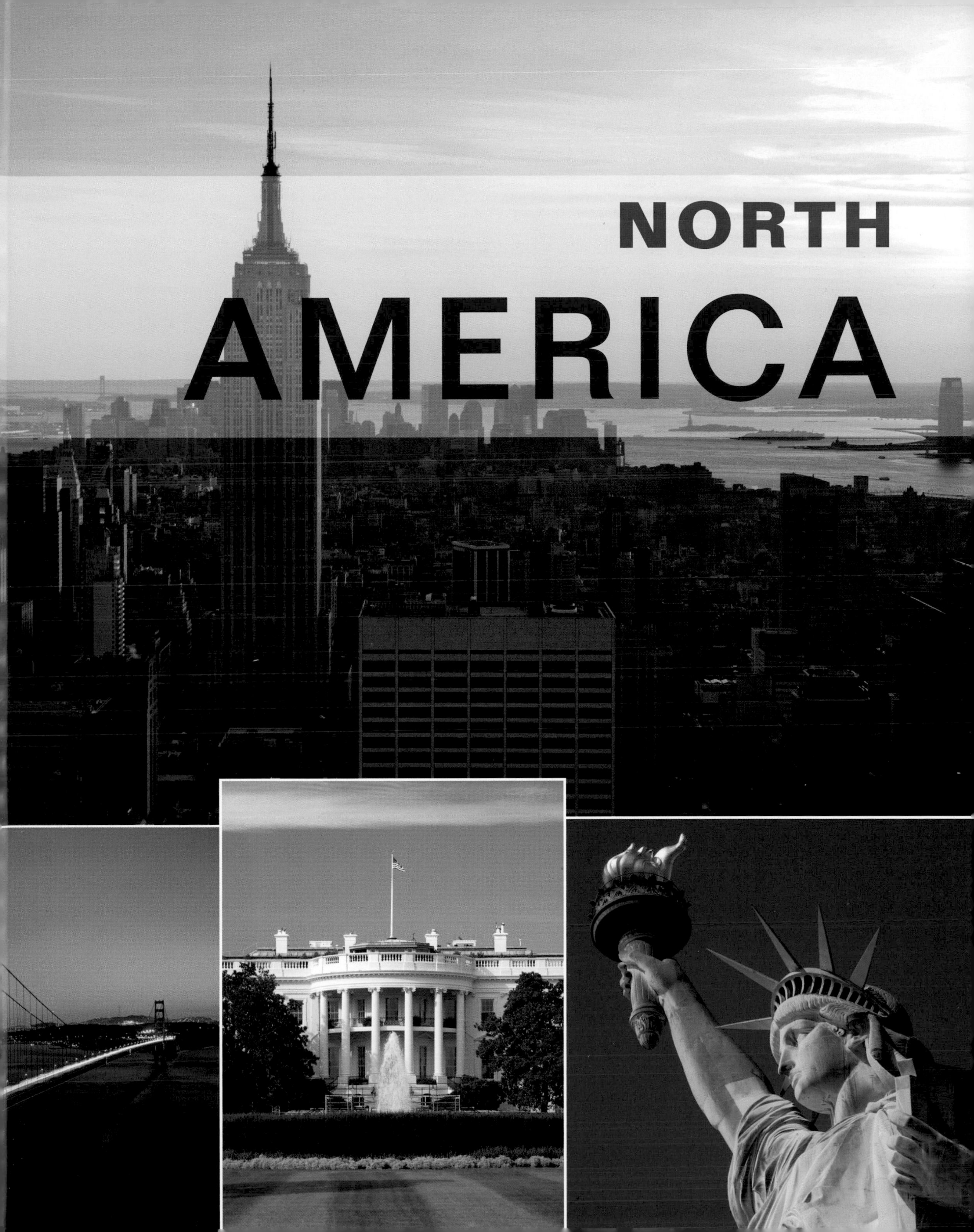
NORTH
AMERICA

CANADA, VANCOUVER

Totem Poles, Stanley Park

ON A WOODED PROMONTORY IN VANCOUVER HARBOR, AN EVOCATIVE GROUP OF CARVED POLES IS GATHERED, AS IF IN CONVERSATION, AMONG THE CEDAR TREES. STANLEY PARK'S TOTEM POLES STAND IN DRAMATIC CONTRAST TO THE DOWNTOWN SKYSCRAPERS AT WHICH THEY GAZE.

Brockton Point is one tip of the peninsula of Stanley Park, an area of protected natural forest in the heart of Vancouver, opened in 1888 and named after Lord Stanley of Preston, then Governor-General of Canada. At the time, the area occupied by the park was still home to a number of First Nation people, but the totem poles that now stand near the point are unrelated to them. In 2008 this cultural anomaly was finally corrected with the installation of three gateways created by carvers of the Musqueam people, one of the groups who traditionally used the land.

Stanley Park's totem pole collection originated in the early twentieth century, when Vancouver's Art, Historical and Scientific Association planned to set up an "Indian Village" as a park attraction. The village never materialized, but more poles were commissioned or loaned over the years; some of the originals have now been removed to museums and replaced by replicas or new carvings. They were erected on their present site in 1962, and are now one of British Columbia's most visited landmarks.

Ancestral stories Unique to the native peoples of the Pacific Northwest Coast, these monumental tree-trunk carvings are not merely decorative, but nor are they objects of worship. Each is made in the particular

TIME LINE

1888
Opening of Stanley Park.

1922
Purchase of four poles from Kwakwaka'wakw in Alert Bay, set up in the park at Lumbermen's Arch.

1950
Ellen Neel commissioned by Totemland Society to make and sell model totem poles at Ferguson Point.

1962
Collection moved to its present position.

2001
Gift store and interpretative center opened near poles.

Opposite: The mythical Thunderbird spreads his wings on the Kakaso'las, carved in 1955 by Ellen Neel, who is thought to have been the first female professional carver.

Right: The Thunderbird house post is a 1987 replica of a pole by the Kwakwaka'wakw artist Charlie James, whose bold colors and shapes initiated a new and influential style.

style of the carver's own community, and the vertical arrangements of figures tell stories that preserve the community's traditions and culture. They require interpretation—just as the pictures in a book go along with the text, these carvings illustrate the words of a storyteller. The figures are those of the shamanic spirit world, and many take the shapes of animals or birds, such as Grizzly Bear, Raven, Wolf, and Beaver.

Traditionally, some were mortuary poles, holding boxes to contain a chief's remains. Others were components of buildings, such as that of Chief Wakas. Topped with the Thunderbird, it represents the chief's talking stick and the characters in a story that belonged to him—Killer Whale, Wolf, Raven, and others. In the 1890s it stood at the front of his house, with Raven's open beak forming the ceremonial entrance and his outstretched wings painted across the walls. The shorter Thunderbird house post was one of a pair that supported a huge roof beam inside a ceremonial house. At its base, Grizzly Bear holds a human figure between his knees.

Below left: The legendary Quolus bird perches on Red Cedar-Bark Man, an ancestor who bestowed the first canoe on the Kwakwaka'wakw people.

Below right: Surrounded by the conurbation of Vancouvor, Stanloy Park preserves a portion of the area's primeval landscape.

CANADA, TORONTO

CN Tower

ON A CLEAR DAY THE VIEW FROM THE SKY POD AT THE TOP OF THE CN TOWER IS SAID TO STRETCH 100 MILES/160 KM. THE TOWER SOARS ABOVE THE SKYSCRAPERS OF DOWNTOWN TORONTO AND HAS BEEN A KEY FEATURE OF THE CITY'S SKYLINE SINCE IT WAS TOPPED OFF IN APRIL 1975.

The Canadian National Railway Company had extensive interests in telecommunications in the 1960s, but broadcasting in Toronto was becoming increasingly problematic. As new office buildings shot up in the city, signals from the existing transmission towers bounced between them, and television viewers had to put up with fuzzy pictures or even found themselves watching two channels at once. In 1968 CN proposed the erection of a new tower that would get around this problem by dwarfing the forest of skyscrapers. To achieve its aim, it would need to be at least 984 ft/300 m tall. The completed structure, opened to the public on June 26, 1976, far exceeded this, at nearly twice the height of the Eiffel Tower.

Building in the sky Work began in February 1973 on a hexagonal concrete shaft surrounded by three tapering buttresslike supports. The concrete was poured into a huge "slipform" mold, which moved upward on hydraulic jacks as the concrete hardened. Plumb lines hanging from the slipform ensured that the growing structure stayed perfectly vertical.

Finally, at the very top of the tower—above the observation decks, the revolving restaurant, the broadcasting station, the satellite dishes, and the vertiginous

CN Tower

FACT FILE

Overall height
1,815 ft/553.33 m.

Height of glass floor
1,122 ft/342 m.

Height of Sky Pod
1,465 ft/447 m.

Height of 360 Restaurant
1,151 ft/351 m; the restaurant completes a full rotation every 72 minutes.

Steps
2,579 steps in metal staircase up to the Sky Pod.

Opposite: The tower, delicately colored by means of its new intelligent iighting system, dominates the city skyline on a summer evening.

Right: Ownership was transferred to the Canada Lands Company in 1995 but, to avoid a name change, "CN Tower" is now said to stand for "Canada's National Tower."

Below: You can look straight down to the ground through the glass floor of the main deck.

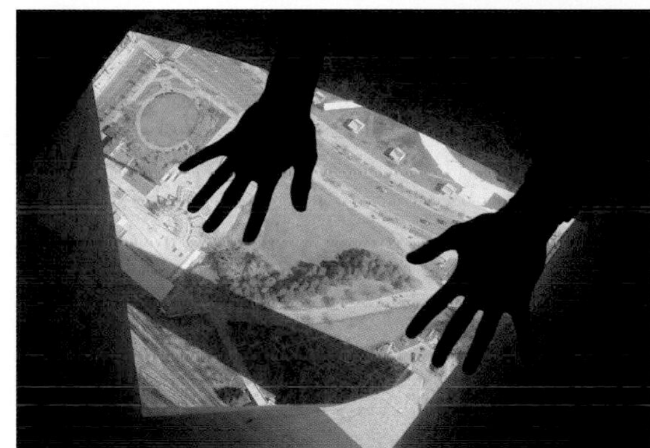

Sky Pod—the 335-ft/102-m steel mast was delivered in sections by a Sikorsky Skycrane helicopter, which the public affectionately nicknamed Olga. Her daily flying schedule was published in the local newspaper so that her many fans could watch her at work.

Going up The CN Tower is now Toronto's signature structure and its greatest visitor attraction. Six high-speed elevators zoom up and down all day, reaching the main deck level in under a minute. If you've coped with the view through the glass panel in the elevator floor, you can defy your vertigo again looking between your feet on the glass floor of the main deck, or go outside to the observation deck to feel the strength of the wind and enjoy the view over to Niagara Falls. Another elevator will take you even farther up to the Sky Pod, the world's highest man-made observatory. A computer-programmed LED system, installed in 2007, illuminates it each evening in patriotic red and white and is used to honor special occasions and causes with themed color displays.

USA, PHILADELPHIA, PENNSYLVANIA

Liberty Bell

IT WAS INSTALLED TO HONOR RELIGIOUS TOLERATION, BUT OVER THE YEARS THIS SILENT BELL BECAME A SYMBOL OF ALL FORMS OF LIBERTY—INDEPENDENCE FROM BRITISH RULE, THE ABOLITION OF SLAVERY, AND, IN THE MODERN AGE, OF THE ASCENDANCY OF THE UNITED STATES AS A GUARDIAN OF THE FREE WORLD.

In 1751 London's Whitechapel Foundry received an order from the Pennsylvania State Assembly for a "good bell of about 2,000 lb [900 kg]." Philadelphia's State House was nearing completion, and the commission was to replace the original city bell, which hung in a nearby tree and was rung at times of danger or celebration. The new bell arrived the following August, in good time to be hung in the new State House steeple, but disaster struck when the rim cracked the first time the bell was sounded.

Two local Philadelphia founders, Pass and Stow, were employed to recast the bell: they added copper to the metal to make it less brittle, but the resulting sound was compared to two coal scuttles clashing. They tried again. Returned to its original composition, the bell was hung in the steeple on a yoke of American elm and was tolled to summon the State Assembly and to mark significant events.

Independence The bell's most famous peal—on July 4, 1776—is legend rather than fact. No bells were actually rung when the Declaration of Independence was signed, but in 1847 a short story by George Lippard created that myth and it caught the public imagination.

By the time the story was published, the bell had fallen permanently silent. It had cracked again, and the

TIME LINE

1752
New State House bell, weighing 2,080 lb/940 kg, arrives in Philadelphia.

1753
Pass & Stow recast bell, which bears inscription: "Proclaim LIBERTY throughout all the Land unto all the Inhabitants Thereof."

1785
Bell mounted inside Independence Hall.

1848
Bell displayed on a pedestal in the Assembly Room.

1865
President Lincoln's body lies in Independence Hall with Liberty Bell at his head.

1893
Première of Sousa's *Liberty Bell March* in Chicago.

Opposite: For the 1976 Bicentennial, the bell was moved into a new glass pavilion, and it moved again in 2003 into the Liberty Bell Center, where it can be seen against the backdrop of Independence Hall.

Right: The Liberty Bell originally hung in the steeple of Independence Hall, but in 1777, when Philadelphia feared attack by the British, it was removed and hidden so that it couldn't be melted down for munitions.

crack expanded catastrophically in 1846 as it was being rung to celebrate Washington's birthday.

Liberty The bell acquired its name in the 1830s, when it was sarcastically bestowed by pamphleteers berating Philadelphians for their lack of action in the abolitionist cause. Long after the sarcasm had lost its sting the symbolism stuck, and the bell's fame grew. It went on display in the Assembly Room and later toured the country, promoting the causes of freedom and national unity. It was mobbed by admiring crowds along the way, while an immense souvenir industry grew up around it. But its travels were worsening the cracks, and chunks were being broken off as mementos. The bell took its last trip, to the Panama-Pacific Exposition in San Francisco, in 1915.

During World War II, Philadelphians enlisted in front of the Liberty Bell. Its image was used on war bonds and later, during the Cold War, on savings bonds. The Whitechapel Foundry offered to recast the bell in 1958, but their offer was declined: by then the crack had become an intrinsic part of this globally famous icon.

Below: Philadelphia's State House (right) later became known as Independence Hall, in honor of the signing of the Declaration of Independence in the Assembly Room (left).

USA, WASHINGTON D.C.

National Mall

"AMERICA'S FRONT YARD," THE GREAT STRETCH OF TREE-LINED LAWN THAT RUNS STRAIGHT AS A DIE FROM THE CAPITOL TO THE WASHINGTON MONUMENT AND ON TO THE LINCOLN MEMORIAL, IS THE SCENE OF NATIONAL CELEBRATIONS, PROTEST MARCHES AND RALLIES, FESTIVALS, PICNICS, AND EARLY MORNING RUNS.

Pierre Charles L'Enfant, who was commissioned to lay out the new federal capital of the United States in 1791, had a grandiose vision. He envisaged an orderly network of streets and avenues connecting elegant circles and plazas. The city's great public buildings were to be the Congress House (the Capitol) and the President's House. Running west from the Capitol, L'Enfant planned an impressive "grand avenue," which would culminate in a great equestrian statue of George Washington to the south of the White House. But the grand avenue was not fully realized, and during the nineteenth century the open space disappeared beneath troop encampments, munitions factories, vegetable plots, and railroad tracks. However, in 1901 it became the centerpiece of a plan to give Washington D.C. a formal processional route that would rival the set pieces of European cities, such as Paris and Rome. The McMillan Commission drew up a scheme for a grass sward shaded by avenues of American elms and lined with public buildings.

The Castle Civic building had already begun along the Mall. The Smithsonian Institute Building, completed in 1855, was funded by a curious bequest by a British scientist, James Smithson, to set up in Washington "an Establishment for the increase and diffusion of

Left: The Abraham Lincoln Memorial, in the form of a Greek Doric temple, stands at the west end of the Mall, facing the Washington Monument and the Capitol.

Right: The oldest building on the Mall is the Castle, the original Smithsonian Institute Building, designed in a nineteenth-century version of Norman style.

Far right: Inside the Lincoln Memorial sits the four-times life-size figure of the president, sculpted by Daniel Chester French and completed in 1920.

Center: In 1912 the Mayor of Tokyo presented 3,000 flowering cherry trees to the city of Washington as a token of friendship, and they were planted beside the Tidal Basin.

Below right: From the top of the Washington Monument, the Mall can be seen stretching past the World War II Memorial and the Reflecting Pool to the Lincoln Memorial by the Potomac River.

TIME LINE

1791
Pierre Charles L'Enfant draws up plans for Washington D.C.

1802
Area is named as "The Mall" on map of city.

1855
Completion of the Smithsonian Institute's "Castle."

1884
Completion of Washington Monument.

1901
McMillan Commission plan for formal processional way.

1922
Lincoln Memorial opened.

1943
Completion of Jefferson Memorial.

1965
National Mall officially established.

knowledge." The result was the Castle, a Gothic Revival confection designed to evoke the collegiate architecture of the oldest British universities. It is now the headquarters of the world's largest museum complex.

Washington Monument Meanwhile, near the spot where L'Enfant had wanted a statue of Washington—which turned out to be too swampy to support a large structure—the vast Washington Monument stood partially built at about a third of its eventual height. Donations had run out in 1854, and after a fund-raising drive, the interruption of the Civil War, and arguments about its design, work on the obelisk eventually resumed in 1879—using stone from a different quarry, and of a slightly different color. When it was ceremonially topped off with a pyramid of solid aluminum in 1884, it was the tallest structure in the world.

The monument immediately became an enormously popular attraction, even though there were 896 steps to climb. After 1888 visitors could ride in a steam-powered elevator—but only if they were male, because the contraption was considered too dangerous for women. The amazing view from the top remains uninterrupted today, because the monument is still the city's highest building.

Lincoln Memorial From the top of the Washington Monument the view to the west sweeps over the World War II memorial and the long, formal Reflecting Pool to

Left: Fireworks bursting over the Washington Monument and the Capitol are the traditional climax of the annual Independence Day celebrations in Washington D.C.

Below: The Korean War Veterans Memorial, dedicated in 1995, includes 19 life-size statues by Frank Gaylord, representing a squad on patrol drawn from all the armed forces.

the Doric temple commemorating Abraham Lincoln. The brooding figure of the President sits inside, flanked by the texts of his most famous speeches: his second Inaugural Address and the Gettysburg Address.

Proposals for a memorial to Lincoln were put forward soon after his death, but the grandiose 1867 plan, which called for dozens of colossal statues, proved too costly and was abandoned. Henry Bacon's austere and dignified white marble building eventually opened to the public in 1922. A familiar sight in the everyday life of all Americans from its use as a motif on the penny and the $5 bill, it has been the backdrop to many momentous public events, most famously Martin Luther King Jr.'s "I Have a Dream" speech in 1963, at the height of the American Civil Rights Movement.

Jefferson Memorial The perfect rhombus laid out in the McMillan Commission plan, with the National Mall as its east–west spine and the White House to the north, gained its southerly point with the completion of the Jefferson Memorial in 1943, picturesquely sited on the shore of the Potomac River Tidal Basin. The area is planted with cherry trees, and a cherry blossom festival is held here as the flowers open each spring.

McMillan had suggested a pantheon on this site, honoring many distinguished citizens. While this didn't happen, when John Russell Pope designed Jefferson's

Above: A bronze statue of Jefferson by Rudulph Evans stands inside his memorial, which has passages from the President's writings, including part of the Declaration of Independence, engraved on its interior walls.

monument, he did indeed model it on the Roman Pantheon, in the Neoclassical style Jefferson himself had loved and used for his house at Monticello and his designs for the University of Virginia. The building was to house a bronze statue of the President, but because there was no bronze to be had in the middle of World War II, a painted plaster cast had to suffice for the opening ceremony. The statue itself arrived in 1947, and gazes out between the Ionic columns of the open rotunda toward the White House.

History of the Nation L'Enfant's original vision for the Mall was as a growing monument to the country's founders and leaders. Many other memorials occupy this green oasis in the center of the capital, such as those commemorating Franklin D. Roosevelt, Korean War veterans, and Vietnam veterans, and collectively they symbolize the history of the country.

The Mall is a national arena, where the public gather to celebrate, mourn, protest, and honor. But it is also a city park, where the locals come to take a break and eat their sandwiches, and an essential destination for sightseeing tourists. With about 25 million people visiting each year, the National Mall is wearing out. It is currently the subject of a major refurbishment plan to restore and preserve this grand space and the many structures within it for future generations.

Right: The whole length of the National Mall was opened to the public for the swearing-in ceremony during the inauguration of President Obama on January 20, 2009.

USA, WASHINGTON D.C.

The White House

AT 1600 PENNSYLVANIA AVENUE, ONE OF THE WORLD'S MOST FAMOUS ADDRESSES, THE PRESIDENT OF THE UNITED STATES BOTH LIVES AND WORKS. THE WHITE HOUSE IS A HOME, A MUSEUM, AN ADMINISTRATIVE HUB, AND THE SYMBOL OF THE EXECUTIVE ARM OF THE UNITED STATES GOVERNMENT.

One of the first buildings to be commissioned for the new federal city of Washington D.C. was the President's house, for which nine architects (including, possibly, a pseudonymous Thomas Jefferson) submitted proposals. In July 1792 George Washington selected a Greek revival design by James Hoban, even though he thought it too small and plain. Hoban was Irish, and his design is said to have been inspired by Leinster House in Dublin.

The house, duly enlarged though not quite complete, was ready for John Adams to move into on November 1, 1800. Just 14 years later, invading British troops stormed the building and, after eating the dinner that had been prepared for President Madison, set the house on fire. Following the rebuilding, the walls of the house were whitened with a mixture of lime, casein, glue, and lead, though it was not officially named the White House until 1901.

Roosevelt's legacy The new name was part of Theodore Roosevelt's reinvention of the building. Its multiple functions had inevitably outgrown it, and his wife, Edith Roosevelt, complained that she felt she was "living over the store." Victorian clutter was swept away, bathrooms and electric light installed, and a "temporary" office building—the West Wing—replaced some greenhouses.

TIME LINE

1791
Pierre Charles L'Enfant draws up plans for new federal capital.

1800
John Adams becomes first President to move in.

1814
British troops set fire to building, but walls survive.

1824
South portico added.

1829
North portico added.

1901
Building of West Wing; Oval Office and Cabinet Room added in 1909.

1913
Rose Garden planted by President Wilson's wife, Ellen Wilson.

1948–52
House gutted and rebuilt.

1961
White House acquires museum status; interiors restored by Mrs. Kennedy.

1995
Pennsylvania Avenue closed to traffic in front of house.

Opposite: The bow-fronted south portico, seen from the National Mall. The second-floor balcony, which visually slices across the columns, was added by Harry S. Truman in 1948.

Right: The West Wing houses the offices of senior presidential staff, with the Oval Office in one corner, overlooking the garden, on a site originally used for hanging out laundry.

The Oval Office became a central part of this extension in 1909, moving to its current position in 1934.

Successive presidents put their own marks on the White House, but it also suffered periods of neglect. In 1948 Harry S. Truman found himself living in a building in danger of collapse, and it was gutted and rebuilt around a steel framework. Much of the historic character of the interior disappeared, but in 1961 Jacqueline Kennedy embarked on a major restoration using period wallpapers, fabrics, and furniture. Her televised *Tour of the White House* was watched by millions and established her as an arbiter of American taste. The house was declared a museum, and subsequent occupants have treated it as such, making only minor changes to the structure and largely preserving the authentic decor.

Below: The north portico was added for Andrew Jackson in 1829. It allowed visitors' carriages to draw up to the front entrance under cover.

Right: Renovated by Mrs. Kennedy, the State Dining Room has bison heads (rather than lions) on its mantelpiece at Theodore Roosevelt's insistence.

USA, KEYSTONE, SOUTH DAKOTA

Mount Rushmore

IT BEGAN WITH AN IDEA FOR ATTRACTING TOURISTS TO THE BLACK HILLS OF SOUTH DAKOTA, AND CERTAINLY SUCCEEDED, WITH OVER TWO MILLION VISITORS NOW ARRIVING EVERY YEAR. BUT THANKS TO THE AMBITION OF ITS CREATOR, THIS TOURIST ATTRACTION ACQUIRED A WEIGHTIER STATUS AS A NATIONAL MONUMENT.

South Dakota's state historian, Doane Robinson, dreamed of carving the natural pillars known as the Needles into giant statues of legendary local figures, to put the Black Hills on the tourist map. But Gutzon Borglum, the sculptor who agreed to carry out his vision, had loftier ideas. He wanted to represent the birth and development of the nation, for which he chose four presidents: Washington, Jefferson, Lincoln, and Theodore Roosevelt. And he rejected the Needles. Instead, in 1925, he settled on the sunny southeastern face of Mount Rushmore, sacred to the Lakota Sioux and the region's highest peak. Permission was obtained, but not funding. Luckily, two years later, President Calvin Coolidge came to South Dakota to learn to fish, and while there he was persuaded to grant federal finance to create a "national shrine."

Reshaping the mountain Over the next 14 years, nearly 400 workers drilled and dynamited the rock face under Borglum's direction, removing 450,000 tons of granite—which still lies where it fell at the foot of the cliff. The ambitious original design included the Declaration of Independence, the Constitution, and other key documents, and the four figures were to have been portrayed to the waist, but the project ran out of money and—after Borglum's death in 1941—impetus.

FACT FILE

Cost
$990,000.

Size
Heads 60 ft/18 m tall; eyes 11 ft/3.3 m across; mouths 18 ft/5.5 m; noses 20 ft/6 m long (Washington's is a little longer).

Height
5,500 ft/1,675 m above sea level.

Opposite: The heads were unveiled as they were completed: Washington on Independence Day 1934, Jefferson in 1936, Lincoln in 1937, and Theodore Roosevelt in 1939.

Right: George Washington's head seen in profile. In 2010 the Mount Rushmore monument was digitally scanned to create a computer model, accurate to the nearest centimeter.

It was an extraordinary undertaking to reshape a mountain, and even in the 1920s there were protests that the plan was a violation of the natural environment—a cause dear to one of its subjects, Theodore Roosevelt, and to the local Native Americans. The Lakota Sioux had been granted the Black Hills in perpetuity in 1868, but as soon as gold was found a few years later the territory was seized back from them. Many remain unreconciled to the Monument. Nevertheless, on a nearby—equally sacred—mountain an even larger project, the Crazy Horse Memorial, has been in progress since 1948, commissioned by the Lakota people from a sculptor who previously worked for Borglum on Mount Rushmore.

Instantly recognizable and fascinatingly huge, the Monument figures largely in popular culture. In the most famous of many movie appearances, it was a dizzying backdrop in Hitchcock's *North by Northwest* in 1959 (though a studio mock-up was used). It is a Legoland model and has appeared on magazine and album covers, United States coins, and South Dakota license plates.

Below: Using Borglum's 1:12 scale model as a guide, workers created the heads by drilling closely spaced holes to precise depths, breaking off the remaining rock, and smoothing the surface.

USA, NEW YORK, NEW YORK

Statue of Liberty

THE STATUE OF LIBERTY ENLIGHTENING THE WORLD WAS CREATED TO CELEBRATE THE HIGH IDEALS OF DEMOCRACY REPRESENTED BY THE UNITED STATES IN THE NINETEENTH CENTURY. BUT FOR MILLIONS OF EUROPEAN IMMIGRANTS WHO PASSED HER ON THEIR WAY TO ELLIS ISLAND, LIBERTY TOOK ON A MORE PERSONAL MEANING.

Each new arrival saw the great statue as a welcoming, motherly figure offering the hope of freedom and new opportunities. A poem written by Emma Lazarus to help raise funds for the pedestal contained the lines that encapsulated this new symbolism:

"...Give me your tired, your poor,
Your huddled masses yearning to breathe free,
The wretched refuse of your teeming shore.
Send these, the homeless, tempest-tossed to me,
I lift my lamp beside the golden door!"

Irving Berlin's 1949 musical *Miss Liberty* concluded with a setting of these famous words. As a child, Berlin had been one of those immigrants welcomed by Liberty's beacon: he escaped with his parents from the Russian pogroms, reaching New York Harbor in 1893, before the statue had even begun to acquire its patina of verdigris.

A gift from France It was the jurist and politician Edouard René de Laboulaye who suggested in 1865 that a monument to the country's independence would be an appropriate gift from its historical allies, the French. At the time, under the repressive regime of Napoleon III, the idea was little more than wishful thinking, but a decade later Laboulaye founded the Union Franco-Américaine, and fund-raising began on both sides of the

TIME LINE

1811
Fort Wood constructed on Bedloe's Island.

1876
Torch-bearing arm displayed in Centennial Exhibition.

October 28, 1886
Dedication of statue, marked by New York's first ticker-tape parade.

1924
Statue designated as National Momument.

1956
Island officially renamed Liberty Island.

Opposite: The beautiful blue-green verdigris that covers the statue began to spread in the early twentieth century. Congress voted for it to be painted over, but the public had better taste and protested against it.

Right: Liberty's original torch had lights installed but was not bright enough to function as a harbor light, and the addition of glass panes in 1916 created leaks and led to corrosion. It was removed in 1984.

Atlantic: it was agreed that the French would fund the statue and the Americans the pedestal.

Frédéric-Auguste Bartholdi, inspired by Laboulaye's idea, had been working on the design since 1870, and created the torch-bearing arm so that it could be displayed to drum up interest in the project; it then languished in New York for several years before the money was raised to complete the pedestal. Meanwhile, the head (for which Bartholdi's mother was the model) was shown at the Paris Exposition Universelle in 1878.

Technical achievement Finally completed in 1886, the colossus was as much a feat of engineering as of art. Bartholdi's figure of Libertas, the Roman goddess of freedom, was created using the repoussé technique, which involved hammering thin copper sheets into molds. The sections were then assembled over a steel armature, designed by Eiffel et Cie, which had enough flexibility to allow the figure to sway slightly in the wind and to accommodate any movement of the copper skin as it expanded in the sun.

Far removed from the bare-breasted Marianne of revolutionary France, Bartholdi's version of Liberty is chastely draped in full-length robes, and wears a sun-like rayed diadem on her head. The broken chains at her feet were discreetly hidden under her robes to avoid too much association with the divisive issue of slavery so soon after the end of the Civil War. She is *Liberty Enlightening the World*, with her raised torch representing progress—and providing a guiding light into a safe haven—and the tablet in her left hand is inscribed with the date of the Declaration of Independence.

Below left: A staircase winds up inside the figure, amid the steel framework that supports the shell.

Below right: The base of the statue is a star-shaped granite fort, built in the early nineteenth century to defend New York Harbor against attack by the British.

USA, NEW YORK, NEW YORK

Empire State Building

INSPIRED BY THE SLENDER PROFILE OF A PENCIL, THE EMPIRE STATE BUILDING WAS THE FIRST SKYSCRAPER TO EXCEED 100 FLOORS, AND ITS SOARING SPIRE MADE IT THE WORLD'S TALLEST BUILDING FOR OVER 40 YEARS. IT STRUGGLED TO FIND TENANTS, BUT IT WAS AN IMMEDIATE SUCCESS AS AN ICON OF NEW YORK CITY.

The invention of the safety elevator and the development of steel-frame construction in the late nineteenth century heralded the skyscraper, and in New York buildings raced skyward. Two magnates of the burgeoning auto industry were the fiercest rivals in this expensive competition—Walter P. Chrysler of the Chrysler Corporation and John J. Raskob of General Motors. When the economy lay in ruins in 1929, they were among the very few who still had fortunes to stake on record-breaking towers, and both produced distinctive and beautiful buildings that still define the New York skyline.

Building higher The Empire State Building's midtown site on 34th Street and Fifth Avenue had previously been occupied by the Waldorf-Astoria Hotel, which was moving to the more fashionable Park Avenue. Raskob and his partners in the newly formed Empire State Corporation acquired the site in 1929 and hired the architectural firm of Shreve, Lamb & Harmon.

The Chrysler Building was already under way, but its ultimate height was a secret. Raskob is said to have stood a pencil on end and asked William F. Lamb, "How high can you make it so that it won't fall down?" As the Chrysler Building grew, Lamb added further floors, which were finally topped with a 230-ft/70-m spire that

TIME LINE

1929
Acquisition of site.

January 22, 1930
Beginning of excavation.

March 17, 1930
Start of construction.

November 13, 1930
Completion of masonry.

May 1, 1931
Official opening by President Hoover.

1950
Installation of broadcasting antenna.

1976
Colored floodlights installed.

1986
Building declared National Historic Landmark.

Above: The building's midtown location puts it at a distance from most New York skyscrapers, making it a distinctive feature of the city's skyline.

Above: The main tower is set back from the street, and full-height indentations and further tapering at the top create an elegant, streamlined shape.

Raskob planned to promote as a mooring for transatlantic airships. (In the event, the updraft around the building made this too dangerous.)

Lamb's design was prepared in just two weeks, but it is a triumph of restrained Art Deco style. It is clad in limestone, with prominent vertical nickel-steel window frames that glint in the sun. At street level, the facade has finely ribbed stonework and Egyptian-style motifs.

Fast work There could be no financial return until the building was occupied, so the company needed it to be completed at record speed. Mass-produced and prefabricated parts were used where possible. Lamb's metal window frame design allowed the edges of the stone cladding to be left unworked, and he installed a vertical rail system to transport materials up inside the frame, with trucks filled from hoppers in the basement. The girders, fabricated in Pittsburgh, were riveted in place within 80 hours of leaving the steel plant, and the frame grew by an average of 4.5 floors per week—the record was 14 stories in 10 days. Up to 3,500 people worked at

Right: The lavish triple-height lobby is clad in polished marble, with a gilded ceiling and wall panels in metal relief.

Left: The nickel-steel bands that border the windows were a practical feature intended to eliminate the need to dress the edges of the stone, but they are also crucial to the building's appearance, enhancing its slender vertical lines and creating its unique shimmering appearance with their subtle reflections.

breakneck speed, taking their lunch breaks on site—two sandwiches, coffee and a piece of pie were sent up for each man. The building went up in less than 15 months.

Sky boys The fact that it was being built at all after the stock market crash made the tower an emblem of survival and hope for America. Photographers and moviemakers climbed the frame with their cameras, aware from the beginning that this building would be important, to record the sure-footed exploits of the "sky boys."

These apparently fearless construction workers balanced on the girders at ever greater heights, and their nonchalance fascinated passersby, who gathered to watch them from the street below. Riveters worked in teams of four: the heater tossed each red-hot rivet over to the catcher, who caught it in an old paint can, fished it out with tongs, and placed it in a hole; the bucker-up supported the rivet while the gunman hammered it into place. The very last rivet to go into the frame was allegedly of solid gold.

City icon It was opened on May 18, 1931. President Hoover ceremonially switched on the lobby lights, and

FACT FILE

Cost
$40,948,900, including land.

Height
1,454 ft/443.2 m to top of lightning rod; 103 floors.

Number of steps
1,860.

Weight of steel frame
60,000 tons.

Number of windows
6,500.

Elevators
73: journey from lobby to 86th floor can take less than one minute.

Above: Floodlights on the top floors are colored for special occasions: in this case purple and gold for the visit of Elizabeth II in 2002.

visitors took the elevators to the observation deck and the 102nd floor. But in the depths of the Depression there were few tenants and the gleaming new edifice was known as the "Empty State Building": the company didn't begin to make a profit from rents until 1941. As a tourist attraction, however, it was an immediate success, with over a million visitors in the first year.

For the New York World's Fair in 1964, new floodlights were installed on the top 30 floors, and colored lights arrived in the 1970s, allowing for commemorative schemes on special occasions. In 2004 the lights were extinguished for 15 minutes to mark the death of Fay Wray, who played the unfortunate heroine captured by the monster in the most memorable of the building's numerous screen appearances, *King Kong*, in 1933.

The Empire State Building is currently being "greened" by super-insulating the windows and improving the lighting and ventilation systems; the aim is to reduce energy consumption by 38 percent. None of the changes will be visible on the exterior, however, and the colored light show at the top will stay.

Left: To capture his powerful images of the construction workers, Lewis Wickes Hine, the project's official photographer, endured many of the same risks as the men themselves.

Right: The monster bestrides a virtually unrecognizable Empire State Building in a poster for the 1933 movie *King Kong*.

USA, MERRITT ISLAND, FLORIDA

Kennedy Space Center

BORDERING THE ATLANTIC HALFWAY BETWEEN JACKSONVILLE AND MIAMI IS FLORIDA'S SPACE COAST: A WIDE-OPEN REGION OF BEACHES, DUNES, MARSHES, AND BIG SKIES, WHERE LAND, WATER, AND SKY MERGE AND DAZZLE, AND OUTER SPACE SEEMS LIKE THE OBVIOUS NEXT DESTINATION.

All spacecraft are launched eastward to take advantage of the earth's rotation. Being near the equator—where the spin speed is greatest—makes the most of this helpful boost, and launching from an east coast means that a misfired rocket will land harmlessly in the sea. The Atlantic coast of Florida, an area previously known for its citrus groves, therefore became the favored jumping-off spot when the United States directed its ambitions spaceward.

The National Aeronautics and Space Administration (NASA) was created in 1958, and four years later, with a very ambitious target—the Moon—in its sights, it established its Launch Operations Center on Merritt Island near the Cape Canaveral Air Force Station. At the end of 1963, the center was renamed in honor of President John F. Kennedy, whose speech in May 1961 had redefined the goal of the Space Race with the USSR by announcing America's intention to fly humans to the Moon and back within the decade.

The missions Launchpads were numbered from north to south down the coast, and the complex constructed for the Moon launch was designated 39. Pad 39A, completed in 1965, stands at its eastern end near the sea, ringed by salt marshes and creeks. The Apollo

TIME LINE

Oct 1, 1958
Foundation of NASA.

May 5, 1961
First U.S. manned space flight.

July 1962
Inauguration of Launch Operations Center.

1966
Completion of Vehicle Assembly Building.

Dec 21, 1968
Apollo 8, first manned flight to leave Earth orbit, launched from Complex 39.

July 16, 1969
Apollo 11 launched.

April 12, 1981
Launch of first Space Shuttle *Columbia*.

Jan 28, 1986
Explosion of Space Shuttle *Challenger*.

April 24, 1990
Space Shuttle *Discovery* launched to deploy Hubble Space Telescope.

May 11, 2009
Launch of final Space Shuttle mission to Hubble Telescope.

Opposite: Space Shuttle *Columbia* sits on Launchpad 39A being prepared for its maiden flight in 1981. To its left are the fixed and rotating service structures, installed on the pad for the shuttle program.

Right: Apollo 11's Saturn V space vehicle lifts off, with Neil Armstrong, Buzz Aldrin, and Michael Collins. Collins was to orbit the Moon in the command module while Armstrong and Aldrin spent 22 hours on its surface.

lunar missions ran from 1961 to 1972, but the world-changing flight was Apollo 11, which landed the first humans on the Moon on July 20, 1969, having left Florida four days earlier. When Apollo ended, Pad 39A was modified to launch the Space Shuttle. Pad 39B was built as a backup, but was the scene of the disastrous *Challenger* launch of January 1986.

The complex Inland along the 3-mile/5-km Crawlerway, which carries the space vehicles on their mobile launch platforms out to the pads, are the Vehicle Assembly Building (the world's fourth largest building) and the Launch Control Center. Responsibility for a spacecraft rests here until it clears the tower, when it passes to Mission Control in Houston.

Around this great slab of technology, nature thrives. Merritt Island is a national wildlife refuge, with over 300 species of birds and 1,000 different plants. A number of important endangered species, such as the green sea turtle, the West Indian manatee, and the Southern bald eagle, can be found here.

Left: Ospreys nest near the Vehicle Assembly Building.

Right: Space Shuttle *Atlantis* on its mobile launcher platform.

Below: The Crawlerway links the two launchpads with the rest of the complex.

USA, BOULDER CITY, NEVADA

Hoover Dam

AFTER YEARS OF STUDIES, PLANS, AND INTERSTATE NEGOTIATIONS, IN DECEMBER 1928 CONGRESS AUTHORIZED THE CONSTRUCTION OF A DAM ON THE COLORADO RIVER TO CONTROL FLOODING, PROVIDE IRRIGATION, AND GENERATE POWER. THE FOLLOWING YEAR, DESPERATION WOULD SUPPLY THE WORKFORCE.

Flowing from the Rocky Mountains to the Gulf of California, the Colorado is the principal river of the western states. But in its annual cycle it varies from a useless trickle to destructive floods, and early attempts to use it to irrigate the surrounding deserts ended in disaster. The new dam would at last create a stable water supply for the developing region.

In the wake of the Wall Street crash of 1929, the project offered a rare hope of work. As men flocked into Las Vegas with their families, the building schedule was brought forward, leaving no time to build housing for the workers. Down in the Black Canyon some 5,000 people set up home in "Ragtown"—a ramshackle assortment of tents, cardboard boxes, and other scraps—and only barely survived the intense summer heat. In 1932 they were rehoused in Boulder City, a new settlement above the dam in Nevada.

High scalers While the river was at its lowest, diversion tunnels had to be drilled through the sides of the canyon and coffer dams built to protect the site. Most of the work was dangerous and dirty, and 96 men died during the construction. The boldest workers could earn an extra 25 cents an hour as "high scalers," hanging from ropes on the sheer canyon walls. Chosen for their

FACT FILE

Height
726 ft/221 m.

Length of wall
1,244 ft/379 m.

Thickness
45 ft/13.7 m at top, 660 ft/201 m at bottom.

Power generated
Over 4 billion kilowatt-hours per year.

Cost of construction
$165 million.

Opposite: The Hoover Dam is an arch-gravity dam, combining an upstream curve to direct much of the water pressure against the canyon sides with huge weight to resist the rest of the thrust.

Right: To supply water to the generators, four giant penstocks or intake towers (two in Nevada and two in Arizona) stand behind the dam in Lake Mead, which is the country's largest artificial reservoir.

strength and agility, their job was to remove any weak or loose rocks using drills and dynamite. Some had worked as sailors or acrobats, and among the most daring was Louis "One-rope" Fagan, who performed death-defying stunts to entertain the workers below. A bronze sculpture of one of the men now stands near the dam.

Concrete More concrete was used to create the dam than had ever been mixed before. It was produced at the site and transported by rail in huge buckets to be poured into wooden forms. The concrete had to be set in blocks and cooled with iced water running through embedded pipes—cast in one piece it would have taken over a century to cure. The pipes themselves, and the joints between the concrete blocks, were then filled with grout.

Hoover's legacy As the Boulder Dam, it was formally dedicated by Franklin Roosevelt on September 30, 1935. The ceremony avoided any mention of the former President Hoover, who had championed the project—he was by then being blamed for the Depression—but his name was attached to the dam in the minds of many Americans, and it became its official title in 1947.

Right: The dam's Art Deco styling by Gordon B. Kaufmann extends to the intake tower clocks facing each bank, set to the two states' different time zones.

Below: The road along the top of the dam was the main river crossing until the completion of a new bridge and bypass in 2010. Visitors to the dam are still able to drive onto it.

USA, SAN FRANCISCO, CALIFORNIA

Golden Gate Bridge

IS IT THE MOST PHOTOGRAPHED BRIDGE IN THE WORLD? IT'S CERTAINLY BEAUTIFUL ENOUGH, WITH ITS ELEGANT TOWERS AND SLIM SPAN FLAMING RED AGAINST THE CALIFORNIAN SKY. A MARVEL OF ENGINEERING IN 1937, WHEN IT WAS THE WORLD'S LONGEST SUSPENSION BRIDGE, IT REMAINS AN ICON OF SAN FRANCISCO.

Ferries had run across the mouth of the bay since the 1820s, serving the small local population. But the Californian Gold Rush changed everything: by the end of 1849, San Francisco was a boom town of 25,000 people, and it went on growing. Finding gold seemed like the fulfillment of a prophecy, since two years earlier the soldier and explorer John C. Frémont had named the mouth of the bay the Golden Gate, likening it to the Golden Horn of the Bosphorus.

Building the impossible By the late 1920s, the Golden Gate Ferry Company was the largest of its kind in the world, and the lines were becoming intolerable. The need for a bridge was clear, but building one was thought unfeasible. The strait was over 1¼ miles/2 km wide and 500 ft/150 m deep, with high winds and strong currents. The suggested cost was $100 million. But the visionary bridge builder Joseph Baerman Strauss promised his cantilever design would cost less than one-third of that.

His first version was rejected, but Strauss persevered with a new suspension bridge designed with the help of Irving and Gertrude Morrow, who created the towers and Art Deco detailing, and Charles Alton Ellis, who was largely responsible for the structural design. In the depths of the Depression, the voters of a specially

FACT FILE

Length
8,981 ft/2,737 m including approaches.

Length of middle span
4,200 ft/1,280 m.

Width
90 ft/27 m.

Clearance above high water
220 ft/67 m.

Height of towers
746 ft/227 m above water.

Cables
36 in/92 cm diameter, made of 27,572 strands of wire.

Color
International Orange.

Mid-span sway
27 ft/8.2 m.

Suicides
Over 1,300.

Above: The thick blankets of fog that roll into San Francisco Bay through the Golden Gate in summer and fall are often low enough over the water to leave the bridge's towers exposed in clear air.

Right: Architect Irving Morrow devised subtle lighting to illuminate the refined detailing and enhance the soaring height of the towers. His scheme was fully realized only in the 1980s.

incorporated bridge district were persuaded to support $35 million in bonds to finance the project.

Construction began in 1933 and involved sinking the largest foundation piers ever built. Strauss was unusually attentive to workers' safety and installed a safety net: 10 of the 11 fatalities occurred in a single incident when this broke, and 19 other men were saved by it, becoming members of the "Halfway to Hell Club." The bridge opened with a week-long party in 1937.

There are now around 41 million crossings a year. On May 28, 1987, the bridge was closed to vehicles to celebrate its 50th birthday, and about 300,000 people visited it on foot. A sadder statistic is that the bridge is the world's most popular place to commit suicide, because of its height above the water. Efforts are continuing to finance a safety net under the span.

Right: A view normally seen only by bridge workers: Marin Headlands from the south tower.

USA, LOS ANGELES, CALIFORNIA

The Hollywood Sign

MOST PEOPLE CAN REMEMBER WHAT THEIR HOME TOWN IS CALLED WITHOUT A CONSTANT REMINDER FROM A NEARBY HILL, BUT HOLLYWOOD IS VERY ATTACHED TO ITS OUTSIZE NAME TAG. INSTALLED NEARLY A CENTURY AGO BY PROPERTY DEVELOPERS WITH BIG IDEAS, IT'S NOW A UNIVERSAL SYMBOL OF TINSELTOWN.

The sign originally read "HOLLYWOODLAND"; it was commissioned in 1923 by Harry Chandler, publisher of the *Los Angeles Times*, and the movie director Mack Sennett to advertise the luxury houses their real-estate company was building in the hills below. Each sheet-metal letter was 50 ft/15 m tall and 30 ft/9 m wide, attached to a framework of wood and scaffolding poles, and the sign was lit by 4,000 bulbs. It was intended to stand on the hillside for 18 months.

From advertisement to icon The Hollywoodland property company went out of business during the Depression, but the sign survived: it had arrived just as Hollywood was establishing its identity as the capital of the movie industry, and it quickly became an icon of fame and glamour for every hopeful new arrival in search of stardom. Later, as the movie industry recovered from the dark days of the McCarthy hearings and mounting competition from television, the now shabby sign was refurbished—losing the final "LAND"—in 1949. The lightbulbs, however, were not replaced.

The new sign The makeshift structure continued to deteriorate: by the late 1970s, it was in tatters and now read "HuLLYWO D." A campaign was mounted to save it, and nine donors—including Hugh Hefner (Y), Andy

TIME LINE

1907
Nestor Film Company opens first Hollywood studio.

1923
"Hollywoodland" sign erected on Mount Lee.

1932
Struggling actress Peg Entwistle commits suicide by jumping from letter "H."

1944
Ownership of sign passes to city council; land remains in private hands.

1949
Sign refurbished and reduced to "Hollywood."

1973
Wins official landmark status, but continues to disintegrate.

1978
Sign completely replaced, funded by "auction" of individual letters.

2010
Hollywood Sign Trust purchases 138 acres/56 ha of surrounding land to prevent future development.

Opposite: Viewed straight on, the letters appear in alignment, but when seen from below the contours of the hill create the sign's familiar wavy outline.

Williams (W), and Alice Cooper (O)—sponsored one letter each to pay for a complete replacement. The new, more durable steel structure was unveiled in November 1978. The original letters, stored away and long forgotten, turned up for sale on eBay in 2005.

The sign on screen Hollywood's very own icon has naturally made many screen appearances, generally as a target for spectacular destruction in movies, such as *Superman* and *The Day After Tomorrow*, but recently it was threatened with actual demolition by—ironically—property developers. In April 2010 the "Save the Peak" campaign raised $12.5 million to buy the surrounding land and give the sign permanent protection. It's now under 24-hour webcam surveillance, so you can stand behind it (virtually) any time to see the view through the famous letters.

Right: Seen here framed by the trees lining a boulevard in Beverly Hills, the sign stands on a south-facing slope of Mount Lee in the Santa Monica Mountains.

Below: The decaying 1920s sign was completely replaced in 1978: the new enameled steel letters are a little smaller than the originals, at 45 ft/13.7 m tall.

MEXICO, CHICHÉN ITZÁ

Pyramid of Kukulcán

AS THE SUN STRIKES THE SIDE OF HIS TEMPLE AT THE SPRING AND FALL EQUINOXES, THE MASSIVE PLUMED SERPENT KUKULCÁN CAN BE SEEN SLITHERING OVER THE STEPS OF THE PYRAMID AS HE DESCENDS FROM HEAVEN TO EARTH, INSPIRING AWE AND TERROR IN HIS WORSHIPPERS.

The stepped Pyramid of Kukulcán, called El Castillo (the Castle) by the conquistadors, is the spectacular centerpiece of the sacred city of Chichén Itzá on the Yucatán Peninsula. On the north staircase, the side panels end at ground level in two huge stone serpents' heads, which become part of an amazing optical illusion each spring and fall.

Serpent god As the afternoon sun strikes the pyramid, the shadow of the stepped corner is thrown onto the side of the staircase, creating the image of a giant undulating snake's body trailing upward from the carved head. This is the manifestation of Kukulcán, the feathered serpent god, whose cult had its center at Chichén Itzá. He is an aspect of the deity worshipped throughout Mesoamerica in pre-Columbian times and later known to the Aztecs as Quetzelcoatl. His form synthesized the snake, identified with the earth, fertility, and rebirth, with the bird of the air and sky, and he was worshipped as a benevolent god, bestowing the knowledge of astronomy and agriculture on the people.

Chichén Itzá It's thought that the Maya established a settlement at Chichén Itzá around AD 600. The name means "at the mouth of the well of the Itzá" because there are large natural wells nearby, known as *cenotes*, to

FACT FILE

Height of top platform
78 ft/24 m.

Length of side
180 ft/55.3 m at base.

Number of steps
91 in each staircase, plus top platform, adding up to 365.

Number of terraces
9 on each side, divided by stairs to give 18 parts, corresponding to the 18 months of the Maya solar calendar.

Inset panels
52 panels on the faces of the terraces on each side represent the 52-year cycle over which the Maya solar and religious calendars return to alignment.

Opposite: Nine sheer-sided terraces lead up to the platform at the top, which supports a two-story temple with carvings of Kukulcán and Chac, the rain god. Two sides of the pyramid have been restored.

Right: One of the goal rings, twined with carvings of snakes, set high on the walls of the Great Ball Court at Chichén Itzá. These rings may have represented sunrise and sunset, or the equinoxes.

provide fresh water in an otherwise arid region, allowing the early agricultural community of the Itzá people to flourish. In the Classic Maya period, the city became important as a cultural and religious center. The later buildings of the sacred city, now thought to date from around the tenth century, show the influence of Toltec culture, and ruins, such as the Observatory, the Great Ball Court, and the Temple of the Jaguars, are among the most impressive remains on the huge site.

El Castillo The pyramid, which dominates Chichén Itzá, dates from this later phase. Its architecture is based on astronomical data and it is precisely aligned to mark the solstices and equinoxes, functioning like a giant calendar. Like other Mesoamerican step pyramids, it was built on top of at least one older, smaller structure. Excavations in the 1930s discovered a temple chamber, containing a Chac Mool—a reclining human figure used as an altar—and a painted throne in the shape of a jaguar, with spots made of inlaid jade. It used to be possible to squeeze inside and up the narrow staircase of the older temple to visit the chamber, but since 2006 climbing the pyramid has been forbidden. But the many visitors to the site can still try out the "chirping" echoes of the staircases by standing in front of the pyramid and clapping their hands. The sounds are said to resemble the forest call of the sacred quetzal bird, whose gold-green feathers adorned the plumed serpent Kukulkán.

Below: The snake's head at the bottom of the north staircase completes the vision of the serpent god Kukulkán descending to earth at the equinox.

Below: Bas-reliefs cover the walls of the temple at the top of El Castillo, from which the Temple of the Warriors can be seen, flanked by hundreds of columns.

The great landmarks of South America are thrilling and challenging. Thrilling because of their size, originality, and brilliance; challenging physically because they can be remote and demanding to reach, and intellectually because their origins are often mysterious. Relics of lost civilizations, such as Machu Picchu and the Easter Island statues are evidence of sensational technological skills that we now find almost impossible to explain.

SOUTH AMERICA

BRAZIL, RIO DE JANEIRO

Christ the Redeemer

EXTENDING HIS ARMS IN A 92-FT/28-M-WIDE EMBRACE, CHRIST THE REDEEMER PRESIDES OVER ONE OF THE WORLD'S MOST SPECTACULAR CITYSCAPES. EVERY VISITOR TO RIO DE JANEIRO FEELS COMPELLED TO CLIMB UP TO SHARE THE STATUE'S VIEW OF DOWNTOWN RIO, GUANABARA BAY, AND SUGARLOAF MOUNTAIN.

The almost vertical granite mountain practically in the center of the city rises to 2,330 ft/710 m and is known as El Corcovado—the hunchback. Emperor Dom Pedro I led the first official trek to the top in 1824, and 60 years later his successor Pedro II opened the rack railroad, which still carries visitors up through the Tijuca Forest to marvel at the view from the summit.

The idea of erecting an outsize religious statue on this key site gathered momentum for years but was vetoed in 1889, when Brazil became a secular republic. However, in the country with the highest number of Roman Catholics in the world, it was only a matter of time. In 1921 the Catholic Circle of Rio began raising donations from the faithful.

Art Deco lines The Brazilian engineer Heitor da Silva Costa worked on the design, but his first proposal, a mannered figure of Christ holding a large cross and a globe, was rejected. His second, produced in collaboration with the sculptor Paul Landowski, was successful: in a streamlined, semiabstract Art Deco style, with the arms outstretched in blessing (and also resembling a cross), it had far more impact and elegance. Landowski produced his maquettes in Paris, and in 1927 full-size models of the head and hands were shipped to Brazil.

TIME LINE

16th century
Peak named Pinnacle of Temptation by Portuguese, later renamed Corcovado.

1824
First ascent of mountain.

1859
Father Pedro Maria Boss suggests religious monument on mountain.

1921
Completion of railroad to summit.

1922
Laying of foundation stone.

1931
Inauguration of statue.

2002
Installation of elevator and escalator.

2007
Statue named as one of the New Seven Wonders of the World.

Below: Countless movie scenes set in Rio have used an aerial view of the statue as an instantly recognizable establishing shot.

Opposite: The statue—seen here unveiled after its 2010 restoration—is faced with a mosaic of soft yet durable soapstone.

Above and below right: Paul Landowski is said to have spent almost two years working on the face and hands of the statue.

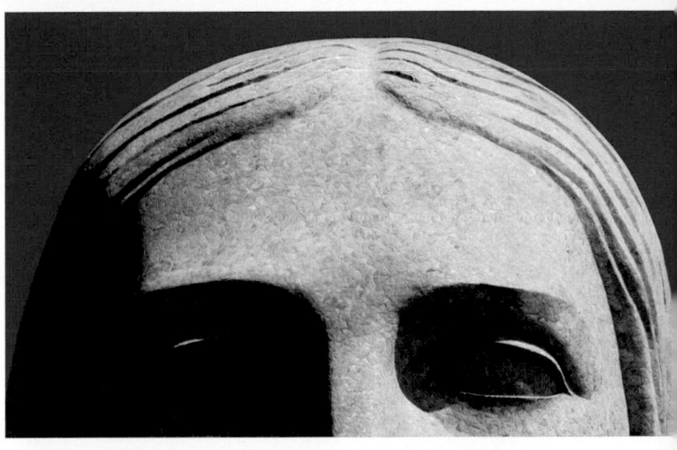

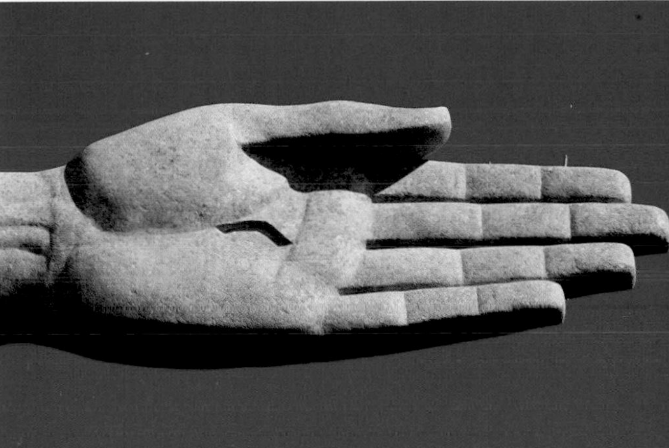

The statue was constructed in reinforced concrete, and to face it da Silva Costa devised a mosaic of soapstone, which gives it a pearly gray appearance. The millions of small triangular pieces required were cut by the ladies of the Catholic Circle, who wrote the names of their loved ones on the backs of some of the stones.

The inauguration ceremony was held on October 12, 1931. During it, floodlights were to be lit remotely from Rome by Guglielmo Marconi, via shortwave radio, but bad weather foiled this ambitious plan and the lights had to be turned on in Rio in the ordinary way.

Restoration To celebrate the monument's 75th birthday in 2006, it was declared a sanctuary, and baptisms and marriages are now solemnized in a little chapel at its base. After being struck by lightning—which damaged Christ's fingers and singed his eyebrows—and daubed with graffiti, the monument disappeared under scaffolding in 2010. During restoration, 79 gallons/300 liters of water were removed from each arm, the leaks were repaired, and better lightning protection installed.

BRAZIL, MANAUS

Teatro Amazonas

EXCEPT FOR THE FACT THAT IT IS 900 MILES/1,500 KM UP A JUNGLE RIVER, THE TEATRO AMAZONAS IS A STANDARD ISSUE LATE-NINETEENTH-CENTURY GRAND OPERA HOUSE. ITS ARCHITECTURE IS AS METROPOLITAN EUROPEAN AS ITS SETTING IS EXOTIC SOUTH AMERICAN.

From the 1880s, high-quality building materials and craftsmen were shipped across the equator and then up the Amazon to Manaus. Steel walls were imported from England, roof tiles from Alsace, eighteenth-century-style fixtures and fittings from Paris, and marble for the stairs, statues, and columns from Italy. Thirty-two chandeliers of traditional Venetian Murano glass with North American lighting technology brought a touch of modernity. Italian artist Domenico de Angelis painted wall panels and ceilings, while Crispim do Amaral from France decorated the curtain with a Europeanized view of local river scenes.

Capital Operatic status symbols and the spectacles they house are usually too extravagant to pay their way, and Teatro Amazonas followed the standard pattern. The rubber barons who instigated the building in 1882 soon called on subscriptions that eventually amounted to $10 million of public funding for a decade-and-a-half construction project. They aimed to make a booming frontier town into the world's most unlikely cultural capital.

Boom and bust For a few years it worked. Plaques in the modern mirrored bar commemorate visits by Enrico Caruso and Anna Pavlova on their world tours. But within a few years of the opening performance of *La Gioconda* by Amilcare Ponchielli, on January 7, 1897,

TIME LINE

1882
Opera house proposed by rubber plantation owners.

1897
Opening-night performance of Ponchielli's *La Gioconda*. By World War I, the theater had fallen into disuse.

1982
The worn-out opera house appears in Werner Herzog's *Fitzcarraldo*, which begins with the hero in the Teatro Amazonas listening to Enrico Caruso singing from Verdi's opera *Ernani*.

2001
Opera house reopens.

Opposite: The opera house brought European culture to the Amazonian heartlands. Behind its Neoclassical facade, electric lighting completed a nineteenth-century high-tech marvel.

Right: The building overlooks the confluence of the Negro and Amazon rivers. Its domed roof is decorated with 36,000 ceramic tiles.

Below: The 700-seat interior has been restored to its original velvet plush and electrically lit grandeur.

there was an economic collapse. When the seeds of the local rubber trees proved fertile in more accessible and less ambitious colonies, the Manaus economy collapsed. The rubber boom, which had brought electricity here before it had arrived in many European cities, deflated. The generators shut down and the new-fangled lights went out on the famous opera house for 90 years.

The show goes on In the latter part of the twentieth century, Manaus regenerated itself as a duty-free area and, hungry for status, the city administration restored the opera house to its Belle Époque splendor. Deep in the jungle the chandeliers still twinkle, the pink marble floors are glistening, and the sheened mahogany walls pick up the reflections of champagne flutes. A bell sounds and ushers in top hats show the formally dressed bourgeoisie to their seats. Once again the lights dim as the conductor leads the Amazon Philharmonic Orchestra (reliant on Belarus, Bulgarian, and Russian players) into another overture.

ARGENTINA/BRAZIL

Iguazú Falls

THE IGUAZÚ WATERFALLS SUMMARIZE A SUBCONTINENT: NEAR AT HAND THEY ARE COMPLEX, AT A DISTANCE THEY ARE GRAND AND THEATRICAL; THEY ARE DEEP IN THE JUNGLE AND ABUNDANT IN WILDLIFE; THEY HAVE A MIXED NATIVE INDIAN, SPANISH, AND PORTUGUESE NOMENCLATURE.

More than anywhere else in a high-volume continent, the air is filled with loud noises. The days and nights reverberate to the oscillating jungle screech of insects, macaws, parrots, and howler monkeys. Moving toward the falls through forest trails dense with ferns and flowers, a distant thrum becomes a roar when the visitor steps into a multiplicity of watery amphitheaters.

Two-thirds of an inland cliff measuring 2,950 yd/2,700 m has water flowing over it in a total of 275 cascades that unify into a single crescent downloading sheets of water into a gorge some 260 ft/80 m deep. Go close up and there is an incessant undifferentiated white noise, the soundtrack to one of the most breathtaking displays of the power of nature.

Names and nations Travelers approach the drama from Foz do Iguaçu in Brazil, or Puerto Iguazú in Argentina, or Ciudad del Este in Paraguay, hence a post-colonial babel of names deriving from the original Tupi-Guaraní Indian words *ig* ("water") and *wasu* ("great"). Downstream, the three countries are visible to one another and are linked by the Amizada ("Friendship") Bridge between Brazil and Paraguay, and the Tancredo Neves Bridge between Brazil and Argentina. The best view of the falls is from the Brazilian side.

FACT FILE

Size
The falls are roughly 2,950 yd/2,700 m wide, of which 875 yd/800 m lie in Brazil, the rest in Argentina.

Drops
275 cascades and falls range from 197 ft/60 m to 269 ft/82 m—the longest is the Devil's Throat.

Flow rate
An average of 61,660 cu ft/1,746 cu m per second, a figure that was much higher until the construction of the Salto de Caixas Dam, which regulates the flow.

Flora and fauna
2,000 plant species include orchids, begonias, and bromeliads. Animals include jaguars, ocelots, tiger-cats, giant anteaters, Brazilian otters, tapirs, black-capped capuchins, howler monkeys, and broad-nosed caimans.

Above: The breathtaking cataracts bewilder the senses. The summer air is almost unbearably humid, the vegetation sweet and fulsome, the sound of water overwhelming, and the panoramas immense.

Right: The falls are an ever-changing spectacle, where vertiginous plunges are sometimes punctuated by mist-shrouded ledges, where water vaporizes and rainbows emerge from the spray.

Legends of the falls The tales in this part of the world are of delicacy and violence. One legend holds that the air is so humid, and the land so fertile, that you can hear the petals of rare orchids unfurling. Another story is of the god of the Iguazú River, who wanted to marry the beautiful Naipí. She fled with her lover Tarobá in a canoe and in an outburst of rage the thwarted god jolted the river landscape with thunder and fire and condemned the pair to an eternal cacophonous fall.

Geology and drama The geological story is of a volcano that blew some 200,000 years ago to form a tiered and segmented giant step. The ancient eruption created a basalt rock face so hard that the broad Iguazú River erodes it at a rate of less than a finger's width each year. It created a long-running natural theater, where the most intense climax is the Devil's Throat, an unbroken wall of water curtaining across a 1,650-ft/500-m vista in a 260-degree arc. This wonder of the natural world is simply too large for the spectator to absorb in a single view.

ARGENTINA, SALTA PROVINCE

La Polvorilla Viaduct

THE "TRAIN TO THE CLOUDS" TRAVELS SO HIGH ABOVE SEA LEVEL THAT IT HAS AN ONBOARD MEDIC IN CASE OF ALTITUDE SICKNESS AMONG THE PASSENGERS. THEY ARE ON THEIR WAY TO CROSS AN EXTRAORDINARY VIADUCT, AN ENGINEERING MARVEL THAT PERHAPS LOOKS EVEN MORE IMPRESSIVE FROM THE VALLEY BELOW.

There's not a lot to see in the little town of La Polvorilla, high in northern Argentina: its famous landmark lies 10 miles/16 km away, on the narrow-gauge railroad built a century ago to link Salta Province with the Chilean border. The line is now a heritage route, traveled by 30,000 visitors a year, but it also provides the only public transport for some of the small towns along the way.

Climbing the Andes The General Belgrano Railway, C-14 branch, was the vision of an American engineer, Richard Fontaine Maury. It was intended to serve the copper mines of the Sierra de Cobre ("copper hill") and the local production of borax, but it was a huge engineering challenge for Maury to take a railroad line across the Andes. Steep gradients had to be avoided because this is not a rack-and-pinion mountain railroad. Instead, the engine pulls the train up a series of zigzags and around spirals to gain its amazing height, running through 19 tunnels and over 29 bridges and 13 viaducts on its 135-mile/217-km route.

Train to the Clouds Under construction for decades and beset by financial problems, the line finally opened in 1948. The viaduct at La Polvorilla, completed in 1932, is now the train's principal destination, since

TIME LINE

1907
Construction of the line receives official approval.

1921
Work begins.

1925
The first stretch is opened.

1932
La Polvorilla Viaduct is completed.

1935
Additional funding is obtained after work grinds to a halt.

1948
The line is officially opened on February 20.

1972
La Polvorilla becomes an international tourist attraction, and the Train to the Clouds comes into operation.

2008
After several years' closure for restoration, the line reopens on July 16.

Opposite: The viaduct is crossed at the highest point of the train journey into the mountains, at 13,800 ft/4,200 m.

Right: Standing underneath the viaduct and looking up at the train as it crosses is almost as dizzying as the ride itself.

the borax and copper mines long ago chose alternative transport. The route has been rebranded as the Tren a las Nubes (the Train to the Clouds) because clouds do indeed form around the bridges as the line clambers up the mountains. Every Saturday in summer, a little train decked out in spanking-new, red and yellow livery carries travelers who want to experience the doubtful thrill of riding over an impossibly delicate-looking viaduct, 250 yd/224 m long, apparently assembled from Erector. The valley bottom is a worrying 200 ft/63 m below. Local traders turn out in force to meet the train.

Averaging 22 mph/35 kph, the journey there and back from Salta takes 15 hours: fortunately, during the train's recent refurbishment the carriages were fitted with comfortable seats.

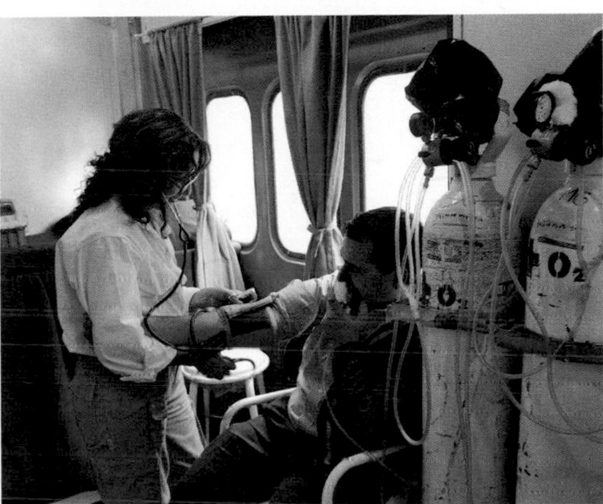

Below: The train rattles through an austere, largely uninhabited landscape, dry and wind-scoured.

Right: Oxygen supplies and health checks are available for any passengers who succumb to the thin air.

BOLIVIA, POTOSÍ

Cerro Rico

THE CONQUISTADORS WENT TO SOUTH AMERICA TO FIND GOLD, BUT THE TREASURE THAT TURNED OUT TO BE THE MOST IMPORTANT TO THE COURSE OF WORLD HISTORY WAS SILVER. THE SPANISH COINS MINTED FROM THE SILVER MINED IN POTOSÍ BECAME THE FIRST GLOBAL CURRENCY.

Cerro Rico's name literally means "rich mountain," and it certainly made Spain rich—for a while. There is a legend that the Incas were the first to find silver, but abandoned their mine when they heard a voice warning them that it was "destined for other masters." Once the Spanish arrived, excavation began on a large scale. Potosí, the world's highest city, was founded at the foot of the mountain, and its name became a proverbial expression of wealth.

Spanish silver The city's own mint was set up in 1572, enabling the silver to be converted on the spot into the high-value coins that became the stuff of legend: pieces of eight. More silver poured out of Potosí than the world had ever seen before—ships full of ready money en route to Spain were tempting prizes for pirates—and the large, weighty coins made European fortunes and transformed world trade.

Some of the hundreds of millions of Spanish "dollars" that went into circulation became the basis of the economy of the fledgling United States, and they remained legal tender there until 1857. But the huge supply of colonial silver deluded the Spanish monarchy into ever more extravagant borrowing to fund its empire-building ambitions, until the country was trapped in a vortex of debt, inflation, and bankruptcy.

TIME LINE

1544
Silver ore discovered by the Spanish, allegedly when a fire lit by a llama herd heated the ground and molten metal oozed out.

1574
First coins produced by Potosí mint.

ca. 1580
Introduction of industrial "patio" silver extraction process.

1827
First Bolivian Republic coinage struck at Potosí, following independence in 1825.

1873
Silver demonetized by U.S. Coinage Act, leading to fall in value.

Opposite: Looming over Potosí, a once wealthy city still rich in colonial architecture, the conical peak is now in danger of collapse after five centuries of excavations.

Right: Mining techniques have changed little; in their hellishly hot surroundings, the miners set up figurines in honor of the devil—known, with grim humor, as "Tio" ("Uncle").

In the mine In Potosí the human cost was cruelly high. Miners worked, ate, and slept underground four months at a time, without ever emerging into daylight or fresh air. The mine owners exploited the local system of forced labor, and when overwork, accidents, and silicosis had exhausted the supply of local recruits, they brought in African slaves. The silver was extracted by grinding the ore in hydraulic mills, mixing it with mercury (which the workers did with their bare feet), and later driving off the mercury with heat: mercury poisoning was rife.

They still mine the fabled mountain today, though the scale of silver extraction is small, and conditions remain severe. Eight million people are said to have died there since the treasure was discovered.

Right: Large cargoes of pieces of eight minted in the Spanish colonies were prey to treasure-seeking pirates in the Atlantic.

Below: In the 1770s the mint was installed in a prestigious new building. It later served as a prison and is now a museum.

PERU, ANDEAN MOUNTAINS

Machu Picchu

THE SACRED CITADEL IN THE MOUNTAINS IS THE MOST EVOCATIVE OF PERU'S MONUMENTS. IT CAPTURED THE COLLECTIVE IMAGINATION WHEN A REAL-LIFE INDIANA JONES CALLED IT THE "LOST CITY OF THE INCA," AND GENERATIONS OF ENTHUSIASTIC TRAVELERS HAVE SINCE CLIMBED THE INCA TRAIL TO FIND IT.

Supposedly built after 1450 for the ninth Inca emperor, Pachacuti, the city was never found by the conquistadors as they looted their way through Peru, so it survived virtually intact. Although it is less than 50 miles/80 km from Cuzco, it is effectively hidden away on its mountaintop; after the fall of the Inca, the abandoned settlement was enveloped by rain forest and known only to the circling condors and a few local inhabitants, some of whom made their homes in the Inca buildings. But in 1911 the American explorer Hiram Bingham III discovered it in true adventure-story style, and told the world. Now the world beats a path—whether it's the strenuous four-day trek known as the Inca Trail or the hairpin bends of the road up from Aguas Calientes—to Machu Picchu, and it has become a top tourist destination.

Ideal site Perched on a saddle between the mountains of Machu Picchu ("old mountain") and Huayna Picchu ("young mountain"), the site had plentiful water, land to grow food, and perfect natural defenses. The rock face falls vertically 2,000 ft/600 m to the Urubamba River, and when the cliffside trail was created up the mountain, a gap was left that could be bridged with two tree trunks—the Inca Bridge—which simply had to be pulled away to make the track impassable by outsiders.

Above: The slender peak of Huayna Picchu, which overlooks the ruined Inca city, is the site of a cavern known as the Temple of the Moon.

Right: Steep mountain slopes around the settlement were expertly terraced by the Inca to provide abundant space for growing crops.

FACT FILE

Altitude
7,970 ft/2,430 m.

Climate
Average temperature 50°F/10°C, annual rainfall 85 in/216 cm.

Natural vegetation
Humid subtropical lower montane forest.

Local fauna
Includes spectacled bear, dwarf brocket deer, ocelot, Andean condor.

The citadel There are 140 buildings, made from beautifully cut blocks of stone fitted tightly together, and over 100 flights of stone steps. Fountains, channels, and drains formed a sophisticated water supply.

The spiritual center is a stone called the Intihuatana, or "hitching post of the sun." At midday on the equinoxes, the sun stands directly above it, and it probably functioned as a kind of astronomical clock. Shamanistic legends say that those who touch their forehead to the stone may have their vision opened to the spirit world.

The outer slopes of the site are exquisitely terraced. Planted with crops, these could have fed several times the number of people who lived in the houses, so it has been suggested that they were also used for growing coca for the residents of Cuzco, or even that they were some kind of experimental agricultural station. Perhaps, like us, the Inca simply appreciated the beauty of these serene level spaces high on the mountain, like a tranquil landscape garden in the middle of the jungle.

Right: The trail to the summit of Huayna Picchu leads up dizzying flights of steep Inca steps—the descent can be treacherous.

PERU, CUZCO

Sacsayhuamán

HOW THEY BUILT IT IS A MYSTERY. THE REMAINS OF THE GREAT WALLS STILL STAND HERE BECAUSE THE STONES ARE SIMPLY TOO LARGE TO BE MOVED. YET THEY WERE SLOTTED TOGETHER LIKE THE MOST CAREFULLY CUT JIGSAW, SO PERFECTLY FITTED THAT NOT EVEN A BLADE OF GRASS CAN BE INSERTED BETWEEN THEM.

Lying on a hill to the north of the Inca capital of Cuzco, Sacsayhuamán is often referred to as a fortress because it is so strongly built and appears to guard the city. In fact, the structure may have been a ceremonial site, where rituals in honor of the sun were enacted.

Teeth of the puma Sacsayhuamán's most famous features are its plaza, where thousands of people could have assembled, and the three massive parallel walls that border it, zigzagging for about 440 yd/400 m along the side of the hill. There is a theory that the sacred city of Cuzco was planned in the shape of a puma, with the hill of Sacsayhuamán representing the puma's head and the zigzag walls its teeth.

All the stones are perfectly fitted together, each one laboriously shaped by pounding with hard cobblestones until its sides exactly matched the profile of its allotted space. Yet some of the blocks are the size of a truck: the weight of the largest is estimated at around 150 tons. The chronicler Garcilaso de la Vega, though he was born in Cuzco to an Inca princess and a Spanish conquistador, could not explain how the walls were built. Writing in 1609, he attributed them to "enchantment."

Manpower Inca building involved the construction of large ramps, up which the blocks were dragged, and

TIME LINE

ca. 1200
Foundation of Inca Kingdom of Cuzco.

Mid-15th century
Expansion of Inca empire.

1533
Capture of Cuzco by Spanish conquistadors under Pizarro.

1536–37
Siege of Spanish-occupied Cuzco by Manko Inca Yupanqui.

1559
Stones taken from walls of Sacsayhuamán to build Cuzco Cathedral.

1983
Site added to UNESCO World Heritage List.

Opposite: The zigzag walls of the terraces, said to represent the teeth of the puma, are the most impressively built and contain the largest stones on the site.

Right: A doorway at Sacsayhuamán shows the unrivaled masonry skills of the Inca, who used only stone tools to shape the blocks and constructed their walls without mortar.

sheer numbers: Sacsayhuamán may have needed a workforce of 30,000 men. Like the ancient Egyptians, the Inca used a system of conscripted labor called *mit'a*: each village was obliged to supply a number of men to work on public projects; after a few months of exhausting toil they would be replaced by the next cohort.

Inca ceremonies The Inca, who told their Spanish conquerors that the walls of Sacsayhuamán were the work of giants, adopted and expanded for ceremonial use a building occupied from the twelfth century by the earlier Killke people. When complete, it had numerous storage rooms, towers, and high walls, and was the scene of much of the fighting when Cuzco was besieged in 1536. After defeating the Inca, the Spanish helped themselves to its stones to build splendid houses in the city.

The spectacular remains are now the backdrop to a modern interpretation of Inca sun worship: the Inti Raymi festival held on June 24. Processions, music, dancing, and the (feigned) sacrifice of a white llama draw thousands of tourists to Cuzco every year.

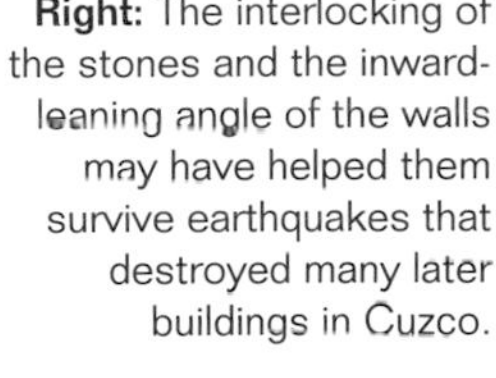

Right: The interlocking of the stones and the inward-leaning angle of the walls may have helped them survive earthquakes that destroyed many later buildings in Cuzco.

Far right: The huge stone walls of the fortress are the setting for the Inti Raymi, an annual evocation of Inca ritual in honor of the sun god Inti, from whom the Inca ruler claimed direct descent.

CHILE

Easter Island's Moai

TINY RAPA NUI IS THE MOST REMOTE INHABITED ISLAND IN THE WORLD, YET ITS MONUMENTAL EFFIGIES ARE AMONG THE MOST RECOGNIZABLE OF MAN-MADE LANDMARKS, GAZING OUT ACROSS THEIR TREELESS DOMAIN. THE HISTORY OF THESE MONOLITHS AND THEIR MAKERS IS RICH AND STRANGE.

On Easter Sunday 1722 the Dutch explorer Jacob Roggeveen landed there, and named it Easter Island. The inhabitants he encountered were the descendents of Polynesian explorers who probably first settled the island between 700 and 900. But he also found another, more surprising population—hundreds of vast, stylized, stone figures, with oversize heads and deep-set eyes under beetling brows. They stood on platforms around the coast, sacred ancestor figures watching over their clans.

Mostly carved between 1200 and 1500, they seem to have been symbols of lineage-based authority and repositories of *mana*, or spiritual power. Some were 33 ft/10 m tall and weighed over 80 tons, and there is still debate over the methods used to transport them from the quarries where they were carved. Some Rapa Nui people believe that they were moved by *mana* itself. It is generally assumed that they were dragged on log rollers or sleds.

Environmental catastrophe So there must have been trees, and the history of the island is now often quoted as a cautionary tale of ecological disaster. Pollen residues show that it was once clothed in palm trees, which stabilized the soil and provided plentiful roosts for birds. The first settlers used the trees to make canoes, for

TIME LINE

700–900
Arrival of Polynesian settlers.

1200–1500
Main period of moai carving.

ca. 1600
Carving of moai ceases and quarries are abandoned.

1722
Jacob Roggeveen and his crew are the island's first European visitors.

1774
Captain Cook visits and finds some moai face down; toppling of statues continues until 1830s.

1862
Peruvian slave traders abduct half the population and introduce smallpox.

1864
Roman Catholic missionaries arrive.

1888
Island annexed as special territory of Chile.

1996
Listed as UNESCO World Heritage Site.

Opposite: Most moai were carved from dark volcanic tuff, though a few are of harder basalt. Some wear cylindical "hats," called *pukao*, of red stone.

Right: Fragments of white coral and black or red stone found on the island have been identified as pieces of eyes, originally inserted in the statues' faces.

building, and for fuel. But the growing population used up the trees, and the pollen record stops in 1650. No longer able to make large canoes for fishing and hunting porpoise, the people ate all the birds. Without trees, there was no fruit and no fuel, the soil turned to dust, and crops diminished; the population crashed.

The toppling After their "discovery" in 1722, outside contact made the islanders' fragile situation worse: whalers, slave traders, and missionaries brought warfare, disease, and reeducation. By 1875, only 111 inhabitants were left alive. Years earlier, the moai had been toppled, as if the ancestors had failed; the islanders turned to the shamanistic Birdman cult and later to Christianity. But about 50 moai have now been reerected and their emotive power is undiminished. As the island's most visited features, they still safeguard its people's livelihood.

Below left and right: The statues were erected on ceremonial stone platforms called *ahu*. Most stood on the coast, with their backs to the sea.

Europe's long and complicated cultural evolution can be told through its abundance of iconic landmarks. Ancient monuments, breathtaking architecture, pioneering triumphs of engineering, audacious artworks, and pious memorials testify to the richness and diversity of European culture. Each one is also an emblem of national identity, freighted with the symbolism of patriotism or civic pride, and regarded with affection by those who live around them.

EUROPE

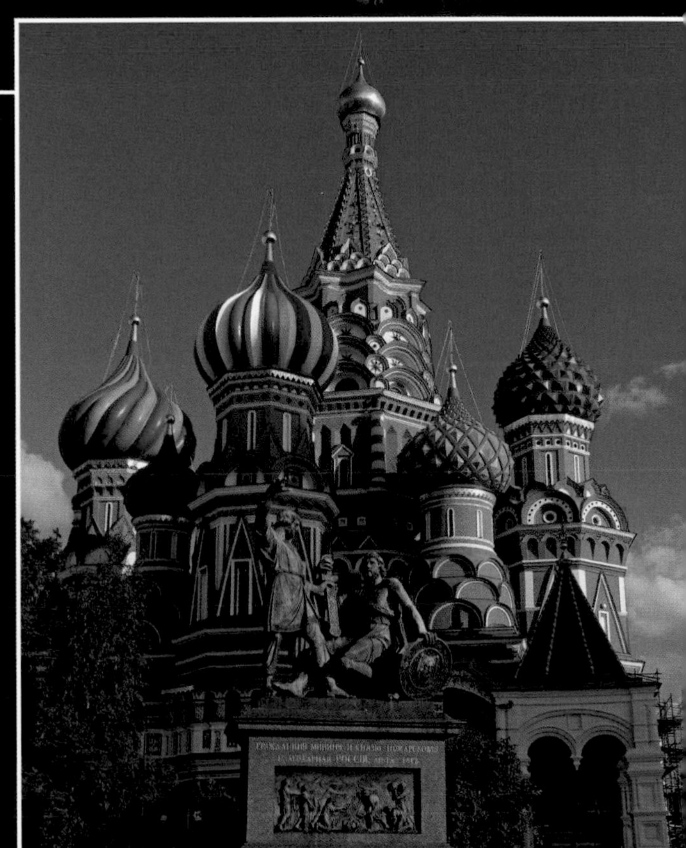

ENGLAND, KENT

White Cliffs of Dover

THE EARLIEST-KNOWN REFERENCE TO THE BRITISH ISLES, PROBABLY DATING FROM THE SIXTH CENTURY BC, COMES IN A DESCRIPTION OF TRADERS' SEA ROUTES AROUND EUROPE; THE NAME IT USES IS "ALBION," WHICH IS THOUGHT TO DERIVE FROM THE WHITE CLIFFS OF DOVER—THE SAILOR'S FIRST VIEW OF THE COUNTRY.

On a clear day you can stand on Cap Gris Nez in France and see the British coast around Dover, and it's a strikingly white strip of land between the blue sky and the deeper blue sea. This was a tantalizing sight for Julius Caesar, William of Normandy, Napoleon Bonaparte, and every other prospective invader considering how to cross and where to land.

Dover's obvious strategic importance is evident on the cliff top. Where Dover Castle now stands are the remains of an Iron Age hill fort and a Saxon settlement. William the Conqueror built a castle here soon after the Battle of Hastings, though most of the great fortress that dominates the cliff today dates from the twelfth century, and it was garrisoned without a break until 1958. Medieval tunnels beneath it were expanded during the Napoleonic Wars to hide 2,000 troops ready to surprise an invading force, and in 1940 the tunnels became the operations center for the evacuation of Dunkirk.

National icon The formidable cliffs stretch along the Kent coast like a white wall, and while they didn't keep out every unwelcome arrival, they reinforced Britain's idea of itself as strongly fortified against its enemies. For those returning to Britain, on the other hand, they were a reassuring first sight of home and therefore

Above: Over 330 ft/100 m high in places, the white cliffs form about 10 miles/ 16 km of the Kent coastline, running both east and west of Dover.

Right: South Foreland lighthouse was built in the 1840s as a guide to ships negotiating the treacherous Goodwin Sands just outside Dover Harbour.

FACT FILE

Height
Up to 350 ft/107 m.

Location
East and west of Dover facing Strait of Dover; Shakespeare Cliff marks Britain's nearest point to France.

Erosion
Chalk cliff face wears away at an average rate of 0.39 in/1 cm per year.

just as strongly symbolic. More sadly, the cliffs were the last sight for emigrants and exiles. The blend of patriotism and wistful nostalgia they inspired reached its peak in 1941, in a song written by two Americans who had never actually been to Dover. "(There'll be Bluebirds Over) the White Cliffs of Dover" was a huge hit, particularly for Vera Lynn, since it managed to wrap up all that yearning for home with hope for the end of World War II—the bluebirds, never seen in England, were borrowed from the equally yearning lyrics for "Somewhere over the Rainbow," recorded two years earlier.

Chalk hills Dover Cliffs are white because they are made of chalk: soft limestone mainly composed of seashells and plankton skeletons, which is constantly eroding to reveal fresh white surfaces. They are full of fossils, from sharks' teeth to sponges and corals. Until the end of the last Ice Age, the chalk hills stretched unbroken across what is now the English Channel, but quickly rising sea levels flooded over the land bridge, and the water cut through the soft chalk to create the cliffs.

Right: Traders and travelers have landed at the port of Dover since the Bronze Age. Today it is the world's busiest ferry port.

ENGLAND, LONDON

Big Ben

WESTMINSTER'S SUPERACCURATE CLOCK STARTED TICKING ON MAY 31, 1859, BUT IT WAS A WHILE BEFORE THE DEEP BONGS OF THE GREAT BELL BECAME PART OF THE CITY'S SOUNDSCAPE. PURISTS INSIST THAT ONLY THE BELL IS CALLED BIG BEN, BUT TO MOST PEOPLE THE NAME MEANS THE CLOCK AND ITS TOWER AS WELL.

The first clock tower on the site was built in 1288, just as Parliament was becoming established in Westminster, then the seat of royal power. A second tower replaced it in 1367, equipped with England's first public chiming clock. But that didn't make Westminster chimes an essential part of London life: by the eighteenth century the clock had been replaced by a sundial, and Charles Barry's initial designs for the new palace had no clock tower at all—London's premier landmark was a late addition.

Westminster's new palace On the night of October 16, 1834, two stoves under the floor of the House of Lords overheated, causing a fire that swept through the medieval palace and destroyed both Houses of Parliament. Despite King William IV's offer of Buckingham Palace as a new home for Parliament, its members decided to rebuild their old one.

The following year a public competition was launched to choose a design for the new building, and the winner was the neo-Gothic vision submitted by Barry, with detailed designs by the great genius of the English Gothic Revival, Augustus Pugin. Inspired by his studies of medieval architecture in Britain and northern Europe and his fierce Catholic faith, the precociously brilliant Pugin had initiated a resurgence of medieval style in buildings of all

TIME LINE

October 16, 1834
Destruction of old Palace of Westminster.

1843–59
Construction of bell tower.

1856
First casting of Big Ben.

1858
Recasting and installation.

1859
Clock starts.

1863
Big Ben starts to chime the hours.

December 31, 1923
First broadcast of chimes by the BBC.

1976
Big Ben is silent for three weeks during repairs.

Left: The clock faces were originally lit by gaslight. A light shines in the top of the tower when Parliament is in session in the evening.

Right: Each clock face is made up of panes of milk glass, like a stained glass window, and set in an iron frame 23 ft/7 m in diameter.

kinds, from churches to waterworks. Pugin's drawings of the Westminster clock tower, with its four-faced clock, were his last work before his death in 1852.

The clock tower Standing at the northeastern end of the Palace of Westminster, the tower of Big Ben is the most famous of a lively forest of towers and turrets shooting up from the steeply pitched roofs. Though only slightly shorter than the massive Victoria Tower at the other end, it is far slimmer, broadening at the top to frame the clock faces, which were also designed by Pugin. Above them, the spire is built on an iron framework, which also supports the bells. Below the clock, the weights that drive it hang in a shaft extending down to ground level. Another shaft contains the 334 stairs to the belfry (there is no elevator), which have to be climbed three times a week to wind the clock.

The clock The specification for Parliament's new clock stipulated that the chime for each hour should be correct to one second. Most clockmakers considered this

Left: Big Ben hangs in the center of the belfry, with the four quarter bells around it. It's still unknown whether the bell was named after Sir Benjamin Hall or a heavyweight boxer of the time called Benjamin Caunt, also known as Big Ben.

Below left: The movement, which weighs about 5 tons, is among the largest mechanical clocks in the world.

impossible for such a large tower clock, but an irascible barrister and amateur horologist, Edmund Beckett Denison, took on the challenge and invented a new mechanism for the escapement; in 1852 the contract for building the clock went to Dent & Co., which had a high reputation for the quality of its marine chronometers.

The pendulum beats every two seconds and fine adjustments are made using a stack of predecimal penny coins lying on top of it: adding or taking away one penny changes the clock's speed by 0.4 seconds per day. It is famously accurate.

Big Ben Before the clock could be installed the bells had to be hung in the belfry above it: four quarter bells and the Great Bell to strike the hours. In 1856, as the tower neared completion, the original Big Ben was cast by the Warner foundry in Stockton-on-Tees. Denison had designed this too. It weighed 16 tons and was inscribed with the name of Sir Benjamin Hall, who was overseeing the building works. The bell was brought to London and hung in Westminster Palace Yard for testing. It cracked irreparably.

FACT FILE

Height of tower
316 ft/96 m.

Clock faces
Each face is 23 ft/7 m in diameter, with 2-ft/60-cm Roman numerals, including a "IV" instead of the "IIII" seen on most clocks. The pendulum is 14 ft 4 in/4.4 m long and weighs 683 lb/310 kg.

Great Bell
Big Ben weighs 13.5 tons and is 7 ft 6 in/2.29 m high and 9 ft/2.74 m wide; it chimes the musical note E.

Replica tower
First erected in 1892, a 20-ft tall/6-m replica of Big Ben known as "Little Ben" stands close to London's Victoria Station.

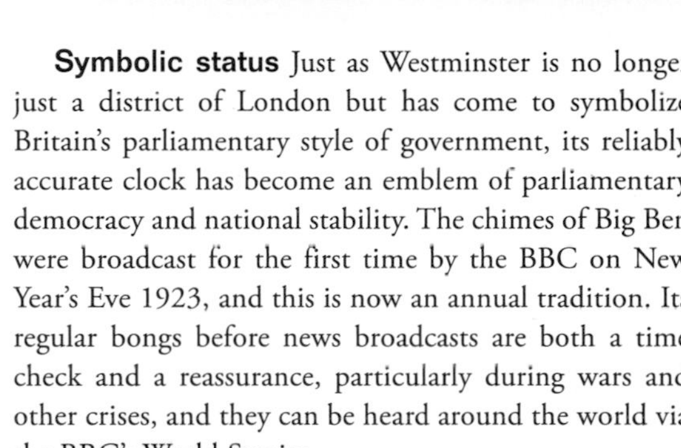

Right: Pugin's delicate Gothic ornament on the spire of the Clock Tower was restored and regilded in the 1980s. The portcullis seen among the heraldic shields is the device Barry used to identify his anonymous submission in the competition to design the new buildings in 1835. It was later adopted as an emblem of the Palace of Westminster.

The bell was broken up and recast by the Whitechapel Foundry in May 1858. Now somewhat smaller, at 13.5 tons, it was pulled to Westminster on a trolley by 16 white horses. Traffic stopped for the procession, the streets were decorated with bunting, and enthusiastic crowds cheered and waved. By now, the tower was complete and the bell could no longer be hauled up the outside as originally planned; it had to be pulled up sideways inside the shaft—an operation that took 36 hours.

Two months later, this bell also cracked. Denison blamed the founders and they blamed Denison for using too heavy a hammer. A legal case ensued and Big Ben was silent for over three years, until a lighter hammer was substituted, with the bell turned so that an undamaged section was struck. The damage produced its slightly imperfect but utterly distinctive tone. The Great Bell has chimed the hours dependably ever since 1863, with only one major interruption in 1976, when metal fatigue caused the chiming mechanism to break, flinging pieces of ironwork across the clock room and even through the ceiling into the room above.

Symbolic status Just as Westminster is no longer just a district of London but has come to symbolize Britain's parliamentary style of government, its reliably accurate clock has become an emblem of parliamentary democracy and national stability. The chimes of Big Ben were broadcast for the first time by the BBC on New Year's Eve 1923, and this is now an annual tradition. Its regular bongs before news broadcasts are both a time check and a reassurance, particularly during wars and other crises, and they can be heard around the world via the BBC's World Service.

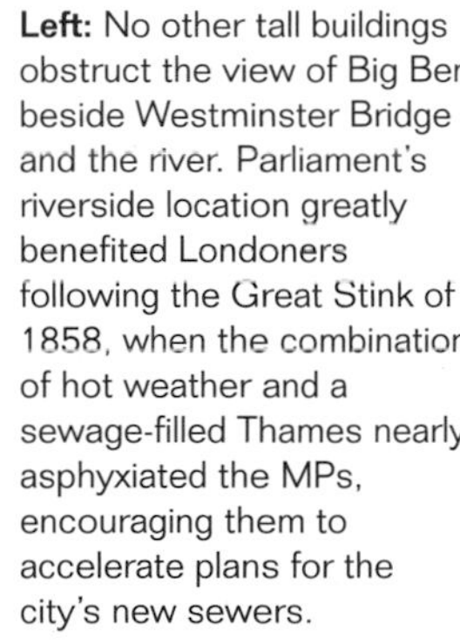

Left: No other tall buildings obstruct the view of Big Ben beside Westminster Bridge and the river. Parliament's riverside location greatly benefited Londoners following the Great Stink of 1858, when the combination of hot weather and a sewage-filled Thames nearly asphyxiated the MPs, encouraging them to accelerate plans for the city's new sewers.

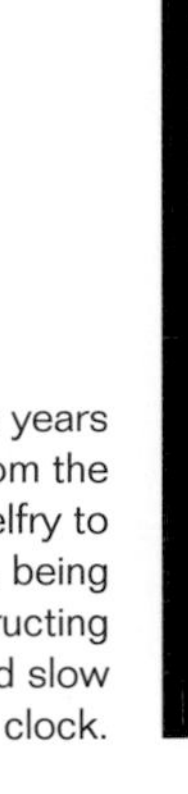

Right: Every five years cleaners abseil from the balcony outside the belfry to clean the clock faces, being careful to avoid obstructing the hands, which could slow or stop the clock.

ENGLAND, LONDON

Eros, Piccadilly Circus

IT'S SAID THAT IF YOU HANG AROUND LONG ENOUGH IN PICCADILLY CIRCUS, YOU'LL SEE EVERYONE YOU KNOW. THAT MIGHT TAKE A WHILE, BUT IT IS A POPULAR MEETING PLACE AND ITS CENTERPIECE, KNOWN TO ALL THE WORLD AS EROS, IS A LONDON LANDMARK THAT SUITS ITS ODDLY CONTRADICTORY SETTING.

Anthony Ashley Cooper, seventh Earl of Shaftesbury, was a Victorian philanthropist who devoted his career to improving the lives of the poor: he campaigned for the care of the mentally ill, children working in factories and mines, climbing boys, ragged schools, and better housing. Immediately after his death in 1885, a plan arose to erect a memorial "in one of the most frequented public thoroughfares in London." The new road being built from Piccadilly Circus toward Bloomsbury was to be called Shaftesbury Avenue, and the memorial would stand at its end.

Unfortunately, the creation of Shaftesbury Avenue had distorted the elegant Piccadilly Circus laid out by John Nash in 1819. It was now an ungainly shape, with two triangular plots in the center. While the Memorial Committee deliberated, one triangle became the site of a public lavatory. That left the other for Lord Shaftesbury.

Shaftesbury Memorial Fountain The monument, created by Alfred Gilbert, was unveiled in 1893. Those expecting a respectful portrayal of the great man saw instead a large octagonal bronze fountain topped by a naked winged youth. The fountain splashed and dripped hopelessly, obliging the flower sellers who sat on its steps to put up umbrellas; many people hated it, some

FACT FILE

Artist
Alfred Gilbert (1854–1934).

Date
1892–93

Figure
Cast in 98% aluminum alloy, 8 ft/2.4 m high, weighing 420 lb/190 kg. The figure was cast in about 15 main pieces, plus separate castings for the main wing feathers.

Base
Octagonal bronze fountain carved with marine motives in Art Nouveau style. A replica of the monument stands in Sefton Park, Liverpool.

Opposite: Half a dozen major streets of London's West End lead into Piccadilly Circus, making the steps around the statue of Eros a popular meeting place.

Right: Gilbert identified the figure as Anteros, brother of Eros and the embodiment of "reflective and mature love." His model was a 16-year-old boy, Angelo Colarossi.

vandalized it, and most doubted that the naked boy was an appropriate memorial for the charitable earl. It appeared to be Eros, the mischievous Greek god of love.

Trying to win the public over, the committee named the figure *The Angel of Christian Charity*. Gilbert explained he was a symbol of "blindfolded love sending forth indiscriminately, yet with purpose, his missile of kindness." Few took much notice: Eros he remained.

West End icon For the redevelopment of Piccadilly Circus underground station the statue was removed in 1925 and didn't reappear for seven years. Londoners began to miss it. It was taken away again during World War II, and when it returned in 1947, several thousand people came to see their Eros reerected. He now presided over an edgy mixture of architectural stateliness and twentieth-century bling, as flashy neon advertising hoardings spread over the surrounding buildings, and the evening crowds passed through on their way to the theaters of Shaftesbury Avenue and the restaurants, bars, and strip joints of Soho. Eros, the beautiful boy with sex on his mind, was now a symbol, not of a charitable nobleman, but of the louche nightlife of the West End. London's daily newspaper, the *Evening Standard*, recognized the statue's iconic status by making it its logo.

In the 1980s the road layout changed and Eros was moved out of the traffic. His steps are always crowded with people, some just sitting there to watch the world go by—and maybe see someone they know.

Below: Relocated away from the center of the circus, the fountain is once more accessible to pedestrians.

Below right: Large-scale illuminated billboards are a traditional feature of Piccadilly Circus.

ENGLAND, LONDON

Tower Bridge

THERE ARE NUMEROUS ROAD BRIDGES ACROSS THE RIVER THAMES, BUT ALL EXCEPT ONE ARE WEST OF LONDON BRIDGE. DOWNSTREAM, NINETEENTH-CENTURY PLANNERS FACED A MAJOR PROBLEM: HOW TO CARRY TRAFFIC ACROSS THE RIVER WHILE ALLOWING SHIPS TO ENTER THE BUSY PORT OF LONDON.

The commercial development and dense population of East London made a new river crossing vital. People and goods faced long, slow journeys into the city and out again to get across. In 1876 a competition was launched to find a solution, but of over 50 designs none was successful. The design that was eventually approved eight years later was by one of the judges, Horace Jones, working with the engineer John Wolfe-Barry. Jones was appointed architect, but he died in 1887 and his work was completed by his assistant George Stevenson. The bridge opened in June 1894.

Bascule bridge The bridge combines two suspension sections at the sides with a central double-leaf bascule (a word derived from the French for "seesaw"), which lifts to allow tall ships to pass through. When Tower Bridge was built it was the largest bascule bridge in the world. Supporting it are two massive concrete piers topped with steel-framed towers. Jones had planned to face these towers with red brick, but their ornate cladding of granite and Portland stone in Gothic revival style was Stevenson's attempt to match the nearby Tower of London, which gave the bridge its name.

The bascules, operated hydraulically, were originally powered by steam engines. Oil and electricity replaced

FACT FILE

Length
801 ft/244 m.
Length of middle span
200 ft/61 m.
Width
Carriageway 35 ft/10.5 m, plus 12-ft/4-m walkways either side.
Clearance above high water
28 ft/8.6 m closed; 139 ft/42.5 m open.
Height of towers
293 ft/89.3 m.
Operation
The record number of lifts in 24 hours was 64, in 1910.

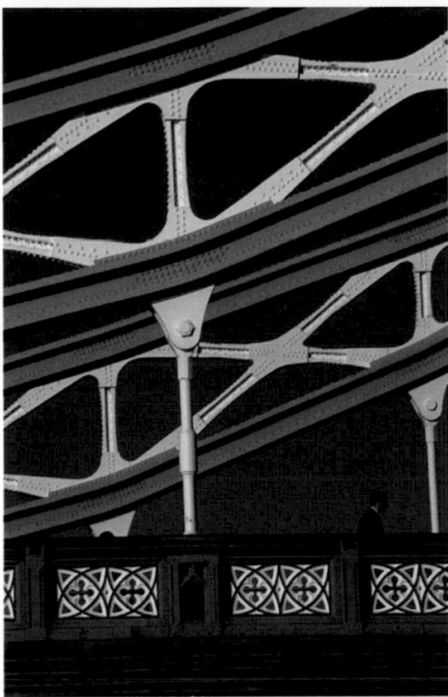

Right: The two side sections are suspension bridges, anchored in abutments on each bank and through ties across the top walkways.

Far right: The medieval style of the towers gives the bascules the appearance of castle drawbridges being raised and lowered.

Left: The whole process of lifting the center of the bridge, waiting while a vessel goes through, and lowering it again, takes about five minutes.

Right: Although the bridge bears the arms of the City of London, which maintains it through a charitable trust, its northern end is outside the city limits.

steam power in 1976. Each leaf weighs over 1,000 tons but is counterbalanced to make lifting easier.

In the 1890s the Pool of London was still thick with wharves and cargo ships, and the bridge was raised and lowered over 6,000 times a year, but these days it's a scheduled event that tourists and enthusiasts linger on the riverside to watch. The bridge requires 24 hours' notice from approaching craft, and now keeps its fans informed of its movements via Twitter. Mishaps have been rare, but in 1952 a bus was crossing the bridge when the bascules began to rise: the quick-thinking driver accelerated and the bus safely jumped a 3-ft/1-m gap. The driver got a £10 reward.

View from the top High above the road the walkways provide fine views over London: they are reached via elevators in the towers and were intended as the pedestrian route across. But they didn't save much time, and people preferred to wait with the traffic. The walkways closed in 1910, partly from lack of use but also because they became the haunt of pickpockets and prostitutes. They are now open again as exhibition spaces.

Right: The bridge's red, white and blue color scheme dates from 1977, when it was painted to celebrate Elizabeth II's Silver Jubilee.

ENGLAND, LONDON

30 St Mary Axe

LONDON'S MOST DISTINCTIVE SKYSCRAPER ACHIEVED ICON STATUS ALMOST AS SOON AS IT ROSE LIKE A ROCKET FROM THE MIDDLE OF THE CITY, AND IN ONLY A FEW YEARS ITS IMAGE HAS BECOME AS FAMOUS AS THAT OF BIG BEN. EVEN A GLIMPSE OF A FEW OF ITS TRIANGULAR WINDOWS IS ENOUGH TO IDENTIFY IT.

Few office buildings in the world have won such instant fame, and Londoners themselves seem really rather fond of their new landmark, quickly nicknaming it the Gherkin. The incongruous image of a little pickled cucumber seems so much friendlier than that of a torpedo or a fat cigar, which are really more descriptive, and ruder epithets like "Towering Innuendo" and "Crystal Phallus" didn't catch on. Those who work in the building find it exciting, and tenants like its architectural prestige.

The demise of the old Baltic Exchange, damaged by a bomb in 1992, created an opportunity to erect a completely new building in the heart of the City of London. (The lavish granite and marble Edwardian building was dismantled and later exported to Estonia, where there are plans to reconstruct it in its spiritual home—the Baltic—in Tallinn.)

Green design The new design, by Foster + Partners and Arup, was promoted as the UK's first environmentally progressive commercial building. It has a circular plan with a lightweight steel frame that is all on the outside, keeping the interior free of pillars, and each floor is rotated by five degrees from the one below. There are no services at the top, but a light-filled, airy open space. Instead of the usual penthouse executive office, this is a

FACT FILE

Architects
Foster + Partners.

Engineers
Arup.

General contractor
Skanska.

Completion
2004; winner of the 2004 RIBA Stirling Prize.

Height
639 ft/195 m, 41 stories.

Floor area
822,360 sq ft/76,400 sq m.

Primary occupant
Swiss Re, an international reinsurance company.

Opposite: Seen from the south bank of the Thames, the Gherkin dwarfs older city landmarks, such as the Tower of London gatehouse and the old Port of London Authority building.

Right: The Gherkin's aerodynamic shape avoids the wind-tunnel effect created at ground level by straight-sided tall structures.

Below: Critics of the building have accused it of taking no notice of its neighbors.

restaurant with fantastic views and—despite the building's curvaceous shape—the only curved piece of glass in the whole structure, forming the little dome at the top.

Light and air Six lightwells spiral up through the floors to maximize natural light and ventilation, and the double-skinned facade provides passive solar heating. The windows are programmed to open in the right weather conditions, although many of the tenants prefer their air-con and don't open them. There's more incentive to breathe fresh air at street level, where the smaller footprint of the new building has created space for a paved plaza, lined with the engraved granite benches of Ian Hamilton Finlay's *Arcadian Dream Garden*.

While it replaced a century-old building, the Gherkin stands on a spot with a far longer history, overlooking the medieval church of St Andrew Undershaft and a few minutes' walk from the Norman Tower of London. Preparing the site revealed the grave of a teenage Roman girl, who has been reinterred under the plaza.

ENGLAND, WILTSHIRE

Stonehenge

MEDIEVAL CHRONICLERS COUNTED STONEHENGE AMONG THE WONDERS OF THE WORLD, AND IT STILL REVERBERATES WITH SPIRITUAL POWER AND MYSTERY. ITS VAST STONES AND THE COMPLEXITY OF ITS ENGINEERING AND DESIGN MAKE IT PREEMINENT AMONG SURVIVING PREHISTORIC MONUMENTS.

The great stone circle stands in a complex landscape of ceremonial monuments: nearby are the early Neolithic Woodhenge and another Neolithic henge at Durrington Walls, the massive stone circle at Avebury, and Silbury Hill, the largest man-made mound in Europe. Approaching Stonehenge is the Avenue, a 1¾-mile/3-km processional route leading from the River Avon, and there are burial mounds and barrows all over the area.

Building at Stonehenge continued for at least 1,500 years. Huge stones were transported, shaped, and erected by a workforce equipped with basic stone tools and antler picks. How did they do it? And why? What was there about this corner of England that made it such a focus of endeavor, ritual, and belief? The lack of conclusive answers only adds to the mystique of this iconic site.

Neolithic circles The earliest structure was a circular bank and ditch, perhaps ringed with wooden posts, made around 3000 BC. Traces of cremations have been found that are thought to be associated with it.

The first stone circle, at least 500 years later, was of bluestones from the Preseli Hills in Wales, 150 miles/240 km away. It is assumed that men dragged the stones to the sea and transported them on rafts; another theory

TIME LINE

ca. 3100 BC
Stage 1: Circular bank and ditch.

ca. 3000 BC
Stage 2: Wooden structure built within earthwork; evidence of cremation burials.

ca. 2600 BC
Stage 3 I: Bluestones erected; entrance aligned with midsummer sunrise; Avenue added from river.

ca. 2600–2400 BC
Stage 3 II: Dressed sarsen stones erected as outer circle and inner trilithons.

ca. 2300–1930 BC
Stage 3 III–IV: Bluestones rearranged inside outer circle and in center; "Altar Stone" possibly erected.

AD 1915
Bought by Cecil Chubb, and given to the nation in 1918.

1928
Surrounding land purchased by National Trust to prevent development.

1986
Inscribed by UNESCO as World Heritage site.

Opposite: The fields around the monument were long used for agriculture but the area has now been restored to native chalk grassland.

Right: The huge lintels are held in place by mortise and tenon joints, making Stonehenge unique among prehistoric stone circles.

is that they were moved by glacial action. This circle was later replaced by the much larger sarsen stones, brought from the Marlborough Downs 25 miles/40 km away. An outer circle of 30 upright stones was joined by lintels; inside this stood five even larger pairs of stones, topped by massive lintels to form "trilithons." Finally, in the Bronze Age, the bluestones were reused as a ring inside the outer circle, with the rest standing inside the horseshoe of trilithons. They seem to have had ritual importance, perhaps connected with healing.

What is Stonehenge? It has been surmised that Stonehenge was an observatory, a solar calendar, or a temple to the sun or the mother goddess, or even that it was built by extraterrestrials. A current theory is that it represented the realm of the dead, with the Avenue as a funerary processional way symbolizing the journey from life to death. Modern Druids associate it with the Celts (although it long predates them) and hold ceremonies there, notably at the summer solstice, and it is a focus for all kinds of alternative and New Age beliefs and rituals.

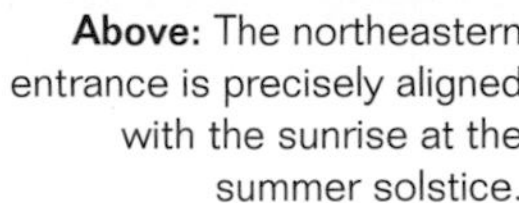

Above: The northeastern entrance is precisely aligned with the sunrise at the summer solstice.

Right: The five inner trilithons were arranged in a horseshoe shape opening toward the entrance.

ENGLAND, BATH

Royal Crescent

IN THE EIGHTEENTH CENTURY, BATH TRANSFORMED ITSELF FROM A RAMSHACKLE HEALTH RESORT INTO THE MOST DESIRABLE ADDRESS IN BRITAIN. FASHIONABLE SOCIETY'S CLAMOR FOR ELEGANT HOMES LED TO A BUILDING BOOM, OF WHICH THE ULTIMATE SHOWPIECE IS THE MAGNIFICENT SWEEP OF THE ROYAL CRESCENT.

The Bath-born architect John Wood had ambitions to recreate a Roman city in the spa town, and laid out squares and terraces on a heroic scale. His plans culminated in the monumental King's Circus, begun in 1754. But his son, John Wood the Younger, introduced something even more original. Having completed his father's Circus, he added Brock Street heading west to an open hillside, where his spectacular Crescent was constructed between 1767 and 1775. With 30 houses arranged in a wide semiellipse around a lawn, it looks out over the slope below like a great country house. It was the first time such an unenclosed design had been seen in an urban setting.

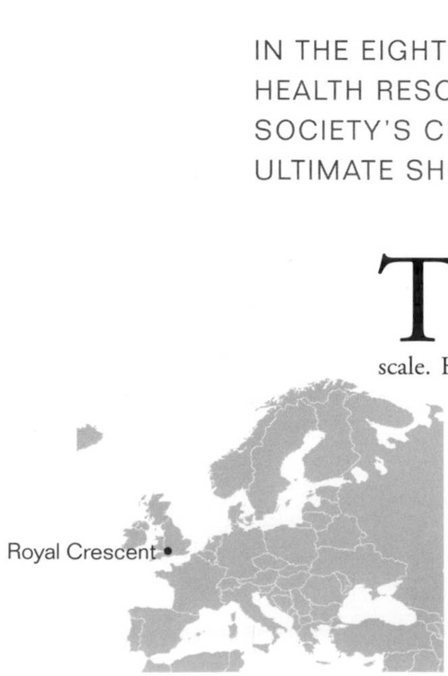

For a visitor rounding the corner into the Crescent today, the effect is still sensational. The scale is spacious and the houses still look out on green open space, with a distant view over trees to the Somerset hills. Until World War II sheep and cattle grazed in the field below the Crescent, and a ha-ha marks the edge of the central lawn.

Classical frontage The design unites the houses behind a facade of giant Ionic columns rising above a completely plain first floor. However, as with other Bath streets the plan was speculative, and the individual plots were sublet to builders who created their own internal

Above: The view from below is largely the same today as in the 1760s. A Victorian church spire used to intrude on the roofline but it was destroyed in World War II.

Below right: The houses at each end of the crescent have five-bay return fronts, with coupled columns at the corners: a detail repeated on the central house.

Right: Wrought iron snuffers attached to the gates allowed the link boys to extinguish their torches when they had lighted the residents to their doors.

TIME LINE

1688–1703
Queen Anne's repeated visits to take the waters make Bath fashionable.

1704
Beau Nash becomes Master of Ceremonies in Bath.

1767–74
Royal Crescent built.

1942
Nos. 2 and 17 gutted by wartime bombs.

1967
Bernard Cayzer donates No. 1 to Bath Preservation Trust to create a museum.

1971
Nos. 15 and 16 become Royal Crescent Hotel.

arrangements behind the strictly uniform frontage. This method of development led to very varied back elevations, with jutting utilitarian extensions—an effect described as "Queen Anne in front, Mary Anne behind."

Residents In the eighteenth century many of the houses were rented for the social season, though some had permanent occupants. A few are still single dwellings, while most are divided into apartments; No. 1 is a museum and a hotel occupies the center. However, the uniformity of the facade remains largely undisturbed, including the color of the paintwork, although one yellow front door became a local *cause célèbre* in the 1970s.

The Crescent became the Royal Crescent in 1795, when Frederick Duke of York (the grand old Duke of York who had 10,000 men) moved in. Other noted residents have included Christopher Anstey, author of the 1766 satire *The New Bath Guide*, Elizabeth Linley, who eloped with the playwright Richard Brinsley Sheridan, and Isaac Pitman, the inventor of shorthand.

ENGLAND, SHROPSHIRE

Iron Bridge

IT DOESN'T SEEM A VERY DISTINCTIVE NAME NOW, BUT IN 1779 "IRON BRIDGE" WAS QUITE ENOUGH TO IDENTIFY A NEW RIVER CROSSING BECAUSE IT WAS THE ONLY ONE IN THE WORLD. IT WAS SUCH AN IMPORTANT ATTRACTION THAT A WHOLE TOWN GREW UP AROUND IT—AND THEN BORROWED THE NAME FOR ITSELF.

Beneath its green, rural surface, the English county of Shropshire conceals a wealth of minerals: for early miners rich seams of lead, coal, and iron were easy to reach in the deep cleft of the Severn Gorge, and by the mid-seventeenth century 100,000 tons of coal were being produced each year. Most went down the river for export, but some fueled growing industries in the area: pottery, lead, and ironworking. The coal from the gorge made ideal coke for smelting iron, and in 1709 Abraham Darby began using it in his patented Coalbrookdale foundry method, making cast-iron cooking pots.

Sixty years later, furnace technology had advanced sufficiently for production on an altogether larger scale. Darby's grandson, Abraham Darby III, made cast-iron railroad tracks, and in the 1770s began work on the components for the world's first cast-iron bridge.

Building without precedent The plans for the bridge were drawn up by Thomas Pritchard, a local architect more at home with designing chimneypieces and funerary monuments than large-scale projects using revolutionary materials. Since no one had built an iron bridge before, there was no pattern to follow. But Pritchard's father was a joiner, so he knew how to work with wood, and that is how the Iron Bridge was made.

TIME LINE

1709
Abraham Darby begins using coke instead of charcoal to smelt iron, reducing its cost.

1750s
Rise of industry in Coalbrookdale increases need for river crossings, with six ferries operating.

1776
Act of Parliament passed permitting the bridge to be erected.

1779–80
Iron Bridge built.

January 1, 1781
Bridge opened to traffic.

1802
Cracked southern stone abutment removed and replaced with iron arches.

1835
Tollhouse enlarged.

1935
Bridge closed to vehicles.

1972
Reinforced concrete counter-arch created under river to strengthen foundations.

Opposite: The elegant Iron Bridge has become a symbol of the Industrial Revolution, and the area is often called the "birthplace of industry," although similar advances were also being made elsewhere.

Right: Some members cracked due to movement of the stone abutments.

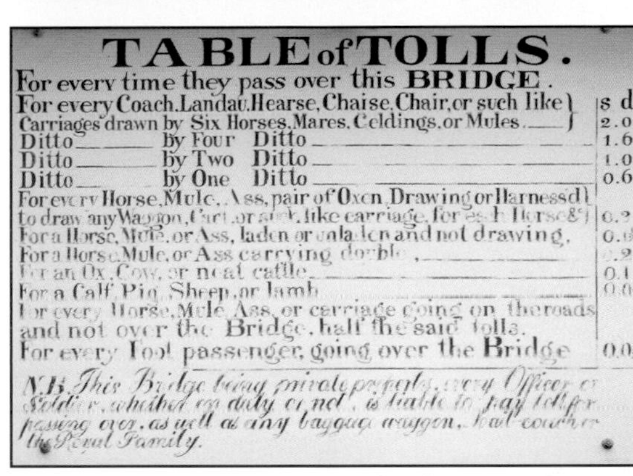

Below right: The tolls were fixed by Parliament in 1776 and were never changed.

Darby did the casting, making each of the 800 pieces separately, and they were put together using mortise-and-tenon and dovetail joints, except at the apex of the arch, where bolts were used. The costs far exceeded the estimate. Pritchard died soon after work began, and Darby remained in debt for the rest of his life.

Tourist attraction When the Iron Bridge opened to traffic, travelers, artists, and rival iron founders flocked to see it, and the little town of Ironbridge grew up to accommodate them—many stayed in the Tontine Hotel facing the bridge, built in 1784 by the project's shareholders and still in business. The bridge survived a great flood in 1795, inspiring growing confidence in cast iron as a building material, and more bridges, aqueducts, and other structures followed in Britain and, in due course, around the world.

Below: The valley today resembles the tranquil scene in an engraving used to promote the bridge in 1780, when in fact the area was full of the smoke and noise of industry.

ENGLAND, GATESHEAD

Angel of the North

AS YOU DRIVE UP THE HIGHWAY TOWARD GATESHEAD AND NEWCASTLE UPON TYNE, THE FIGURE LOOMS OVER THE ROADSIDE TREES, ITS OUTSTRETCHED WINGS APPARENTLY PROFFERING A STIFF HUG. PASSED BY THOUSANDS OF PEOPLE EVERY DAY, LOCALS REGARD IT AS A SIGN THAT THEY ARE NEARLY HOME.

The angel stands on a mound created from the remains of old pithead baths: this place, on the edge of Low Fell, was the site of the Lower Tyne Colliery. Coal had been mined in the region since medieval times, and it fueled a vast expansion of industry in northeast England in the nineteenth century. Iron foundries, shipbuilding, and locomotive manufacture turned Gateshead from a small riverside town into a sprawling center of heavy industry, but much of the twentieth century was a period of slow decline, with the last of the borough's collieries closing in the 1970s.

Regeneration Since the 1980s, arts projects such as the Angel of the North, the Sage auditorium, and the Baltic contemporary art gallery, have been Gateshead's chosen route to regeneration. The colliery site was reclaimed in 1989, and the sculptor Antony Gormley was commissioned in 1994 to make a site-specific work. Four years later, its massive steel sections made their slow and stately road journey under police escort from Hartlepool.

Gormley's angel was manufactured by Hartlepool Steel Fabrications, a company more accustomed to working on bridges and oil rigs, and its ribbed body and wings reflect the idioms of such structures, while being strong enough to withstand the high winds that whip across its

FACT FILE

Sculptor
Antony Gormley.

Engineers
Ove Arup & Partners.

Fabricators
Hartlepool Steel.

Wingspan
175 ft/54 m.

Height
65 ft/20 m.

Weight
200 tons.

Opposite: The extended wings are angled very slightly inward, giving, in Gormley's words, "a sense of embrace."

Right: The angel is made from Corten steel, a "weathering" steel alloy designed to form a stable coat of rust after a few years of exposure, which has produced its warm reddish-brown coloring.

Below: The angel stands on a mound that incorporates the remains of an old colliery's pithead baths.

exposed hilltop. There is no plinth. The figure might just have landed on the grassy mound, or be waiting to take off with those weighty yet gliderlike wings spread to catch the wind.

But it is rooted. To hold it in place between earth and sky, the angel stands on concrete piles sunk into solid rock 72 ft/22 m below the surface—in the ground where miners toiled for three centuries, and Gormley has written that he made his work to bear witness to these men and their vanished industry.

National icon Though isolated between major roads, these days the angel is rarely alone; its feet are worn shiny from being sat on and climbed over. Gateshead Council publishes patterns for knitting your own angel or making one in origami, and a variety of daffodil (tall with a rusty orange flower) has been named after it. The figure is one of Britain's most filmed and photographed monuments, and an instantly recognizable symbol of Tyneside.

ENGLAND, NORTHUMBERLAND

Hadrian's Wall

THE LARGEST ANCIENT MONUMENT IN NORTHERN EUROPE IS A GREAT FEAT OF ROMAN CIVIL ENGINEERING THAT RUNS FROM WALLSEND ON THE EAST COAST OF BRITAIN TO BOWNESS ON THE WEST COAST. THIS VERY EXTENSIVE LANDMARK WAS THE NORTHERN FRONTIER OF THE ROMAN EMPIRE FOR 300 YEARS.

One of the country's national trails now runs alongside the 84-mile/135-km Hadrian's Wall, and it's one of Britain's most popular long-distance walks. But patrolling a wet and windy wall in the wilds of northern England probably wasn't such an enticing prospect for second-century Roman soldiers. Many would have been used to far milder climates, because they were recruited from all parts of the empire.

Emperor Hadrian succeeded Trajan, but unlike him had no desire to enlarge the empire; simply to keep the peace. Until Hadrian's reign Roman ambition had been to rule the whole of the known world, but now the emperor wanted to set limits. Northern Britain was one of the trouble spots he needed to address. He made a personal visit in AD 122, and the wall was probably begun then. Three legions of the army formed the work-force, and it was finished in about six years.

Defenses It was the empire's most heavily fortified border, up to 15 ft/4.5 m high and 10 ft/3 m thick, and faced on both sides with carefully cut stones set in mortar, though the western section was initially more speedily built from turf blocks on a cobblestone foundation. Defensive ditches and earthworks along each side made the structure a serious obstacle for potential attackers.

Security was formidable. The 16 forts along the wall would each have housed around 800 troops. Between them, at each Roman mile (about 1,650 yd/1,500 m) a smaller milecastle gave access to the walkway along the top of the wall. Between each pair of milecastles, two turrets acted as sentry boxes for the duty patrols.

Local impact The wall was not simply a way of keeping the troublesome Picts in the north out of Roman territory. It had gates that probably functioned like customs posts: the people came and went, while the Romans levied taxes. Above all, it was a powerful statement that the Romans were in control of the locals, whom they disparagingly referred to as *Brittunculi* ("little Britons"). Later on, however, many local men patrolled it: it was considered a prestigious job, with posts handed down from father to son. The large numbers of troops posted there were ready customers for local traders, and thriving settlements grew up around the forts.

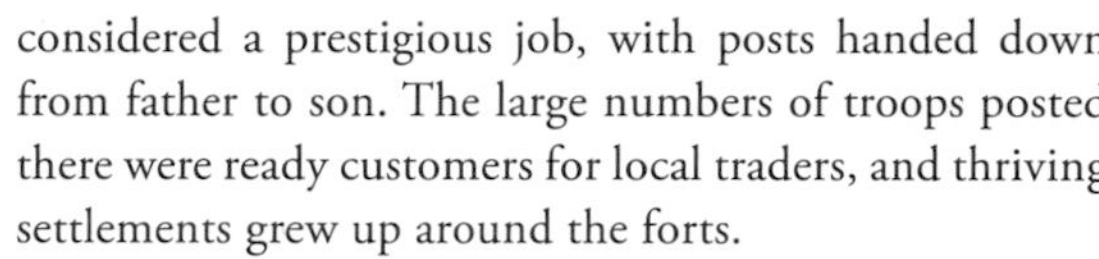

After the Roman period the wall was abandoned and its stones were gradually removed for building material; some found their way into the region's great monasteries, including Jarrow, Lindisfarne, and Monkwearmouth. Today the remains of the wall in some sections are little more than interesting bumps to look for among suburban houses or beside a road. But where it still dips and rises majestically over the Northumberland hills, along the forbidding crags of Whin Sill and past the ruins of Housesteads fort, it is spectacular and evocative.

Below: Much of the stone section of the wall is about 6 ft/2 m wide, with a rubble core between stone facings.

Below: Near the fort of Vindolanda, the wall dips down into Sycamore Gap, named for the lone tree beside the stones.

Above: The wall follows the natural defenses of Windshields and Highshield Crags above Crag Lough.

Top right: The neat Roman stonework would originally have risen far higher, topped with a parapet, probably crenellated, and a walkway.

TIME LINE

55 and 54 BC
Invasions of Britain by Julius Caesar.

AD 43
Roman control of Britain established under Claudius.

117–138
Reign of Hadrian.

122–128
Hadrian's Wall built.

142–154
Antonine Wall built farther north, but soon abandoned.

ca. 410
End of Roman period in Britain.

SCOTLAND, EDINBURGH

Edinburgh Castle

SCOTLAND IS A LAND OF CASTLES: THERE HAVE BEEN WELL OVER 2,000 OF THEM, BUT EDINBURGH'S, TOWERING ABOVE THE CITY ON ITS FORBIDDING ROCK, SETS THE PATTERN, EVEN IF LITTLE OF ITS MEDIEVAL FORTIFICATION REMAINS. IT EVEN HAS A COUPLE OF GHOSTS—A PIPER AND A HEADLESS DRUMMER.

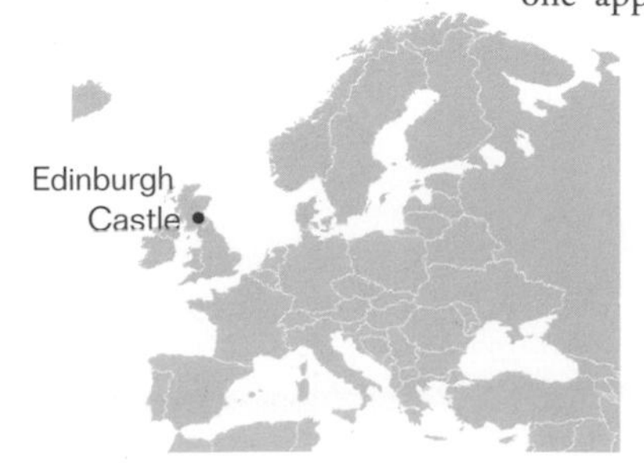

The Castle Rock is the hard basalt plug of an extinct volcano that resisted later glacial erosion, leaving an almost impregnable crag with only one approach route—the ultimate safe refuge. It was known to the ancient Scots as Din Eidyn until it fell to the Angles in AD 638, when it took the English name Edinburgh.

St Margaret's Chapel David I moved his capital here from Dunfermline in the twelfth century, giving the castle royal status. Only one structure remains from this period: the little Romanesque chapel dedicated to his mother on the summit, which is the city's oldest building. When the Earl of Moray's forces captured the castle from the English in 1314—by scaling the precipitous north face of the rock—the chapel was the only building they spared, and Robert the Bruce later left money and instructions for its repair.

Mons Meg The monstrous cannon that sits outside the chapel arrived in 1457 as a gift from Philip Duke of Burgundy. It fired balls weighing 330 lb/150 kg for up to 2 miles/3 km, but really its bark was worse than its bite: firing generated so much heat that it could be used only a few times a day, and it was barely maneuverable on a battlefield. From 1540 Mons Meg was saved for ceremonial use, until the barrel burst in 1681 when greeting

TIME LINE

900 BC
Archaeological evidence of human settlement.

AD 600
Earliest reference to Din Eidyn fortress.

c 1130
Royal castle built by David I.

1356
David II rebuilds castle.

1571–73
Lang Siege, destruction of David's Tower.

1757–1814
Castle used to hold prisoners of war.

1861
One O'Clock Gun fired for first time.

1950
First Edinburgh Military Tattoo.

1996
Stone of Destiny, taken to England in 1296, returned to Edinburgh Castle.

Below: The castle dominates the skyline of Edinburgh, appearing rooted in the living rock.

Opposite: The gatehouse was a picturesque nineteenth-century addition. Over the gate is the inscription of the Order of the Thistle: "Nemo Me Impune Lacessit" ("No one attacks me with impunity.")

Right: Each time the castle was rebuilt it had to accommodate the prevailing style of warfare. While the medieval walls would have had arrow slits, wider openings were necessary for firing cannon.

James Duke of Albany—a rather bad omen for the future king, who managed to reign for only three years.

Royal palace The fifteenth century saw the creation of royal apartments and the great hall, although after the royal family moved down the Royal Mile to Holyrood Palace the castle was mostly used as an arsenal. But Mary Queen of Scots took refuge here to give birth, in a tiny wood-paneled room whose panels are vividly painted to commemorate the event. Before her baby was a year old she was forced to abdicate and he became James VI, later James I of England.

Sieges In all, the castle suffered 13 attacks, culminating in the "Lang Siege," when the garrison held out for nearly two years in support of the deposed Mary Queen of Scots. Bonnie Prince Charlie in 1745 was the last to test its defenses—the castle held out easily—but in the face of the Napoleonic threat the New Barracks was built in 1799, large enough to hold 600 troops. In the event the castle never needed to defend itself against the French—its vaults held prisoners of war instead.

Tradition Soldiers still guard the castle, but the besieging hordes turned into tourists as Victorians went wild for "auld" Scotland. Walter Scott dashingly searched the castle for the crown jewels (missing for a century) and masterminded its tartan-and-bagpipes image. With the gatehouse and great hall restored in baronial style and the One O'clock Gun set up on the ramparts, the annual Military Tattoo on the Esplanade has cemented Edinburgh's status as Scotland's top castle.

FRANCE, PARIS

Eiffel Tower

LA GRANDE DAME TOUT EN FER—THE GREAT IRON LADY—HAS DOMINATED PARIS'S SKYLINE SINCE 1889. IT WAS ORIGINALLY INTENDED TO STAND FOR ONLY TWENTY YEARS. BUT EIFFEL'S GENIUS EXTENDED BEYOND ENGINEERING, AND HE TOOK CARE TO ENSURE A FAR LONGER LIFE FOR HIS GREATEST ACHIEVEMENT.

As Paris planned its International Exhibition for 1889, marking the centenary of the French Revolution, it held a competition to design a spectacular tower to stand at the entrance of the site on the Champs de Mars: at 985 ft/300 m it would be the world's tallest structure. Out of about 700 entries, the design submitted by Gustave Eiffel's engineering company was unanimously chosen for the project.

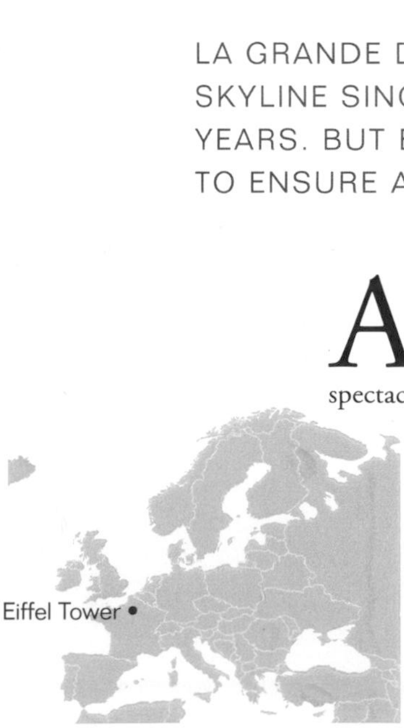

Eiffel's chief engineers Maurice Koechlin and Emile Nouguier were responsible for the radical design—an open latticework of iron girders—which made no attempt to disguise its structure under stone cladding or decorative finishes. A few ornamental features, such as the arches under the first level, were added by the architect Stephen Sauvestre to make the utilitarian style more approachable, but the tower was very much a monument of the industrial age.

Building began in January 1887, but not everyone welcomed the unmissable new landmark. On February 14, 1887, *Le Temps* published a letter signed by about 300 influential artists, including Charles Garnier (architect of the Paris Opéra), Charles Gounod, Alexandre Dumas *fils*, and Guy de Maupassant, comparing it with "a gigantic black factory chimney, its barbarous mass overwhelming and humiliating all our monuments and

Above: The bronze color scheme of the Eiffel Tower was chosen to blend effectively with the colors of the Paris cityscape, over which it looms.

Right: The top level is accessible only by elevator: two sets of electric counterbalanced cabins replaced the original hydraulic elevators in 1982.

belittling our works of architecture ..." They protested that "for twenty years we shall see spreading across the whole city, a city shimmering with the genius of so many centuries, we shall see spreading like an ink stain, the odious shadow of this odious column of bolted metal." (Later, it was reported that Maupassant ate lunch in the tower restaurant every day. When asked why, he replied that it was the only place in Paris from which he could not see the tower.)

Wind resistance It was the bolted metal construction that made the height of the new tower possible. Experience of building bridges had taught Eiffel that the most important consideration was the strength of the wind, and the shape of the curved pylons was developed so that at any height the downward force was equal to the force of the strongest wind at that point, while the open structure minimized wind resistance. The tower sways just 2½–2¾ in/6–7 cm in the wind, but the top can also shift by about 7 in/18 cm, because of expansion

TIME LINE

1884
First drawings.

1887–89
Construction (2 years, 2 months, and 5 days).

March 1889
Tower opened to public.

1898
First telegraph link between Panthéon and Eiffel Tower.

1903–05
Eiffel's experiments with falling bodies.

1909
Completion of military radio-telegraph station.

1912
Franz Reichelt dies after jumping from first level with a home-made parachute.

1921
First radio transmission.

1935
First television broadcast.

1984
Robert Moriarty flies a light aircraft under the arches.

FACT FILE

Height
1,063 ft/324 m (including flagpole).

Footprint of tower
410 ft/125 m square.

Maximum depth of foundations
50 ft/15 m.

Steps to top
1,655.

Iron components
18,038 (plus 2.5 million rivets).

Weight of metal
7,300 tons.

Total weight
10,100 tons.

Paint
60 tons used for each repainting.

Staff
620.

Top left: Looking straight down from the top deck to one of the stone feet designed by Sauvestre.

Bottom left: The view up from beneath the tower shows the symmetry and lightness of the structure.

in the metal components when the sun is shining on one side of the tower.

Erecting the tower There were formidable challenges. The pillars on the riverside had to be supported by air-compressed foundations in underwater steel caissons, and Eiffel devised a system of hydraulic jacks to position each foot at the correct angle to meet the horizontal beams on the first level. The iron components, weighing a total of 7,300 tons, were assembled in Eiffel's workshops and bolted together on site, like Erector. The tower opened on March 31, 1889.

In 1909, when ownership of the tower reverted to the city, there was talk of demolition, but Eiffel had already thought of a way to make it indispensable—by installing scientific equipment at the top, such as barometers, wind gauges, and communications antennae. It was used to transmit wireless telegraph signals, then radio (from 1918), and finally television (from 1957). So it was new technology that ensured the tower's survival into the modern age, giving it time to establish itself as Paris's global icon.

Below: Eiffel acknowledged his debt to 72 French scientists and engineers by inscribing their names around the tower, just below the first deck.

Right: The Eiffel Tower celebrated its 120th birthday in 2009 with an explosion of fireworks during the traditional national celebration on July 14.

Eiffel Tower Brown Now it is carefully preserved, and every seven years 25 painters set up safety nets and harnesses and repaint the whole structure, starting from the top and painting by hand using brushes. The whole job takes 18 months. The original color was reddish brown, but red has also been used, and even yellow; since 1968 the paint has been "Eiffel Tower Brown," specially mixed to blend with the cityscape and applied in three shades—darker at the bottom and lighter at the top to give a consistent appearance.

About six million people visit the tower each year; when nearly two million flocked to it in 1889, Eiffel commented: "I ought to be jealous of the tower, it is much more famous than I am." Having astutely attached his own name to his most notable work, he eventually became very famous indeed.

Below: Eiffel realized the importance of maintaining the tower with meticulous repainting: samples of all the colors that have been used are painted on the first level.

FRANCE, PARIS

Arc de Triomphe

NAPOLEON COMMISSIONED HIS TRIUMPHAL ARCH FRESH FROM HIS GREATEST VICTORY AT AUSTERLITZ. VASTLY LARGER THAN THE ROMAN MONUMENTS THAT INSPIRED IT, THE TOWERING CENTERPIECE OF THE PARISIAN STREET PLAN REFLECTS THE SCALE OF THE EMPEROR'S AMBITIONS. HE DID NOT LIVE TO SEE IT COMPLETED.

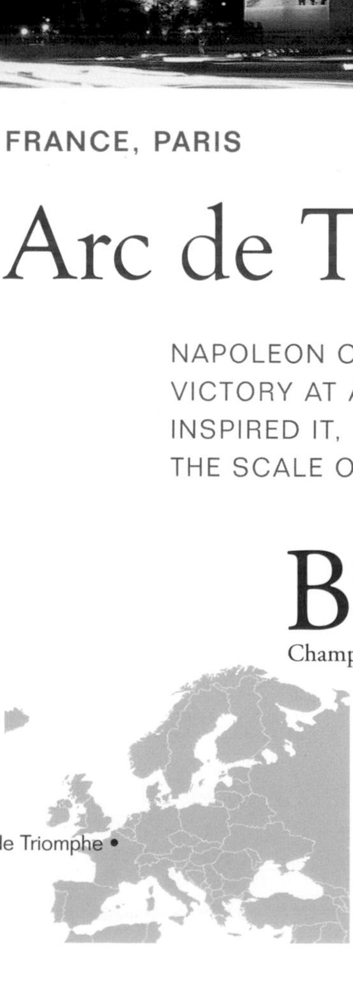

Before the city engulfed it, the spot was a mound known as the Butte Chaillot, where a number of hunting trails met. In the 1770s the Avenue des Champs-Elysées was laid out as an elegant extension of the Tuileries Gardens, and the star-shaped junction was formalized as part of the plan, becoming the Place de l'Etoile ("Square of the Star").

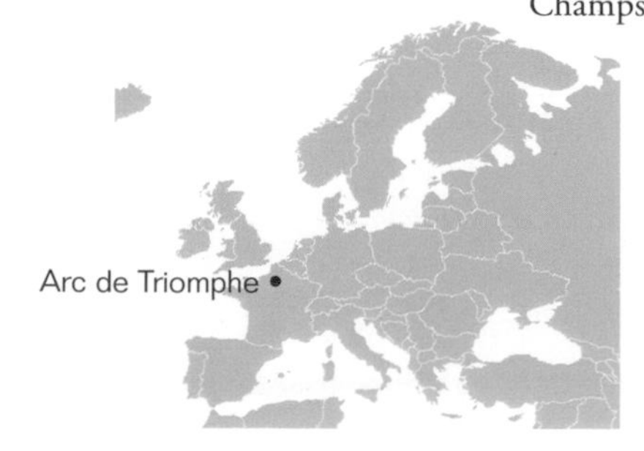

Triumph of Napoleon The battle of Austerlitz in 1805 was Napoleon's greatest military success, and he promised his men that he would lead them home "through arches of triumph." He commissioned the Arc de Triomphe in their honor—and his own. Construction was very slow, and when he married the Austrian Archduchess Marie Louise in 1810, the wedding procession had to pass under a replica arch made of wood and painted canvas. By the time building began in earnest, Napoleon's fortunes were waning, and when he abdicated in 1814 work stopped altogether. The arch was finally completed in 1836, and Napoleon passed under it only once—in his coffin in December 1840.

The battles named around the top are Napoleonic victories, but the arch was dedicated to all of France's war dead, and the subjects of its four major reliefs reflect occasions of national consensus: François Rude's *La*

FACT FILE

Architect
Jean François Chalgrin, completed by his assistant Joust and Guillaume Blouet.

Dimensions
Height 160 ft/50 m; main arch 100 ft/29 m high and 48 ft/14.6 m wide. Size exceeded only by the arch in Pyongyang, North Korea, built in 1982 for Kim Il-Sung's 70th birthday.

Inscriptions
558 generals named inside arch: those underlined were killed in action.

Left: In all, 22 artists worked on the arch, creating France's largest assembly of early nineteenth-century sculpture.

Below: The arch stands at the highest point of Paris's processional way, stretching 5 miles/9 km from the Tuileries to its twentieth-century counterpart, the Grande Arche de la Défense.

Right: A huge tricolor hangs inside the arch on July 14, when it is the rallying point for the annual Bastille Day military parade.

Below right: François Rude's personification of France (modeled on his wife) urges the volunteers of 1792 on to glory.

Marseillaise portrays the Republican volunteers of 1792 and Jean-Pierre Cortot's *Triumph of 1810* shows Napoleon in his pomp, but the two reliefs by Antoine Étex are *Resistance* (the resistance of 1814) and *Peace*, symbolizing the end of the wars and the restoration of the Bourbon monarchy.

Jean Chalgrin's design was inspired by Roman monuments, with the same proportions as the Arch of Titus, but while that is 50 ft/15 m high, the Arc de Triomphe rises to 160 ft/50 m. Its main arch is large enough for the French aviator Charles Godefroy to have flown under it in 1919, with a journalist friend ready to capture his exploit on film. Beneath lies the Tomb of the Unknown Soldier, buried in 1920, on which an eternal flame burns.

Traffic circle The arch now presides over a notorious circus where vehicles jostle ten-abreast. It was originally a junction of five roads, but Baron Haussmann's urban redevelopment in the 1870s increased the number to 12. All are named after military leaders, and the square itself was renamed Place Charles de Gaulle in 1970.

FRANCE, NORMANDY

Mont-Saint-Michel

THE GOTHIC APPARITION RISES ABOVE THE FLAT FIELDS AND SALT MARSHES OF THE NORMANDY COAST, THE ABBEY'S SPIRE CROWNED WITH A GOLDEN FIGURE OF ST MICHAEL. PILGRIMS HAVE BEEN WALKING OUT TO IT ACROSS THE SAND FOR CENTURIES, AND TODAY IT IS FRANCE'S MOST VISITED SITE OUTSIDE PARIS.

Legend tells that Michael, the fiery archangel, appeared to Bishop Aubert of Avranges in 708 and told him to build a shrine on the craggy island in the bay. The bishop was slow to act, even after a second visitation, so Michael appeared a third time and burned a hole in his skull with his blazing finger—that got the work started. Holy relics brought from Italy drew pilgrims to the island, though they were probably following an established route, since many hilltop sites sacred to the Celtic solar god Bel were reassigned to St Michael when Christianity absorbed older pagan traditions.

Tidal island The granite outcrop was originally part of the land, but as sea levels rose after the last Ice Age it was cut off from the coast, except for a small natural land bridge covered by the tide, which rises rapidly by as much as 45 ft/14 m. Early pilgrims had to pick their way across the flats at low water, being careful to avoid treacherous patches of quicksand, and local guides still recreate this hazardous journey for modern visitors.

A permanent causeway was added in 1879, but this has created a buildup of silt carried down the River Couesnon. Work is now under way to replace the causeway with a bridge, allowing the sea to flow freely around the mount so that its island status will be restored.

Left: The abbey church sits on the summit, supported by lower buildings that hug the sides of the rock. The original Romanesque chancel collapsed in 1421 and was rebuilt in flamboyant Gothic style.

Right: At low tide the mount is surrounded by sand, but the causeway has blocked its movement and caused it to build up, threatening to join the island to the coast. A new bridge is planned to replace the causeway,

Abbey and fortress When the Normans acquired the island in the tenth century, they handed it over to the Benedictine order, and the monastery of St-Michel-au-Péril-de-la-Mer was founded in 966. The grateful monks supported William of Normandy's claim to the English throne, and after his conquest the foundation's loyalty was rewarded—among other property it gained a lookalike Cornish island near Penzance, which, with a satellite priory on its summit, became St. Michael's Mount.

As their fortunes grew, the monks of Mont-Saint-Michel carried out an ambitious construction program, building out around the rock to create a platform for the soaring church on the summit. Work continued for almost five centuries, culminating in the flamboyant Gothic choir of 1520. And the pilgrims kept coming, even during the Hundred Years' War, when the mount was besieged—unsuccessfully—by the English. But the Reformation brought decline and the foundation dwindled. At its lowest ebb, the abbey was turned into a prison during the French Revolution.

Today, rescued and restored, the abbey lures visitors as it once drew pilgrims. The walk through the bustling village is likely to be accompanied by the noise of whisks striking copper bowls, because the island is famous for its soufflé omelets. Then it's a stiff climb up—900 steps to the top of the church—into a Gothic maze of vaulted halls, chapels, stairways, and cloisters, with dizzying views out across the salt marshes and the sea.

TIME LINE

5th–7th centuries
Outpost of Romano-Breton culture.

708
St Michael's shrine built.

10th–15th centuries
Abbey constructed by Benedictine order.

1337–1453
Hundred Years' War.

16th century
Pilgrims diminish and monastery declines.

1789
Abbey becomes a prison.

1836
Victor Hugo campaigns for restoration of abbey.

1874
Mount becomes historic monument.

1979
Site listed by UNESCO.

Right: Below the abbey, the village that grew up to cater for hordes of pilgrims is still full of hotels, restaurants, and souvenir stores.

Below: The cloister is at the top of the early thirteenth-century building known as the Merveille, perched on the north face of the mount.

FRANCE, BRITTANY

Île Vierge Lighthouse

THE PURPOSE OF EVERY LIGHTHOUSE IS LITERALLY TO BE A LANDMARK: TO MARK THE LAND THAT WOULD OTHERWISE ENDANGER SHIPS SAILING NEAR ROCKS OR SHOALS. BUT MANY, SUCH AS THIS ELEGANT GRANITE TOWER, HAVE ALSO ACHIEVED ICONIC STATUS. ÎLE VIERGE IS EUROPE'S TALLEST LIGHTHOUSE.

The jagged coast of northwest Brittany is a maze of tiny islands, rocks, and inlets, with strong currents, big tides, and stormy northern weather: a challenge to the most experienced sailor. But Bretons have always lived by fishing, trading, gathering seaweed: the sea is the region's lifeblood, and there were seagoing vessels negotiating the treacherous rocks along this coast more than two thousand years ago.

Warning lights were essential to navigation, but for centuries the Breton way was to light fires to guide ships safely into port, because they feared that lighthouses, though used in other parts of the ancient world, could help invaders as well as their own seamen. The region's first lighthouse, at Stiff on Ouessant, was illuminated in 1700.

First tower By the nineteenth century the fear had passed, and granite towers sprouted along the coast, particularly among the fjordlike inlets of Finistère. Some were placed on rocks that emerged from the sea only at low tide and took years to complete, since the builders could work for just a few hours at a time. On little Île Vierge, at the northwestern tip of Finistère, a square tower 108 ft/33 m tall was begun in 1842, and its fixed white light went into operation in 1845. It turned out to be visible for 18 miles/29 km—not nearly far enough.

Left: The western limit of the English Channel is defined by a line joining the Île Vierge lighthouse to Land's End in Cornwall.

Right: The elegant cantilevered staircase consists of 365 stone steps to the keeper's room; a further 35 lead to the light.

FACT FILE

Height
271 ft/82.5 m.

Diameter at base
43 ft/13.2 m.

Diameter of staircase
16 ft/5 m.

Power of light
650 watts.

Below: The lighthouse is open to the public, and the narrow walkway at the top gives a panoramic view of the surrounding reefs.

Second tower Its replacement, designed by Gaston Pigeaud and Armand Considère, was erected beside it from granite collected locally, faced with stones from Kersanton. The design is a truncated cone enclosing an inner cylinder, with windows that help to tie the two structures together until they meet at the top. Just under the light is a cozy wood-paneled room where the keeper originally slept, ready to refuel the light each night, and leading up to this is the building's most appealing feature: a remarkable helicoidal stone staircase lined with 22,500 turquoise opaline tiles, so dirt-resistant and smooth that nothing can dull their iridescent surface.

The new lighthouse went into operation in 1902. Its light, with four Fresnel lenses and twin beams flashing every five seconds, could be seen for up to 30 miles/50 km. Electrification in 1956 removed the need for the nightly refueling. The light is now automated, but a lighthouse keeper still lives on the island—in the keeper's sturdy house under the old tower.

BELGIUM, BRUSSELS

The Atomium

"THE MOST BELGIAN OF BUILDINGS" AROSE FROM THE FIRST WORLD FAIR TO BE HELD AFTER WORLD WAR II. DESIGNED TO STAND FOR SIX MONTHS, THIS SYMBOL OF THE ATOMIC AGE WAS RESTORED IN TIME FOR ITS FIFTIETH BIRTHDAY AND IS ONE OF BELGIUM'S BEST-LOVED MONUMENTS. AND IT STILL LOOKS LIKE THE FUTURE.

In 1958 science and technology seemed to be the keys to a golden future. The year saw the launch of the integrated circuit, which would transform the development of computers, and the word "aerospace" was coined as Sputnik orbited Earth and NASA was born. Belgium itself was looking steadfastly forward as it emerged from a dark period of its history, eager to portray itself as a young and vibrant nation.

Expo 58 The Brussels fair set out to celebrate the progressive, the positive, and the new, with showcases of groundbreaking technology, such as the Philips Pavilion by the architect-composer Iannis Xenakis for Le Corbusier; it housed an "electronic poem" by Edgar Varèse played through hundreds of speakers in its hyperbolic paraboloid walls. The fair's theme was "A world view—a new humanism": a little optimistic during the Cold War, as the United States and the USSR (in neighboring pavilions) took turns to lob ideological bricks at each other.

The large Belgian section of the fair was dominated by two giant structures. The Arrow of Civil Engineering featured a 262-ft/80-m projection that looked like a paper dart but was in fact made from reinforced concrete, looming over a miniature version of Belgium. But the undoubted star of the show was the Atomium.

FACT FILE

Height
335 ft/102 m.

Diameter of each sphere
59 ft/18 m.

Spheres
Five of the nine spheres are open to the public. They contain a permanent exhibition on Expo 58, temporary exhibition space, the Kids' Sphere hotel, and two restaurants; the top sphere offers views over Brussels.

Opposite: When the Atomium was restored in 2004–06, the weathered aluminum cladding on the spheres was replaced with more durable stainless steel, and looks like new.

Right: At night the spheres sparkle with 2,970 lights.

Below right: Staircases and escalators in the tubes give access to the spheres.

Molecular structure One idea for the fair's centerpiece had been to build an inverted Eiffel Tower—fortunately that was rejected in favor of a more futuristic design by the engineer André Waterkeyn, with interiors by André and Michel Polak. In the 1950s the interconnected spheres and rods used by scientists to represent molecular structure had captured the imagination of commercial designers, and they were appearing as chair legs, coat hooks, and light fittings, on tableware and textiles. The Atomium played with the same idea on a much grander scale—a magnification of 165 billion, in fact. It is a giant model of a unit cell of an iron crystal, with each sphere representing an atom. In the uneasy climate of the Cold War, with both sides testing nuclear weapons, its theme was the peaceful use of atomic energy.

Escalators in the tubes lead to the spheres, which are used for exhibitions and events. There is a restaurant at the top, reached by an elevator that was the world's fastest in 1958, and groups of children can stay overnight in the Kids' Sphere—where they sleep in minispheres.

Below: The structure is a tipped-up cube, with one sphere at each corner and the ninth in the middle.

NETHERLANDS, AMSTERDAM

Herengracht

THE SEVENTEENTH CENTURY WAS AMSTERDAM'S GOLDEN AGE. ITS RICH, SUCCESSFUL CITIZENS COMMISSIONED LUXURIOUS NEW HOUSES ALONG THE ELEGANT CANALS LAID OUT AROUND THE OLD CITY, AND THE MOST PRESTIGIOUS OF THESE WAS HERENGRACHT—THE GENTLEMEN'S CANAL.

The gentlemen in question were the "regents"—the wealthy merchants and bankers who held the reins of power, because they also held the purse strings. From the Middle Ages they had gradually acquired control of Dutch cities, towns, and institutions, creating an oligarchy of interrelated patrician families. They feathered their own nests but also funded public works, such as civic infrastructure, churches, hospitals, and the patronage of the arts.

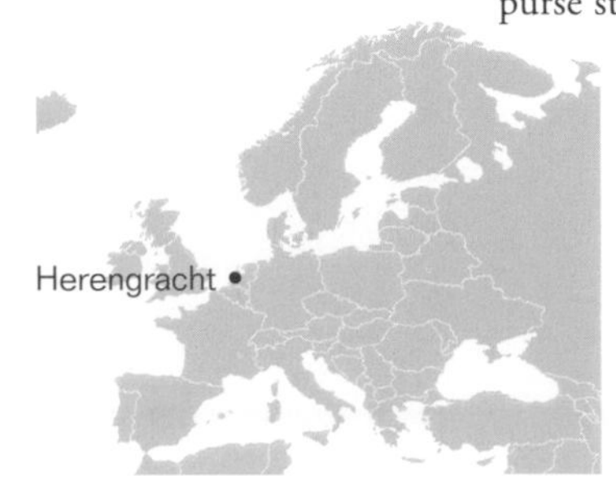

The ideal city At the start of the seventeenth century the regents were seriously loaded. Amsterdam was Europe's richest port and most desirable address, but it was bursting at the seams. With typical care and thoroughness (plus a bit of insider dealing), the regents planned an expansion that would quadruple the size of the medieval city, surrounding it with concentric semicircular canals lined with building plots: larger houses fronting the canals, smaller artisans' homes and workshops in the side streets.

The project was ambitious, because the swampy land between the canals had to be drained and raised, and piles sunk to support the buildings—and even (the ultimate luxury) gardens. But it set the pattern for urban planning until the nineteenth century, and the Grachtengordel ("girdle of canals") remains an intimate,

FACT FILE

43–45
Fortune and Noah's Ark warehouses, ca. 1590: probably the oldest buildings on Herengracht.

168
By Philips Vingboons, 1638: thought to be Amsterdam's earliest bottle-neck gable.

170–172
Bartolotti House, de Keyser, 1615, with step gable and angled facade built to follow the bend in the canal.

386
By Vingboons 1663–65, now a museum devoted to the Grachtengordel.

502
House of Columns, 1672: official residence of the Mayor of Amsterdam.

605
Double house of 1687, now Museum Willet-Holthuysen.

Right: Each house was individually designed for the purchaser of the plot; despite the strict planning controls, this resulted in a wide yet harmonious variety of architectural detail.

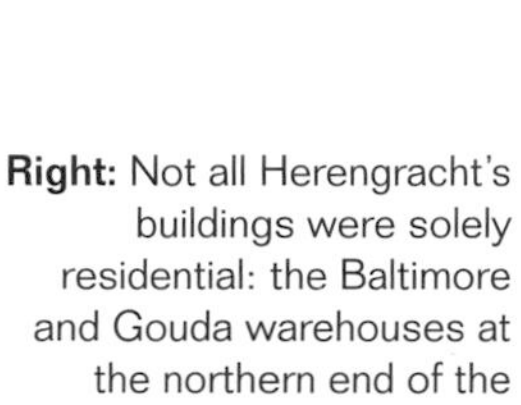

Right: Not all Herengracht's buildings were solely residential: the Baltimore and Gouda warehouses at the northern end of the canal date from the mid-eighteenth century.

Far right: Feline inmates of the privately owned Katten Kabinet enjoy the opulent interiors of a house dating from 1667.

Left: The picturesque junction of Herengracht with Leidsegracht, one of the smaller canals running across the semicircular plan.

Below: Bridges across the main canals link the side streets: the plan of the Grachtengordel resembles a giant spiderweb.

human-scale environment that those who can afford it still love to live in. Strict planning controls were imposed. Each plot was to be precisely 30 Amsterdam feet (26 ft/ 8 m) wide and 100 Amsterdam feet (93 ft/28.3 m) deep; garden buildings and walls were restricted in size. In Herengracht there were to be no trades requiring an anvil (so no noisy blacksmiths or stonecutters), though tradesmen could operate along the other new canals.

So from 1664 the quiet Herengracht filled with magnificent houses. But ostentatious displays were frowned on in this sternly Protestant society, so wealth showed in more subtle ways. Classically proportioned facades were executed in meticulous brickwork with restrained detailing and topped with inventive gables. Inside, luxurious tastes could be more discreetly indulged, with exquisite plasterwork, woodcarving, and paintings.

The Golden Bend The wealthiest residents circumvented the width restriction by buying a double plot, or an adjoining plot at the back where they could create a spacious garden with pretty pavilions and coach houses. Of the hundred or so palatial "double" mansions, about half are clustered on a curving stretch of Herengracht known as the Golden Bend. Now too large and costly to be private houses, most are occupied by banks and insurance companies, though one enjoyably eccentric exception is the Katten Kabinet, a museum of cat-inspired art languidly patrolled by a number of actual cats.

NETHERLANDS

Windmills of Kinderdijk

PAINTED ON COUNTLESS TILES, TEAPOTS, AND TRINKETS, THE WINDMILL IS A CLICHÉ OF THE DUTCH TOURIST TRADE. BUT IT BECAME AN ICON FOR GOOD REASON: WIND-POWERED PUMPS KEPT TWO-THIRDS OF THE COUNTRY FROM DISAPPEARING BENEATH THE SEA.

The Dutch didn't invent the windmill, which was in use in the Persian Empire in the ninth century, and the earliest mills were built to grind corn. But from the fourteenth century Dutch engineers installed and developed windmills as part of ingenious drainage systems to create and maintain productive man-made landscapes, and to power some of the world's earliest industrial operations, such as sawing wood for shipbuilding.

Land reclamation In the low-lying coastal regions of Holland and Utrecht, a constant battle had to be fought against flooding from the time the first dykes were built around AD 1000, but the Dutch also became experts in land reclamation, draining the marshlands by digging canals and regulating the flow of water with networks of sluices and reservoirs. Windmills, powering rotary iron scoops, made it possible to lift water out of the low-lying fields and over the dykes into reservoirs that were emptied into the rivers at low tide. The orderly rectangular fields between the waterways, known as polders, were used as pasture and for growing crops in the fertile, peaty soil. Polders now make up approximately 60 percent of the country—there is an old saying that "God created the world, but the Dutch created the Netherlands."

Left: Flat fields, canals, windmills, and large skies create the quintessential Dutch landscape. The group of historic windmills at Kinderdijk is the largest surviving in the Netherlands.

Decline of wind power In the eighteenth century thousands of windmills dotted the Dutch landscape, but in the age of steam they were gradually replaced. The graceful Kinderdijk mills were erected in 1738–40, and are among the few survivors of over 150 mills in the Alblasserwaard area, which battled to control water levels between the Lek, Noord, and Merwede rivers for over a century until steam pumps were installed in 1868.

The windmills of Kinderdijk are a serene and beautiful monument to an old technology, but one that is now becoming relevant again as we face a post-oil world. Tellingly, they were brought back into regular use during World War II, when there was no diesel available to power the pumps, and they are still maintained in working order in case the modern equipment breaks down.

TIME LINE

11th century
Beginning of the reclamation of land for agricultural use in the peat region of Holland and Utrecht.

1277
Establishment of central administration for maintenance of dykes in Holland.

1360s
Polders of Alblasserwaard created by digging canals to drain into River Lek.

1726
Serious floods prompt decision to build drainage mills to pump water to elevated reservoirs controlled by sluices.

1868
Steam-powered pumping stations installed to replace windmills.

1997
Kinderdijk mills inscribed on UNESCO list of World Heritage Sites.

Below left: The windmills at Kinderdijk are known as "ground sailers" because their huge vanes come within 12 in/30 cm of the ground as they turn.

Below: The bonnet windmill was a Dutch innovation: it meant that only the small top cap had to be turned to face the wind, rather than the whole millhouse.

GERMANY, BERLIN

The Reichstag

AFTER IT WAS SET ON FIRE IN 1933, THE RUINED REICHSTAG BUILDING BECAME AN EMBLEM OF THE DESTRUCTION OF DEMOCRACY, BUT ITS RECONSTRUCTION HAS TURNED IT INTO A NEW SYMBOL OF TRANSPARENCY, WITH LIGHT STREAMING IN THROUGH ITS ICONIC GLASS CUPOLA TO ILLUMINATE THE ASSEMBLY HALL BELOW.

As an institution, the Reichstag originated as the assembly of the imperial estates that made up the Holy Roman Empire, but in the nineteenth century the name was adopted by the parliament of the new German Empire under Wilhelm I. It had its inaugural meeting in 1871 in Berlin, where it decided that its new seat should be built. Ten years of delay followed while Bismarck, the emperor, and the Reichstag members debated how to go about this.

Eventually the architect Paul Wallot was chosen by competition, and the new building was completed in 1894. Though styled as a neo-Renaissance palace, it incorporated some modern engineering, notably in its large central steel and glass cupola. The four towers at the corners were said to represent the four constituent kingdoms of the new empire: Prussia, Württemberg, Bavaria, and Saxony.

Symbolic ruin The building survived Germany's transition from empire to republic, proclaimed from one of its balconies in 1918, but not the fateful arson attack of February 1933, when it was gutted in circumstances that have never been fully explained. The Nazis claimed the fire to be the work of communist plotters and used it to justify the suspension of civil liberties, beginning the trail of events that established Hitler's dictatorship.

TIME LINE

1871
Foundation of German Empire.

1884–94
Construction of building.

November 9, 1918
German Republic proclaimed from Reichstag balcony.

February 1933
Reichstag fire.

1961–89
Berlin Wall.

October 1990
Reunification of Germany and inaugural sitting of Bundestag in Reichstag.

1991
Foster + Partners commissioned to reconstruct building.

June–July 1995
Christo and Jeanne-Claude's *Wrapped Reichstag: a Project for Berlin*, initiated in 1971. Start of rebuilding.

1999
First meeting of Bundestag in new plenary chamber.

Opposite: The focal point of the restored building is the glass dome, which, though uncompromisingly modern, nods to the original nineteenth-century cupola.

Right: The inscription "Dem Deutschen Volke" ("To the German People") was added in 1916, in letters cast in bronze from French cannons seized at Leipzig in 1813.

Under National Socialist rule the Reichstag was left ruinous and unused, but it was fiercely defended by German forces (hundreds of whom died inside) when it became a target for Red Army troops during the Battle of Berlin in 1945. For the Russians, the capture of this crumbling but iconic building encapsulated their triumph over Hitler, despite the fact that the Nazi regime had never used the Reichstag, despising the democratic principles it represented. Yevgeny Khaldei's photograph of a Soviet soldier on the Reichstag roof, raising the Red Flag above the ruined, smoking city, is one of the most famous images of World War II.

The Cold War After the war, with the Bundestag sitting in the new West German capital, Bonn, the Reichstag building was without a function. The cupola had to be demolished in 1954, but the remainder was retained and given a new, bland interior in the 1960s; it was used for meetings, exhibitions, and the occasional concert. Standing virtually on the border between East and West, it was now emblematic of the country's division, particularly after 1961, when the Berlin Wall was erected immediately behind it.

Reconstruction The wall fell in November 1989, and the reunification of Germany meant that the Bundestag would now represent the whole country. It chose to reinstate Berlin as the capital and to return to the old building. But the Reichstag had to be transformed for its new purpose. Another architectural competition was held and the winner was Norman Foster, who wrote: "The most straightforward approach would

Below: Mirrored panels on the central cone reflect natural light down into the debating chamber.

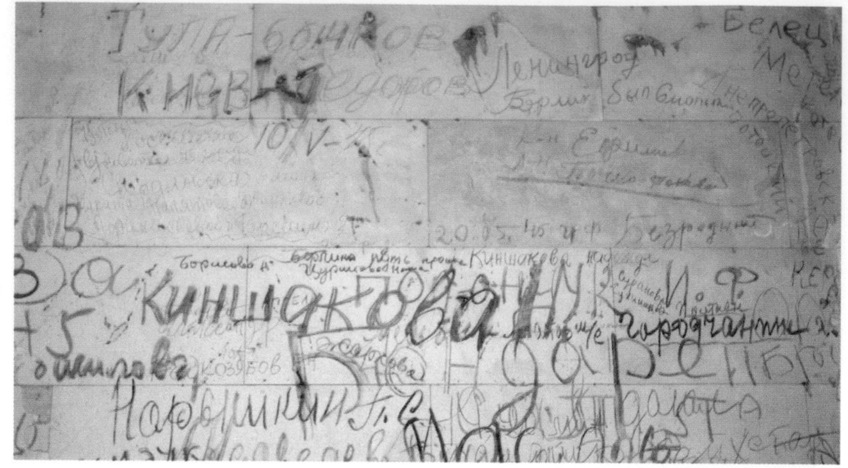

Left: Raw and direct Red Army messages scrawled with charred wood in 1945 have been left on some of the walls as silent testimony to the building's history.

Below left: For *Wrapped Reichstag*, by Christo and Jeanne-Claude, the building was enveloped in silver fabric and blue rope for two weeks in 1995.

have been to gut the Reichstag and to insert a modern building in the place of the odd mix of late nineteenth century and the 1960s fabric which then existed. Yet this would have been in a sense too easy. We believed that history could not simply be swept away."

Among the history that was retained was Russian graffiti dating from 1945, which builders in the 1960s had covered with drywall because it was easier than cleaning the walls. Foster also returned to the original concept of the central cupola, and his modern version has become the signature of the twenty-first-century Reichstag and a new landmark for Berlin.

The transformation began with what seemed like a magician's trick: the disappearance of the entire building under draped fabric for *Wrapped Reichstag*, an environmental work of art by Christo and Jeanne-Claude. As soon as the wrappings came off, work began to create the new building within the shell of the old.

Transparency and functionality The old Reichstag witnessed the dismantling of democracy: the new version is all about transparency. The plenary chamber is

Right: Part of the Reichstag is open to the public, and a spiral walkway winds around the glass dome.

the center of the building, but it's overlooked by the vast glass cupola, where the public can wander around the helical ramp that winds up to the very top, looking out at the view of the city or down (significantly) on their elected representatives. In the center, a mirrored cone reflects daylight down into the chamber. This is the "light sculptor," which sets the green tone of the building by reducing the need for artificial light. It's also a funnel: it extracts waste air but on the way it recovers its heat—so even if the debate below is just a lot of hot air, it's at least helping to warm the offices.

Memorials As well as the Soviet graffiti there are other flashes of history, such as a section of the tunnel that may have been the access route for the fire setter in 1933. In the basement, a room lined with shelves stacked with rusty boxes is Christian Boltanski's *Archive of German Members of Parliament*, commemorating all the elected members from 1919 to 1999: boxes marked with a black stripe denote those who were murdered, and a single black box represents the period from 1933–45, when there was no parliament.

FACT FILE

Architects
Paul Wallot 1884–94, reconstruction Foster + Partners, 1995–99.

Floor area
13,000 sq yd/11,000 sq m.

Height
177 ft/54 m.

Height of cupola from roof terrace
79 ft/24 m.

Diameter of cupola
131 ft/40 m.

Area of glass in cupola
3,560 sq yd/3,000 sq m.

Eagle in plenary chamber
22 x 28 ft/6.8 x 8.5 m, made of nearly 2.5 tons of aluminum.

Left: For Foster's reconstruction, the building was almost entirely gutted, leaving only the outer walls intact.

GERMANY, BERLIN

Brandenburg Gate

BERLIN'S MOST FAMOUS MONUMENT WAS BUILT IN THE NAME OF PEACE BUT CAME TO SIGNIFY VICTORY. IN THE DARKEST PART OF THE CITY'S HISTORY, THE BRANDENBURG GATE WAS AN UNREACHABLE SYMBOL OF DIVISION; NOW IT'S OPEN TO ALL AND HAS TURNED INTO AN ICON OF UNITY.

In 1701 the small walled city of Berlin became capital of the new kingdom of Prussia, and began to grow in both status and size. A new wall was built around it in the 1730s to control the entry of (and charge duty on) incoming goods, with gates on each of 18 roads. The Brandenburg Gate is the only one that still exists today.

It stood at the end of the avenue of linden trees that was planted to shelter the Elector of Brandenburg's route to his palace. This shady boulevard—Unter den Linden—became the grandest street in Berlin when Frederick the Great set about turning his capital into an Enlightenment city, and shortly after his death the gate was given a classical makeover in keeping with its formal processional setting.

The design was based on the ancient Propylaia in Athens, with 12 monumental Doric columns framing the openings. Colonnaded pavilions replaced the old guard houses on each side. On top, Johann Gottfried Schadow's quadriga was driven by Irene, goddess of peace—the Prussians could afford to honor peace after all their military successes. But in 1806 they were defeated by Napoleon, who carried the quadriga off to Paris. When the Prussians entered Paris after Napoleon's fall, they found the sculpture still in its packing cases and

TIME LINE

1791
Gate built to a design by Carl Gotthard Langhans.

1793
Bronze quadriga installed.

1806
Quadriga captured by Napoleonic troops; returned in 1814.

1933
National Socialists march through gate to signal rise to power.

1958
Wartime damage repaired in collaboration between East and West Berlin.

1961–89
Berlin Wall.

1990
Reunification of Germany.

Left: The gate's central section is based on the Athens Propylaia.

Below: After World War II the gate was the only building left standing around Pariser Platz.

Right: Driving her quadriga, or four-horsed chariot, Victoria holds a staff bearing the Iron Cross surmounted by the Prussian eagle.

Below right: Crowds gather by the Brandenburg Gate on November 10, 1989, to witness the dismantling of the Berlin Wall.

brought it back to Berlin. The goddess became Victoria, and was given the Iron Cross of Prussia to hold.

The Wall The gate became world famous in 1961 as a symbol of the Cold War when the Berlin Wall curved around it, leaving it marooned in no man's land. For nearly 30 years no one passed through, and on his 1963 visit John F. Kennedy couldn't even look through, as the East hung red banners across the openings. But in the 1980s the political landscape began to change. Standing in front of the gate on June 12, 1987, Ronald Reagan issued a challenge to the eastern bloc—"Mr. Gorbachev, open this gate. Mr. Gorbachev, tear down this wall!"—and in 1989 the wall came peacefully down.

Engineers worked through the night to open the checkpoints so that on December 22 Helmut Kohl could walk through into East Berlin, followed by thousands of flag-waving, champagne-cork-popping Berliners. Now restored and floodlit, the gate presides over elegant Pariser Platz and is once more at the heart of Berlin's grandest landscape, the emblem of the new Germany.

GERMANY, COLOGNE

Cologne Cathedral

NORTHERN EUROPE'S LARGEST GOTHIC CHURCH DRAWS IN EVERY MODERN VISITOR TO COLOGNE, JUST AS IT DID IN THE THIRTEENTH CENTURY, WHEN IT WAS CONCEIVED AS A PILGRIMAGE CENTER TO HOUSE THE CITY'S GREATEST TREASURES: THE RELICS OF THE THREE KINGS—THE VERY FIRST CHRISTIAN PILGRIMS.

Exotic and magnificent, the Magi had a long, arduous journey to worship the baby Jesus, and their revelatory experience was emulated throughout Christendom. By the Middle Ages, pilgrimages to major shrines were a significant feature of European life, and the possession of an important holy relic could transform the fortunes of a religious foundation, even a whole city. In 1164 Cologne became the resting place of just such a prize, when the remains of the Three Kings themselves arrived in its old cathedral, having been captured in Milan by Frederick Barbarossa.

Shrine of the Magi A fabulous golden reliquary was commissioned, encrusted with bejeweled figures of prophets and apostles, and three gold crowns were placed on the skulls. By 1225 the shrine was ready. But it was apparent that Cologne's basilica would not be adequate to house it. Dating from 818 and enlarged over the centuries, the old cathedral stood on the site of a Roman house where the city's earliest Christian community had worshipped in the fourth century, but in 1248 it was partly demolished and the foundation stone was laid for a completely new Gothic cathedral.

Six centuries of building The choir at the east end went up first, within a forest of intricate pinnacles and

TIME LINE

873
Old cathedral completed.

1164
Archbishop Rainald of Dassel brings relics of the Three Kings to Cologne.

1248
Old cathedral destroyed by fire during demolition; new cathedral founded, with plan attributed to Gerhard von Rile.

1322
Choir consecrated, and Three Kings reliquary installed in it.

1517
Reformation in Germany triggered by Luther's 95 Theses.

1842
New foundation stone laid to restart building.

1880
Opening ceremony attended by Emperor Wilhelm I.

Right: The magnificent golden shrine of the Three Kings, 7 ft/2.2 m long, is the largest reliquary in the Western world.

Right: One of the cathedral's greatest treasures is the Gero Cross, from before 976.

Left: The cathedral, together with the nearby Romanesque church of Great St Martin, towers over the old town.

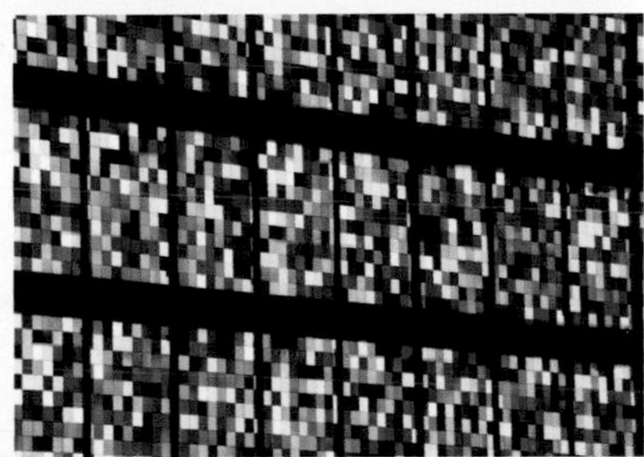

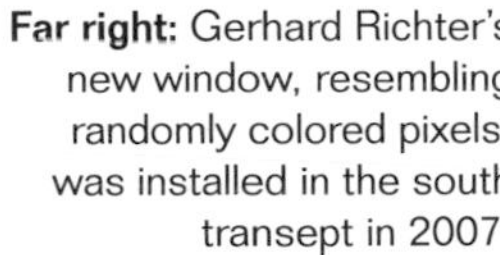

Far right: Gerhard Richter's new window, resembling randomly colored pixels, was installed in the south transept in 2007.

buttresses; it was consecrated in 1322 and sealed off by a temporary wall so that it could be used while work continued on the west end. But the pace of building slowed, then ground to a halt after the Reformation. Parts of the building fell into disrepair and it was even used as a barn when French Revolutionary forces seized Cologne in 1794. It took the Gothic revival of the nineteenth century to make people notice the cathedral's greatness and raise funds to complete it: by then the fifteenth-century wooden crane that had stood on the half-built south tower for 400 years had become a city landmark in itself. It was removed in 1868, and when the two towers were done the great building was finally complete.

For a few years, until it lost the record to the Washington Monument, the cathedral was the world's tallest building. Its openwork spires rise to 515 ft/157 m; inside, the nave seems impossibly lofty. The discovery of the original medieval plans meant that despite taking over 600 years, the whole building remains faithful to its Gothic conception. On completion in 1880 it was celebrated as a national as much as a religious monument, and it still dominates the skyline of Cologne.

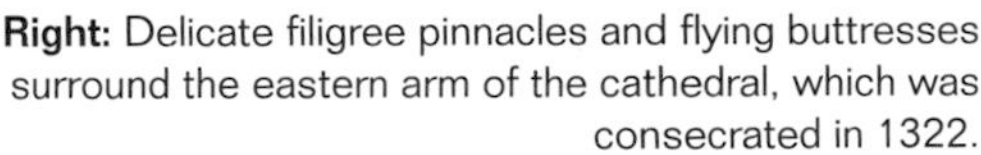

Right: Delicate filigree pinnacles and flying buttresses surround the eastern arm of the cathedral, which was consecrated in 1322.

GERMANY, RHINE VALLEY

Rock of Loreley

WHEN SAILORS COME TO GRIEF IN TREACHEROUS WATERS, THEY INVARIABLY BLAME A WOMAN. WATER NYMPHS AND MERMAIDS STARTED LURING MARINERS TO THEIR DOOM AS SOON AS THERE WERE BOATS TO SINK, AND A LANDMARK ROCK ON THE RHINE INEVITABLY ACQUIRED A BEAUTIFUL BUT DANGEROUS SIREN OF ITS OWN.

The Loreley rock certainly looks daunting. This sheer-sided 433-ft/132-m slate peak forces a bend in the river, which winds around it narrow and deep, creating fast currents that require concentration and skill to negotiate. Nowadays, a protective mole around the harbor of St Goar acts as a warning, and a road around the foot of the rock makes its downward plunge to the river seem less extreme to the onlooker, but the passage is still perilous. Skippers need a special license to take their boats along this stretch of the river, or must take aboard a river pilot to steer them through.

Murmuring voices The rock stands on the east bank of the Rhine near the town of Sankt Goarshausen, in an area replete with history and legend. There are several theories about the meaning of the name "Loreley": it's said to come from a local dialect word *lureln* ("murmur" or "hum") and the Celtic *ley* ("rock"), but it may be connected with lurking, or luring, or merchants, or elves and fairies. (The rock really did murmur once: the sound was said to come from a waterfall, but the effect seems to have been lost when a rail tunnel was cut through it.)

Creating a myth According to the medieval minnesingers, the "Lurlenburg" was the hiding place of the fabled treasure of the Nibelungs. But the story that

Above: Downstream from Burg Katz, amid striking scenery, the Rhine narrows and turns sharp left as it negotiates the intransigent Loreley rock on the inside of the bend.

Top and middle right: Over 2,000 years of settlement along the Rhine, the cliff at the river's narrowest and deepest point has accrued a cultural significance focused on the mythical Loreley.

Right: Portrayed on countless souvenirs, in this case with a charming disregard for scale, the 19th-century Loreley acquired the musical skills and fatal allure of a siren.

TIME LINE

Mid-9th century
"Mons Lurlaberch" documented in records of Fulda Monastery.

1811
Brentano's *Rhine Fairy Tales* include the story of Loreley.

1823
Publication of Heine's "Die Lorelei."

1835
First publication of Baedeker's *Rhinereise.*

2002
Upper Middle Rhine Valley inscribed on UNESCO World Heritage List.

defines the Loreley rock today is that of the fair-haired girl who, abandoned by her lover, throws herself from the rock in despair and is transformed into a siren whose beauty and song lure sailors to their death. Though it sounds like authentic folklore it actually has its roots in the fervid nineteenth-century Romanticism that this dramatic landscape inspired.

The beautiful temptress made her first appearance in "Lore Lay," a ballad written in 1801 by Clemens Brentano, but when Heinrich Heine turned the story into a lyrical poem in 1822 she achieved real fame. In Brentano's narrative, which has a Christian slant, the local bishop absolves the bewitched woman and sends three knights to escort her to a nunnery, but in despair at her predicament she throws herself from the rock, taking the three knights to their deaths with her. Heine's version dispenses with all but the archetypal image: the siren combing her blonde hair as she sings, while a distracted boatman is sucked beneath the water.

The poem was set to a simple folklike tune by Friedrich Silcher, and the Loreley entered the realm of "tradition." Every child learned her song, and tourists—clutching their newly published Baedeker guides—sang it as they passed the rock on their Rhine cruises. Today the tune hangs in the air around the Loreley Visitor Center, the Loreley Open Air Theater, the Loreley Restaurant, and other enterprises eager to benefit from the lady's allure.

GERMANY, BAVARIA

Neuschwanstein Castle

IT WAS THE MOST AMBITIOUS CREATION OF A RECLUSIVE KING LOST IN ROMANTIC DREAMS OF MEDIEVAL CHIVALRY, BUT HE COULD NOT COMPLETE IT AND HARDLY LIVED IN IT. IN THE TWENTIETH CENTURY ITS CRAGGY SETTING AND SOARING TURRETS BECAME THE INSPIRATION FOR THE FANTASY CASTLES OF WALT DISNEY.

As a child, Ludwig II of Bavaria had been at his happiest while staying in the mountains at Hohenschwangau, the medieval castle restored by his father. Identifying with the old legend of the Swan Knight Lohengrin, he became obsessed with Wagner's opera on the subject: after seeing a performance in 1861, he determined to become Wagner's patron and build an opera house worthy of him. As soon as the 18-year-old Ludwig became king, he welcomed Wagner to Munich to begin the new project, but his ministers, fearing Wagner's influence on the king, banished the composer to Switzerland. Ludwig felt he had lost his greatest friend. Meanwhile, Bavaria was drawn into war between Austria and Prussia, losing its independence to the victorious Prussia, and Ludwig's forthcoming marriage to his cousin Sophie was called off. In despair, Ludwig retreated to the mountains and his dreams of castle-building. By 1869, when Prussia conscripted Bavaria's army into the Franco–Prussian war, Ludwig had lost all connection with public life and his duties as king.

Medieval fantasy Neuschwanstein is a synthesis of Ludwig's romantic vision of kingship, his childhood experience of Hohenschwangau, and his obsession with Wagner. Murals of the legends of Lohengrin, Tannhauser,

TIME LINE

1845
Birth of Ludwig in Nymphenburg Castle.

1864
Ludwig becomes king of Bavaria and meets Wagner.

1868
The medieval castle ruins on the site are demolished to prepare for the new building.

1886
Ludwig dies by drowning in mysterious circumstances.

Right: The castellated Gatehouse was the first part of the project to be completed, and Ludwig lodged there from 1873, supervising every detail of the building.

Left: Designed to look picturesque from every angle, the castle follows the contours of the cliff top.

Below: A swan tows the boat carrying the grail knight Lohengrin in the mural in Ludwig's drawing room.

and Parsifal cover the interior walls, and the decoration mingles Byzantine, Romanesque, and Gothic elements. However, the building used modern materials and cutting-edge technology, including flushing lavatories and central heating. Ludwig may have been eccentric but he wanted to be comfortable.

Sited on a vertiginous cliff top overlooking the Pöllat Gorge, the asymmetric plan sought to imitate a medieval castle with centuries of later additions, including elements such as the "Knights' House" and the "Bower." The vast Throne Hall and the Hall of the Singers were elaborate celebrations of kingship, chivalry, and courtly love. The whole conceit is a stage set for Ludwig's private fantasy, based on the drawings of the designer Christian Jank, who had worked on the scenery for *Lohengrin*.

Unrealized ambitions It was Ludwig's dearest wish that Wagner would visit the castle, but by 1884, when the king finally moved into the still unfinished building, the composer was dead. In the end only about 15 of the projected 200 rooms were completed. By 1886 the costs of this and Ludwig's other building projects had all but bankrupted him and he was threatening suicide; the Bavarian government refused his demands for money and voted to depose him. He was taken from Neuschwanstein under the care of a psychiatrist; two days later both were found drowned.

GERMANY, DRESDEN

Frauenkirche

THE BAROQUE "STONE BELL" CROWNING DRESDEN'S FRAUENKIRCHE WAS A PRINCIPLE CITY LANDMARK FOR TWO HUNDRED YEARS. AFTER ITS DESTRUCTION, ITS TUMBLED, BLACKENED STONES BECAME A POIGNANT WAR MEMORIAL, AND NOW THEY HAVE A NEW LIFE IN THE WALLS OF THE REBUILT CHURCH.

At the beginning of the eighteenth century Augustus the Strong, Elector of Saxony, converted to Catholicism in order to become king of Poland, and commissioned the opulent Hofkirche in Dresden, where his heart was eventually buried. Dresden, however, was a staunchly Protestant place, and its citizens were meanwhile erecting their own more magnificent church—the unforgettable Frauenkirche.

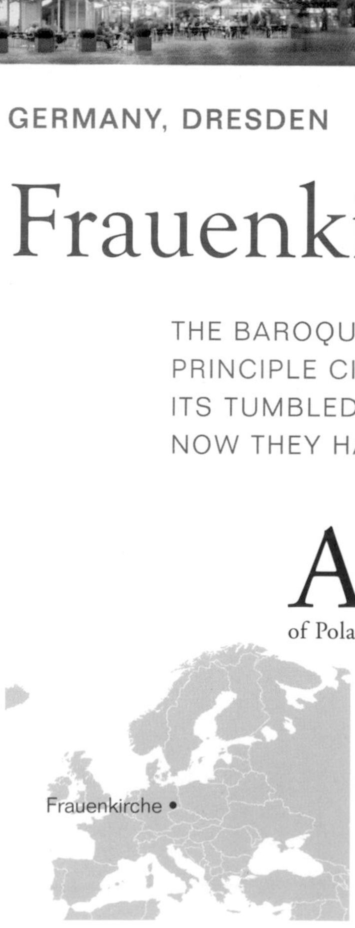

Bähr's church The medieval Church of Our Lady, founded in the eleventh century, had fallen into disrepair, and presented an opportunity to rebuild in a completely new style, in sympathy with Lutheran doctrine. The local architect and master carpenter George Bähr was commissioned to design it, and his Baroque masterpiece has been compared to St Paul's in London and St Peter's in Rome. His octagonal plan, with tiers of semicircular galleries beneath a central dome, put the altar, pulpit, and font right in the center of the church, in full view of the whole congregation.

The comparatively small footprint of the church puts the emphasis on its vertical lines, with a tower at each corner and, of course, the dome, almost as tall as its width, with a curving base that gives it the appearance of a bell. Built entirely of stone and crowned with a lantern,

TIME LINE

11th century
Foundation of Frauenkirche, outside city walls.

1480s
Church, by now absorbed by the city, rebuilt in Gothic style.

1559
Becomes Lutheran foundation following Reformation.

1722–43
New church designed and built by George Bähr.

February 13–15, 1945
Fire-bombing of Dresden; church collapses.

1990
Launch of rebuilding fund appeal.

1996
Consecration of new crypt.

October 30, 2005
Consecration of church following completion.

Opposite: Stones of the old building were left in their blackened state and where possible returned to their original places in the walls.

Right: Barack Obama and Angela Merkel stand in front of the altar, which was reconstructed mainly from original materials, in 2009.

it has no internal supports and was initially thought to be unstable; nevertheless it survived, the jewel of the Dresden skyline, until February 1945.

Destruction The firestorm created by the Anglo-American bombing of Dresden created temperatures of over 1,800°F/1,000°C around the church. The pillars exploded and the dome collapsed. Just a few parts of the altar and chancel remained standing and, with the piles of fire-blackened stones, they were left on the site for the next 45 years, a stark memorial to the lost city and the hundreds of thousands who died in the inferno.

Rebuilding After Reunification a grass-roots movement to restore the church gathered momentum, and the fund-raising became an international effort. The architect Eberhard Burger followed Bähr's original plans faithfully, except for a modern support system for the dome, and nearly 4,000 of the old stones were reused. As a crowning gesture of reconciliation, the golden cross on the new lantern was a gift from Britain, made by the son of a pilot who had taken part in the Dresden raid.

Below: The five encircling galleries give the whole congregation a good view of the altar, pulpit, and font.

DENMARK

Jelling Stones

TWO IMPRESSIVE RUNE STONES STANDING OUTSIDE THE DOOR OF JELLING CHURCH RECORD THE TENTH-CENTURY DEEDS OF TWO KINGS AT THE BEGINNING OF DENMARK'S NATIONAL HISTORY. THEY MARK THE MOMENT WHEN THE COUNTRY'S PAGAN VIKING CULTURE GAVE WAY TO THE CHRISTIAN ERA.

A few thousand people live in the peaceful little town of Jelling in southern Denmark; in the center there are some stores, a couple of banks, a library, and a café. And then there are two huge tenth-century burial mounds and, between them, two massive stones carved with runes, one of which is fondly described as "the birth certificate of Denmark." This is one of the country's most important historical sites.

The two stones stand outside the door of Jelling Church, a white-painted stone building dating from around 1100, surrounded by a neat and pretty graveyard full of plots edged with perfectly clipped hedges. It is as if two weatherbeaten and rather unruly Viking warriors had turned up to a church tea party. But the stones were here first.

Royal history Jelling was the seat of King Gorm the Old, whose redoubtable Queen Thyre was credited with defending Denmark against the invading Germans. When she died, Gorm erected the smaller of the two stones as a memorial to her, as is explained simply and affectionately in the runes carved on it:

> King Gorm made this monument in memory of his wife Thyre, Denmark's adornment.

He may have raised the burial mounds at the same time.

TIME LINE

ca. 936–958
Reign of Gorm the Old.

958–985/6
Reign of Harald Bluetooth.

ca. 960
Christianity introduced into Denmark by Harald; wooden church built at Jelling.

ca. 1630
Gorm's stone moved from an unknown location to stand beside Harald's.

1820
First excavation of burial mounds.

1994
Mounds, stones, and church inscribed on UNESCO World Heritage List.

2008–10
Glass cases, designed to protect stones from further weathering, under consideration by Jelling Church Council.

Opposite: The larger pyramid-shaped monument is the biggest surviving rune stone in Scandinavia, and still stands in its original location.

Right: The Crucifixion scene on Harald Bluetooth's stone is the earliest depiction of Christ in the Nordic world. The design would originally have been brightly colored.

Gorm's son Harald Bluetooth was responsible for the larger stone, which is far more ambitious. Elaborately illustrated, it makes momentous claims for Harald himself as well as remembering his parents:

> King Harald commanded this monument to be made
> in memory of his father Gorm and his mother Thyre.
> It was this Harald who won the whole of Denmark and
> Norway and made the Danes Christian.

The end of paganism Rune stones are the only written texts to survive from the Viking period. Harald's impressive three-sided stone is considered a key to Denmark's early history. It stands on its original spot, midway between the two burial mounds, while Gorm's stone has been moved to join it. The two pictorial sides encapsulate the tenth-century transition from pagan to Christian beliefs: both are carved in the same interlaced style, but while one depicts the "beast of Jelling" (a lion entwined with a serpent), the other shows the Crucifixion, and is the earliest depiction of Christ in Scandinavia.

Above: Harald's large stone stands midway between the two flat-topped burial mounds, which were both made from stacked turf.

Right: The twelfth-century stone church stands on the site of Harald Bluetooth's wooden building, under which he buried his father.

DENMARK, COPENHAGEN

The Little Mermaid

SHE REALLY IS LITTLE, AND MANY VISITORS TO COPENHAGEN ARE JUST A BIT DISAPPOINTED WHEN THEY SEE HER FOR THE FIRST TIME. BUT THE MERMAID, LOOKING RATHER CHILLY ON HER UNCOMFORTABLE PILE OF ROCKS, CARRIES A HEAVY WEIGHT OF SYMBOLISM ON HER SLENDER SHOULDERS.

Now the official symbol of Copenhagen, the statue embodies two things central to the city's fame and fortune: the sea and Hans Christian Andersen. Its biggest brewery enters the story too.

The Little Mermaid •

Copenhagen has always looked seaward: its name derives from *køpmannaehafn*—"merchants' haven"—reflecting the importance of its harbor, set on the approach to the Baltic Sea. In the twelfth and thirteenth centuries it grew into a major trading port and a center of the herring fishery, and in the seventeenth century King Christian IV made it his capital and principal naval port.

The fairy tale As for Hans Christian Andersen, he is one of Copenhagen's favorite sons, even though he spent much of his time traveling abroad. Like many of the characters in his stories, he was restless and uneasy, yearning for places and people beyond his reach. He wrote his first collection of *Fairy Tales* while living by the harbor, with boats bobbing outside his windows.

In her poignant story, the Little Mermaid listens as her elder sister tells of swimming to the shore to see the lighted houses and hear the noises of the city, and yearns to visit it herself. The statue the story would inspire is tantalizingly placed just offshore—within earshot of the human sounds the mermaid longed to hear.

TIME LINE

1805
Birth of Hans Christian Andersen.

1837
Publication of first volume of *Fairy Tales Told for Children*, including the story of the Little Mermaid.

1875
Death of Andersen.

1909
Royal Danish Ballet's production of *The Little Mermaid*, with music by Fini Henriques and choreography by Hans Beck.

1913
Statue installed in Copenhagen Harbor.

2010
Statue travels to Shanghai for Expo 2010; replaced by *Mermaid Exchange*, a video installation by Ai Weiwei.

Below: The statue was the star feature of the double-spiral Danish "Welfairytales" pavilion at Expo 2010.

Opposite: Eriksen's figure has only a suggestion of fins around her feet, rather than the classic mermaid's tail.

Right: The ballerina Ellen Price was the inspiration for the wistful mermaid who longs to be mortal.

The model It was not exactly Andersen's story itself but an adaptation that led to the statue being commissioned. In 1909 Carl Jacobsen, founder of the huge Carlsberg brewery and all-round cultural godfather of Copenhagen, watched the Danish ballerina Ellen Price dancing the title role in Fini Henriques' ballet version of the story and rather fell for her. He persuaded her to sit for the sculptor Edvard Eriksen, but when she discovered how public and how nude the intended work was to be she declined to pose for the body, which was modeled on the sculptor's wife.

The icon The mermaid was installed in the harbor on August 23, 1913. Since then, she has been visited by millions, lost her head twice (the first time it had to be remodeled, the second time just reattached), had her hair painted red and been dressed in bras and sweaters. Farther up the Langelinie, the *Genetically Modified Little Mermaid* was installed in 2000 by the artist Bjørn Nørgaard: the work exploits the iconic status of the original to open up debate about GM technology.

In 2010 *The Little Mermaid* left her customary perch for the first time ever, and traveled to Shanghai to be the centerpiece of the Danish pavilion at Expo 2010. While she was away, an original copy cast by Eriksen and belonging to his family deputized for her in the Tivoli Gardens. Each year her birthday is marked by bikini-clad Danish "mermaids" jumping into the harbor around her—one for every year of her age. While in China she turned 97 and was feted by synchronized swimmers and three days of musical celebrations.

SWEDEN, MALMÖ

Turning Torso

MALMÖ'S TWISTING SKYSCRAPER, STANDING ALONE IN A SEA OF LOW-RISE BUILDINGS, IS AN EYE-CATCHING LANDMARK FOR VISITORS APPROACHING THE CITY OVER THE SWEEPING ÖRESUND BRIDGE THAT LINKS SWEDEN WITH DENMARK. IT HAS QUICKLY ASSUMED ICONIC STATUS AS MALMÖ'S MOST FAMOUS BUILDING.

Santiago Calatrava, the Spanish architect and structural engineer who designed the Turning Torso, draws on studies of natural forms in his buildings. The Malmö tower had its roots in Calatrava's *Twisting Torso* sculptures, dating from 1985 and 1991, which explored the torsion of a human figure. He explained: "They describe the spine, or how our body stands up. The spine is made up of vertebrae that are represented in the sculptures in a very elemental way, as a series of cubes … Also quite important is how our spine twists, how it turns around an axis, and how it bends and reaches."

New city landmark Calatrava's sinuous tower, which twists through 90 degrees around its own axis between ground and roof, stands in a new residential development that has regenerated Malmö's old industrial western harbor district. The whole area was the showpiece of the "Bo01" European housing exhibition hosted by the city, which set out to create housing that combined ecological sustainability with high-quality architecture and public spaces. The Turning Torso became the project's exclamation mark.

The tower grew, some said, uncontrollably. Originally conceived at half the height and half the budget, once the idea of commissioning Calatrava took hold, the city

FACT FILE

Height of building
623 ft/190 m.

Average floor area
4,300 sq ft/400 sq m.

Total residential space
157,150 sq ft/14,600 sq m, 147 apartments.

Total office space
45,200 sq ft/4,200sq m.

Right: The tower is clad in aluminum panels, which are curved to follow the twist of the building, while the windows are flat.

Left: The tower looms incongruously but spectacularly over the low-rise housing—more typical of Malmö—around it.

Below: Painters are buffeted by winds at the top as they work on the giant steel tubes that connect the spine with the building.

lost its heart to the iconic design and ended up with one of the tallest residential buildings in Europe.

As a local landmark, it has replaced the fondly regarded Kockums Crane, a huge gantry crane that stood in the nearby shipyard for some 30 years and was last used to lift parts of the foundations for the Öresund Bridge. It was being dismantled as construction began on the Turning Torso, neatly symbolizing the area's transition from industrial to residential use.

Living at an angle The plan of the building is an irregular pentagon and, like the sculptures on which it was based, it is divided into segments, each five floors high. Its "back" is supported by an external steel spine. The tower's profile changes unnervingly depending on the direction from which you view it, seeming to bend, narrow, or swell, and from some angles looking uncomfortably top-heavy. The view from directly below is particularly challenging. And the residents have to get used to some odd angles too: to follow the twisting shape, the windows need to lean slightly—inward on the western side and outward on the eastern side, while their sides are about six degrees off the vertical.

In spite of the odd effects induced by living in a leaning tower, people are eager to have such a prestigious address, complete with high-speed elevators, inhouse gym and sauna, and their own space in the wine cellar.

NORWAY, URNES

Urnes Stave Church

FROM THE FERRY ACROSS THE LUSTRAFJORD FROM SOLVORN IT'S A SHORT, STEEP WALK TO THIS ANCIENT CHURCH, STANDING QUIETLY IN A BEAUTIFUL SETTING OF MEADOWS AND MOUNTAINS. THE SOPHISTICATED CARVING IN THE CHURCH AT URNES HAS GIVEN ITS NAME TO A DISTINCTIVE STYLE OF VIKING ANIMAL ART.

Since it's built entirely from wood, the church can be precisely dated, and the timbers were felled between 1129–31. Two earlier churches had stood on this site since Christianity reached Norway in the tenth century, but the powerful and wealthy family who owned the land called in outstanding craftsmen to construct and decorate their new church.

Stave churches These small wooden churches are Norway's unique contribution to surviving medieval architecture. The country's communities were small and scattered but pious, and each needed its local church. More than a thousand were built, until the Black Death arrived in 1349 and virtually all building stopped for the next two centuries. Just 28 stave churches remain, of which Urnes is the oldest and most elaborately decorated. The form derives its name from its basic structure: a braced frame of staves, or vertical wooden posts, resting on stone foundations to prevent them from rotting.

A seafaring people living in a country clothed in forest, Norwegians had long been specialists in wood and knew how to build weatherproof structures using techniques of shipbuilding. There are no nails in this church, and its flexible frame has withstood nearly a thousand years of storms blowing up from the fjord, while the

TIME LINE

10th century
Arrival of Christianity.

1000–50
First church built; earliest Christian burials.

1050–70
Second church built, with elaborate carved portal.

1130
Stave church built.

1323
Earliest mention of Urnes in written sources.

17th century
Redecoration of interior.

1880
Acquired by Society for the Preservation of Norwegian Ancient Monuments.

1900
Restoration to original form.

Opposite: The setting of Urnes church is spectacular, with forested mountains dropping straight down to the fjord in a quintessentially Norwegian landscape.

Right: This animal has been identified in Christian iconography as a lion beset by dragons, but is definitely descended from the Vikings' mythical menagerie.

steeply pitched roof covered with scalelike shingles ensures that snow slides off. The builders were aware of current architectural styles farther afield, but expressed them in wood instead of stone, as in the Romanesque arches constructed from naturally curved lumber.

Urnes style Urnes is most famous for its carvings, some of which were preserved from the earlier church it replaced. The portal in the north wall may have been the main door of the older building; it is carved with stylized serpentine creatures writhing among delicate foliage and an enigmatic four-legged animal with the slender build of a greyhound.

More interlaced animals decorate the intimate, dim interior—the daylight came only through little portholes at first, until a larger window was cut to give the priest enough light to read by. The church is an astonishing survival from a time when Christianity was still mingled with pagan traditions, and its mysteries were being unfolded in an atmosphere of ritual, flickering candle-light and incense smoke.

Below: Columns with cushion capitals follow Romanesque style but are of wood instead of stone.

Below right: The church is very small, accommodating only about 40 people.

RUSSIA, MOSCOW

Red Square

AT THE HEART OF MOSCOW AND THE HEART OF RUSSIA, RED SQUARE IS AN IMPOSING SPACE FULL OF SYMBOLIC POWER. HISTORY REVERBERATES IN ITS COBBLES, AND THE BUILDINGS AROUND IT REFLECT THE RELIGIOUS AND POLITICAL EVOLUTION OF THE WORLD'S LARGEST COUNTRY.

The square is a vast expanse of dark gray cobbles, bordered on one side by the monumental architecture of the Kremlin Wall Necropolis and Lenin's Tomb, on the other by the pseudo-Venetian palace of the GUM department store—an odd mixture of ideological symbolism and commerce, tempered by the exquisite architecture and spiritual significance of St. Basil's Basilica at the southern end. Red Square is most famously associated with political demonstrations and the triumphalism of the annual Victory Day military parade, but it's also a venue for summer concerts, winter ice skating, New Year celebrations, gawping tourists, and Muscovites eating ice cream in the snow.

Red Square •

What's in a name? The sloping open space, measuring about 5.7 acres/23,100 sq m, dates from 1493, when an edict issued by Ivan III led to the razing of the rickety wooden houses that crowded by the Kremlin wall. Medieval Muscovites therefore called it Pozhar ("burned-out place"), but it was also known as Trinity Square, after the cathedral that was later to be replaced by St. Basil's Basilica.

The English translation of Krasnaya Ploshchad as Red Square is misleading, as *krasnaya* ("red") used primarily to mean "beautiful." However, the association

Left: Beyond St. Basil's Basilica, the high Kremlin walls with their 20 towers enclose four palaces and four cathedral buildings. The Kremlin is the seat of national government and the residence of the President.

Right: The monument to Minin and Pozharsky, who expelled Polish invaders from the Kremlin in 1612, is the square's only statue. It once stood in the center but obstructed parades and was moved in 1936.

Below: The entrance to Lenin's mausoleum is dusted down in readiness for the morning's visitors. His embalmed corpse has lain here on public view since 1924; it is said to require daily attention to preserve it, and his eventual burial is a recurring topic of debate.

with the bloody events of the Revolution, the symbolic color of Communism, and even the red brick walls of the Kremlin all give the name of the square an appropriate depth of meaning.

Kremlin and Lenin's tomb One wall of the Kremlin, Moscow's ancient citadel and the seat of government since the beginning of the Soviet era, forms the western side of the square. Spasskaya Tower, over the processional entrance to the Kremlin from Red Square, dates from 1491. The Kremlin Clock on the tower is Moscow's equivalent of the big ball drop at Times Square—the symbolic heart of New Year's Eve celebrations.

Between the Spasskaya and Nikolskaya towers, both topped with Soviet red stars since the 1930s, is the Necropolis, where niches in the wall contain the funerary urns of revolutionary heroes and Soviet leaders. Burials here began after the October Revolution in 1917, when nearly 240 pro-Bolshevik soldiers killed during the storming of the Kremlin were interred in a mass grave,

Left: GUM's facade is illuminated for the New Year and Christmas festivities, and a large ice skating rink is set up in the square in front of the store.

Below left: Lenin's granite mausoleum, designed by the Constructivist architect Alexey Shchusev, was erected against the wall of the Kremlin in 1930.

more or less where they had fallen. Konstantin Chernenko was the last person to be buried here, in 1985.

Occupying center stage is the most famous tomb of all, Lenin's Mausoleum, a severe Constructivist pyramid of granite and labradorite. It was erected in 1930 to replace the original wooden structure when it became clear that the long line of pilgrims wanting to visit Lenin's embalmed body wasn't getting any shorter. People still visit every morning to gaze into his bullet-proof glass coffin.

St. Basil's Cathedral The basilica of St. Basil is the square's most dazzlingly picturesque building, quintessentially Russian yet entirely unique. It was built by order of Ivan the Terrible to celebrate the capture of Kazan and Astrakhan in 1552. The architect, Ivan Barma, known as Postnik, is said to have been blinded to prevent him from repeating such a beautiful design, though this is a legend that has also attached itself to other spectacular buildings, and Postnik did in fact work on a later cathedral. The interior is a maze of dark steps and passages connecting eight small chapels, each under

TIME LINE

1156
Triangular wooden fortifications built on Borovitsky Hill.

1328
Moscow becomes seat of Metropolitan of Rus.

1485–95
Construction of new Kremlin walls and towers.

1493
Edict forbids building between Kremlin and merchant quarter.

1560
Consecration of St. Basil's Cathedral.

1703
Capital moves from Moscow to St. Petersburg.

1918
Kremlin becomes seat of Soviet government.

1941
Soviet troops parade in Red Square before successfully defending Moscow against Nazi forces.

2010
Troops from USA, Britain, and France take part in Red Square parade.

Below: Flanked by the palace frontage of GUM to the east and the Kremlin to the west, the ornate and colorful St. Basil's Cathedral marks the center of the city of Moscow.

Right: The State Historical Museum, a Russian Revival building that echoes the appearance of the Kremlin walls and towers, was founded in 1872 and houses a huge collection.

its own distinctive onion dome, clustered in a star shape around the central sanctuary, which is topped by a spire.

Stalin ordered Red Square to be cleared of churches in 1936. St. Basil's escaped destruction, but Kazan Cathedral, its companion at the other end of the square near the State Historical Museum, was demolished. It was rebuilt in the 1990s.

GUM Now a glitzy shopping mall, GUM was built in 1893 on palatial lines in Russian Revival style. Originally known as the Upper Trading Stalls, in the Soviet era its initials (pronounced "goom") stood for *Gosudarstvennyi Universalnyi Magazin* (State Department Store), but as a model of Russia's new devotion to private enterprise its name has been discreetly changed to Main (*Glavnyi*) Department Store, so that the famous abbreviation can still apply.

The elegant arcaded interior has three levels, linked by bridges and under the cover of a curving glass roof. Most visitors sensibly regard it as an exhibition of impossibly expensive bling rather than as a place where they can actually shop.

CZECH REPUBLIC

Prague Astronomical Clock

IT'S SAID THAT THE MAKER OF THIS GREAT TIMEPIECE WAS BLINDED ONCE HIS WORK WAS DONE SO THAT HE WOULD NEVER BE ABLE TO PRODUCE ANOTHER LIKE IT FOR A RIVAL CITY. PRAGUE'S 600-YEAR-OLD CLOCK IS STILL A MATHEMATICAL WONDER AND HAS EVEN BEEN TURNED INTO AN IPHONE APP.

To celebrate its 600th anniversary in 2010, a three-dimensional light show played over the tower and faces of the Prague Orloj, with high-definition animations showing events in its history. Twenty-first century innovation was honoring the cutting-edge technology of the early fifteenth century, but Prague's beautiful astronomical clock doesn't really need newfangled bells and whistles to give it crowd appeal. It is still the most popular attraction in the city's Old Town Square.

Although it dates from a period of political turmoil in Prague, the clock is a miraculous legacy from the medieval city's golden era, when Holy Roman Emperor Charles IV made it his capital. Prague became the empire's economic and cultural center, and the foundation of Charles University in 1348 turned it into a hub of European learning. Charles also oversaw a vast expansion of the city, but the clock is in the oldest part, overlooking the tenth-century marketplace from the wall of the Old Town Hall, a building erected by Charles's father, John of Luxembourg.

Medieval worldview The clock and astronomical dial—in effect an astrolabe—was made in 1410. It was the work of the clockmaker Mikuláš of Kadaň, based on the calculations of Jan Šindel, professor of math and

TIME LINE

1410
Clock and astronomical dial installed in Old Town Hall.

1490
Calendar dial and Gothic sculptures added.

17th century
Animated figures added beside clock face.

1866
Procession of Apostles added after major repairs.

May 8, 1945
Prague Uprising: German incendiary bombs set fire to Old Town Hall, burning Apostles and calendar.

1948
Clock is restarted after repairs and restoration of figures.

Opposite: Three independent coaxial wheels in the movement control the sun's pointer, the pointer with the moon, which also indicates its phases, and the eccentric zodiac dial.

Right: The clock is on Prague's Old Town Square, an ancient space ringed by an eclectic mix of architecture but dominated by the Gothic church of Our Lady before Tyn.

astronomy at the university. The sun and moon circle around the still earth in the center of the dial, while the sun also moves around the zodiac and the moon indicates its phases. The sun and the golden hand on its arm point to the time in various ways: on a 24-hour dial, as "Bohemian" or "Italian time" (which measures the hours before sunset) and as a period of daylight divided into 12 "unequal hours"—longer in summer, shorter in winter.

Automata Beneath the clock is a calendar flanked by four carved figures: a chronicler, an angel, an astronomer, and a philosopher. But the figures the crowds gather every day to see are the moving ones, which go into action on each hour.

Four seedy seventeenth-century characters stand beside the clock: Vanity admiring his reflection, a miser clutching his bag of gold, a turbaned Turk, and skeletal Death, who rings his bell and eyes his hourglass. Above them the 12 Apostles, added in the 1860s, peer out as they shimmy past their two doorways, and finally a golden cockerel crows to signal the end of the show.

Right: The Apostles process past their little doorways at the top of the clock.

Below: The calendar dial illustrates the months and lists the saint for each day.

AUSTRIA, VIENNA

Schönbrunn Palace

UNESCO CITES THE SCHÖNBRUNN PALACE AS "A REMARKABLE BAROQUE ENSEMBLE AND A PERFECT EXAMPLE OF GESAMTKUNSTWERK." BAROQUE ARCHITECTURE IS ORDERLY, SYMMETRICAL, DRAMATIC, EXUBERANT, IMMODEST; "GESAMTKUNSTWERK" DESCRIBES THE FUSION OF MANY ART FORMS INTO A COHERENT WHOLE.

The mid-eighteenth century Austrian extravaganza is the last word in aristocratic Europeanism, and the buildings and gardens in their totality thus check all the Baroque and *Gesamtkunstwerk* boxes. The palace interior is a shining riot of gilt and glass, polished walnut paneling and gold stucco, white marble and bright wallpaper, red velvet and fine lace. Artistic and craft eclecticism extend through unparalleled examples of embroidery, chandeliers, silverware, carpeting, porcelain, and antique furniture. There is a museum's worth of oil paintings, murals, and frescoes.

Pleasure and paintings The opulence is hardly surprising, for Schönbrunn was the playground and often the home of the Habsburg dynasty until it collapsed in 1918. The showpiece at the heart of a labyrinth of staircases, grand vaulted rooms, and formal courtyards is the 130-ft/40-m long Great Gallery. Arching over tall windows that face crystal mirrors is a ceiling fresco whose message is clear: enthroned in the center is the Empress Maria Theresa surrounded by an allegory of her virtues and pictures of her territories and their riches.

Power and parkland Outside it is no less lush, and the list of conspicuous expenditure must continue. There is an amazing maze, the world's first zoo, the world's

TIME LINE

1683
Turkish invaders destroy the Schönbrunn château.

1688–1700
Architect Johann Bernhard Fischer von Erlach builds the palace's central section.

1743–49
Architect Nikolaus Pacassi completes the residential apartments.

1805–9
Occupied by Napoleon.

1817–1904
Refurbished after the Congress of Vienna. In 1904 the Sundial House is built for the world's largest collection of orchids.

1996
Inscribed by UNESCO as a World Heritage Site.

Above right: The Palm House was built in 1881 as part of a garden laid out in the English style.

Right: The mid-eighteenth-century Vieux-Laque Room helped set a European fashion for chinoiserie.

Above: The main palace seen from the Schönbrunn hill. Beyond the formal proportions of gardens and palace, Vienna is in the background.

Right: Symmetry rules in the view back up the hill from the city side. The Great Gallery is immediately behind the two sweeps of stairways.

largest orangery, a palm house, a theater, a fake Roman ruin, fountains, pools, statues, and archways, all melded together to emphasize the stability and permanence of an empire's first family. While the Habsburgs fell, their grand building project remains intact as a high-toned theme park, the theme being dynastic wealth, taste, and power.

History and Mozart Schönbrunn is also a crucible of European history. The now privatized tourist attraction was first developed as a fourteenth-century monastery, then an imperial hunting ground and then a Habsburg/Austro-Hungarian palace. After World War II it was briefly a British garrison, and in 1961 (when it was owned by the Austrian Republic) the West confronted the East here when John F. Kennedy met Nikita Khrushchev in the Great Gallery. In the current fortunate era of European peace, the palace has evolved into a heritage site with multiple uses from movie set to a venue for Mozart concerts. The Baroque still lives.

AUSTRIA, VIENNA

Riesenrad, Prater

VIENNA'S ANTIQUE WHEEL, IMMORTALIZED ON SCREEN IN CAROL REED'S MOVIE "THE THIRD MAN," HAS STOOD IN ITS FAMOUS AMUSEMENT PARK FOR OVER A CENTURY, AND HAS BECOME A SYMBOL OF THE CITY: A SUITABLE EMBLEM FOR A PLACE WHERE THE PLEASURES OF LIFE ARE PROPERLY APPRECIATED AND PURSUED.

The original Ferris Wheel, created by George Washington Gale Ferris Jr. for the 1893 Chicago World's Fair, was designed as a response to the engineering marvel of the previous international extravaganza—Paris's Eiffel Tower. Ferris's ambitious plan was initially dismissed as impossible, but it worked. And it set a trend that was eagerly copied around the world.

A giant wheel appealed on many levels: it displayed an up-to-the-minute appreciation of contemporary engineering, it was a big statement, it offered unique views of its surroundings, and everyone wanted a ride. Just four years after the triumph at the Chicago fair, the organizers of Vienna's own expo, to be held in 1898 in honor of the Golden Jubilee of Emperor Franz Josef I, decided they must have a wheel of their own.

Jubilee celebration Vienna's Riesenrad ("great wheel") was designed not by Ferris but by an English engineer, Walter B. Basset, who had previously created big wheels in Blackpool and London, and the steel components were fabricated in Glasgow. When complete it was nearly 213 ft/65 m high, with 30 enclosed gondolas. It was erected in 1897 in the Prater, Vienna's historic pleasure garden, where other attractions of the Jubilee Exposition included "Venice in Vienna," complete with

TIME LINE

1897–98
Riesenrad erected for Vienna's Jubilee Exposition.

1914
Mme Solange d'Atalide circumnavigates the wheel mounted on a horse standing on a cabin roof.

1916
Demolition ordered, but not carried out.

1944
Wheel burns down.

1947
Renovated wheel returns to operation.

1949
Release of *The Third Man*, directed by Carol Reed, screenplay by Graham Greene.

Opposite: The wheel has been illuminated at night since 2002. After its restoration only alternate cabins were installed.

Right: The cabins were rebuilt in 1947. Each is suspended from an overhead axle and can hold 20 standing passengers.

canals, and an early version of a roller-coaster ride that jolted through a mocked-up mountain.

Survival The wheel was an immediate success, selling a quarter of a million tickets in its first two seasons. Unlike its predecessors, it escaped dismantling at the end of the fair, and even though a demolition permit was issued in 1916, no money was found to carry out the work; instead, the wheel survived to become an important feature of Vienna's skyline and an essential port of call for visitors to the city. As a treat after their first Communion, Viennese children were traditionally taken by carriage to the Prater amusement park, and a ride on the Riesenrad crowned these visits.

Movie stardom During World War II the wheel was burned down, but it was rebuilt and new cabins were made in 1947. There are now just 15 instead of the original 30, but you can still take a ride and savor the atmosphere of the wheel's greatest moment—as a creaking location for the unforgettably tense exchange between Orson Welles and Joseph Cotton in *The Third Man*.

Right: Six of the cabins are now luxuriously furnished for romantic trysts and parties.

Below: The wheel stands at the entrance to the Prater and is an iconic element of Vienna's skyline.

SWITZERLAND, GENEVA

Jet d'Eau

THE DISTINCTIVE PLUME OF THE JET D'EAU ON LAKE GENEVA GIVES A COMPELLING IMAGE OF SWITZERLAND THAT IS PERSISTENT ENOUGH TO HAVE MADE A FOUNTAIN INTO A WORLD LANDMARK. HOWEVER, IT GOES AGAINST THE STEREOTYPES NORMALLY ATTACHED TO A CAREFUL, LANDLOCKED, AND MOUNTAINOUS NATION.

The Jet d'Eau is electrically powered, unnatural, and ephemeral, which are things the Swiss Alps are not. It is showy, frivolous, and wasteful of energy, three qualities not normally ascribed to Swiss people. So why is the fountain famous?

Hydraulic Perhaps it is an antidote, a safety valve of fun for its own sake, built by a people with control enough to find prosperity in a harsh mountain environment. The fountain certainly began as a safety valve. In the late nineteenth century the Usine de la Coulouvrenière hydraulic power system needed to relieve pressure on its turbines when Geneva's factories and workshops shut down their new power valves each evening. In 1886, as a temporary measure prior to a planned reservoir, an innovative engineer botched an outlet in the River Rhone, and the resulting 100-ft/30-m spout became a magnet that attracted citizens and tourists alike.

Electric Within five years, the fountain was moved downriver and out into Lake Geneva to celebrate the Swiss Confederation's 600th anniversary. This second fountain had a maximum height of 295 ft/90 m. Half a century later, a penchant for high fountains combined with a spirit of post-World War II relaxation to instigate a third fountain. In 1951, when the switch was thrown

FACT FILE

Height
459 ft/140 m.

Volume
132 gallons/500 litres of water emerge per second, with 1,849 gallons/ 7,000 litres in the air.

Speed
Water is ejected at a speed of 124 mph/200 kph.

Time
On a still day, water droplets spend 16 seconds in the air.

Power
A pair of 500 kW pumps, operating at 2,400 V, consume 1MW of electricity.

Opposite: The Jet d'Eau bisects views of the lakeside city and seems to reach even higher than the Alps beyond.

Right: The fountain remains switched on late into the evenings in a light show that has become part of life in Geneva.

on electric motors consuming over one megawatt of electricity, the Jet d'Eau was the highest fountain the world had ever seen, at 459 ft/140 m.

Fountastic Viewed from a nearby stone jetty jutting into Lake Geneva, the force and volume of the jet of water hints at Alpine cataracts. The broader setting, at the point where the Rhone debouches into Lake Geneva, is equally dramatic. The drama has endured, for the Jet d'Eau remains a must-see on any Swiss travel itinerary.

Fountains always fascinate, and the last six decades have seen waters being thrust up ever higher. The list of the world's tallest is topped by the 853-ft/260-m King Fahd Fountain (1985) in Jeddah, Saudi Arabia, followed by the World Cup Fountain (2002) in Seoul, Korea; the Port Fountain (2006) in Karachi Harbor, Pakistan; Fountain Park (1970) in Fountain Hills, Arizona; the Dubai Fountain (2008); and the Captain Cook Memorial Jet (1970) in Canberra, Australia. The Jet d'Eau comes after all these, but when ranked by renown it's still at the top. Size is not all.

Below: Lake Geneva and its famous fountain are pictured here from high up on the spire of St. Pierre Cathedral.

SPAIN, BILBAO

Guggenheim Museum Bilbao

LIKE A HUGE, CHAOTIC SILVER SHIP MOORED BESIDE THE RIVER NERVIÓN IN BILBAO, WHEN THE GUGGENHEIM OPENED IN 1997 IT CHANGED THE WORLD'S PERCEPTION OF THE CITY AND OF ART GALLERIES GENERALLY. THE MUSEUM MIGHT DIVIDE OPINION, BUT IT IS UNIVERSALLY ACKNOWLEDGED TO BE AN ICONIC BUILDING.

Bilbao is an elegant and spacious city with a fascinating medieval quarter, wide streets and squares lined with substantial nineteenth- and twentieth-century buildings, and a history of great industrial prowess, together with commercial wealth derived from trade and banking. A century ago it was the wealthiest city in Spain, a major port with thriving mining, steel, and shipbuilding concerns. However, by the 1980s its heavy industries were becoming obsolete, and unemployment stood at 25 percent. The streets were plagued with decay, pollution, and eruptions of violence.

Urban regeneration The city embarked on a program to overhaul its infrastructure, building new transport systems, homes, and offices, renewing its drains, and cleaning up the pollution and dirt that kept tourists away. The centerpiece of the plan—the building of an overwhelmingly expensive museum of modern art—was an audacious step that many felt was unwarranted and irresponsible. In fact, the museum transformed Bilbao's fortunes: from its opening day it has attracted over 800,000 visitors a year, and cities around the world seek to reproduce the so-called "Guggenheim effect."

Architectural icon The Canadian-American architect Frank Gehry created a sculptural design inspired by

TIME LINE

1991
Guggenheim Foundation signs preliminary agreement to build a new Guggenheim Museum in Bilbao.

1993
Construction work begins.

October 19, 1997
Museum opens with inaugural exhibitions on the Guggenheim Museums and art of the twentieth century, and recent European art.

1998
Over 1.3 million people visit the museum in one year.

2007
The gallery's tenth anniversary is marked by the inauguration of a new artwork, *Arcos Rojos* by Daniel Buren, on the adjacent La Salve bridge.

Right: The interior contours are as fluid as the outside walls. Suspended walkways connect the galleries across the central atrium.

Left: Viewed from across the river, the buiding resembles a vast ship with the wind in its sails.

Right: The gallery's tenth birthday in 2007 was marked by a riverside firework display.

Bilbao's maritime history and the building's riverside location. Constructed in limestone, glass, and titanium, its curving, organic shapes resemble the billowing sails of a ship, and the titanium panels reflect the light like fish scales. The interior walls also billow and curve, while steel walkways lead from the 150-ft/50-m glass atrium into 19 exhibition spaces arranged over three floors. There is a permanent collection as well as temporary exhibitions of contemporary art, but for many of those 800,000 annual visitors the main draw is probably the museum itself.

Critics object that the building overwhelms its function, that it sits uneasily with the rest of the city, and that it is unwelcoming as a public space. Visually, however, it is unforgettable, whether partially glimpsed at the end of a narrow street or seen lying along the riverside, with the water reflecting its shimmering titanium scales.

Right: In front of the entrance sits Jeff Koons' giant floral terrier, *Puppy* (1992), now a city mascot.

SPAIN, BARCELONA

Sagrada Familia

BARCELONA'S MOST CELEBRATED BUILDING, BEGUN IN 1882, IS YET TO BE COMPLETED BUT IS WELL ESTABLISHED AS ONE OF THE WORLD'S ARCHITECTURAL TREASURES. BIZARRELY BEAUTIFUL AND DRIPPING WITH SYMBOLISM, IT WAS THE LIFETIME OBSESSION OF ITS IDIOSYNCRATIC CREATOR, ANTONI GAUDÍ.

In the late nineteenth century building plots in the expanding city of Barcelona—nicknamed "Little Manchester" for its industrial prowess—were becoming expensive, but in 1881 the Spiritual Association of the Devout Followers of St. Joseph found a site it could afford for its new "expiatory temple": it was in a scruffy working-class area on the outskirts, but the association hoped to encourage piety among its humble neighbors as well as donations from prosperous citizens with plenty of sins to expiate.

Francisco de Paula del Villar was contracted as architect, and drew up plans for a modest neo-Gothic building, but he soon argued with the association and resigned in 1882, before even the crypt was completed. Gaudí, more sympathetic to the conservative views of the Devout Followers, was appointed instead; he finished the crypt, then, thanks to a huge anonymous donation that funded work throughout the 1890s, began a reimagining of the church that would take over the rest of his life. His plans were constantly growing and evolving—a sketch of one of the facades was found in his pocket on the day he died.

Catalan modernism Gaudí's early architecture embraced the Gothic revival, combined with traditional Catalan styles, but his intense love of nature, possibly

Left: Each of the three monumental facades will eventually have four bell towers, representing the 12 Apostles.

Right: The central motif at the top of the Nativity facade is the tree of life, with a flock of white doves clustered on its branches.

Below: The bell towers are linked by high, narrow walkways, for close-up views of the mosaic decoration and bird's-eye views of Barcelona.

fostered during long lonely periods of illness as a child, found its way into his work in the era of Art Nouveau and Symbolism. Inspired by trees, fern fronds, bones, shells, leaves, and fruits, his organic, dynamic forms were made possible by the use of modern materials, such as steel reinforcing rods. The devoutly Catholic architect regarded his work as homage to God's creation, and the Sagrada Familia became its greatest expression.

Contrasting facades As his ideas grew in scale and ambition, Gaudí decided to build one side of the church at a time, so that the first completed front and its spires would enable people to understand his vision and set the pattern for the whole—which others might complete after his death. He chose to start with the facade based on the Nativity as the most accessible and appealing theme. Facing east (the direction of the rising sun and birth), it is a mass of curling, billowing, carved foliage, looking more like wax than stone and crowded with figures illustrating the story of the birth of Christ.

Left: Glinting green tiles suggest a leafy canopy, and every facet of the interior is flooded with light from the hundreds of windows, which will gradually be filled with stained glass to create complex washes of color.

The Passion facade to the west (the direction of death) dates from 1954–76 and could hardly be more different. It is spare and plain, with jolting contrasts of light and shadow and angular, stylized figures by the Catalan sculptor Josep Maria Subirachs. There is real pain in the scenes leading up to the Crucifixion: Gaudí intended this to inspire fear.

The Glory facade, the third and largest, was begun in 2002 and is yet to be completed. It will represent the ascension of souls: from death to judgment and glory (or hell); its columns will be mounted on the seven deadly sins and crowned with the seven virtues.

Debts and war Private funding, or the lack of it, has governed the progress of the work. When Gaudí died in 1926, only one of the total of 18 spires he envisaged was in place and the Nativity facade was ten years from completion. Preferring to design in three dimensions rather than on paper, Gaudí had devoted most of his last years to creating a vast scale model in plaster, which stood in his workshop on the site. As the outbreak of war stopped work completely, the future of the church must

TIME LINE

1882
Original plans drawn up by Villar; foundation stone laid.

1883
Gaudí takes over project.

1892
Nativity facade begun.

1923
Gaudí completes models of nave and roof.

1926
Death of Gaudí.

1936
Church and workshop damaged during Civil War.

1954
Passion facade begun.

2001
First stained glass installed.

2010
Building consecrated as minor basilica by Pope Benedict XVI.

Left: Biblical text carved into the door focuses the thoughts of the pious as they enter the church.

Above: Different artists working under Gaudí's direction created the figures on the Nativity facade.

Right: Cranes are currently the tallest structures on the church, but will one day be dwarfed by the main spire.

have seemed hopeless; in 1936 Catalan anarchists destroyed Gaudí's workshop and smashed his models.

The broken pieces were saved, however, and after the war they were painstakingly reassembled. Building has continued with the help of surviving sketches, photographs of Gaudí's models, and computer projections.

Consecration The building was finally ready to become a basilica in 2010, when the roof was completed. The soaring columns and fan vaulting of the old Gothic cathedrals, which echoed the leafy canopies of ancient sacred groves, have here undergone a reverse transformation—back into fluted, branching stems and an explosion of foliage, fruits, and flowers overhead.

The 18 spires of the finished church will stand for the Apostles, the Evangelists, the Virgin Mary, and—the largest—Jesus. This will make the Sagrada Familia the tallest church in the world, but it won't be quite as tall as Montjuïc, the hill overlooking Barcelona. Gaudí wanted his church to be the "last great sanctuary of Christendom," but he didn't want to outdo the work of God.

SPAIN, SEGOVIA

Segovia Aqueduct

ROMAN ENGINEERS DESIGNED THE SEGOVIA AQUEDUCT ACCORDING TO VITRUVIAN PRINCIPLES IN THE FIRST CENTURY AD. A REMARKABLE FEAT OF MASONRY, THE BRIDGE HAS HELD TOGETHER PERFECTLY FOR THE LENGTH OF CHRISTENDOM, AN ENDURING MONUMENT TO THE ENGINEERING SKILLS OF THE ROMANS.

The Roman architect and engineer Marcus Vitruvius set European standards that held until the arrival of modern synthetic building materials. His book *De Architectura* insists that structures must be *firmitas, utilitas, venustas*: solid, useful, beautiful. There are no better adjectives to describe the Segovia Aqueduct.

Solid The structure has maintained its sublime equilibrium without mortar or cement, for the 20,400 granite blocks were each cut with enough precision to have bonded for nearly 2,000 years. The aqueduct's solidity is such that the overall span withstood the destruction of some of the central arches during a Muslim conquest in the eleventh century. Craftsmen in the fifteenth century followed the Roman template and rebuilt the damaged sections to the original style. Two decorative central niches were added to the upper level in the sixteenth century: the north-facing niche once held a statue of Hercules, Segovia's legendary founder; the other niche still contains statues of the Virgen de la Fuencisla (the city's patron) and St. Stephen.

Useful Apart from the statuary, everything else about the Segovia Aqueduct is strictly utilitarian. It supplied the citizenry of Segovia with water from the Fuente Fría some 10 miles/16 km away. Water transported along

FACT FILE

Patrons
Emperors Domitian and Trajan.

Age
Excavations of the footings suggest it dates to AD 50.

Scale
The aqueduct has 166 arches and 120 pillars arranged in two levels; it is 890 yd/813 m long and is made up of 20,400 granite blocks.

Damaged and rebuilt
Partially destroyed by Moors in 1072; repaired by order of King Ferdinand and Queen Isabella after 1484; in 1930 a cement canal replaced the sixteenth-century stone conduit.

Status
Designated a World Heritage Site in 1985.

Above: For nearly 2,000 years, the inhabitants of the Spanish city of Segovia have looked out at—and for most of their history depended on—the sweep of the aqueduct.

Right: The niche at the center of the bridge (viewed from the other side to the main picture) holds sixteenth-century statues of the Virgen de la Fuencisla and St. Stephen.

a canal entered Segovia's southeastern end and flowed across the 890-yd/813-m-long engineering miracle, which remained the source of supply for the old city center, the Segovia Alcázar, until recent times. There is a local saying, *"El acueducto da título a Segovia"*—"The aqueduct is Segovia." Without the aqueduct the city would not exist, and that is a definition of usefulness.

Beautiful Civil engineering doesn't often hit aesthetic heights, but this aqueduct is a notable exception. The sheer sweeping scale of the structure is remarkable. Its state of preservation and antiquity add to the aesthetic effect. The real beauty, however, is that the granite span seems to transcend solidity. This is due to the nature of the arch: the Romans knew all about arches and how they transfer loads downward and outward. The aqueduct's proportions, with its mathematically stacked tiers and tapering pillars, demonstrate how efficiency and utility can be parents to beauty. Art and craft are united in a way that would have made Vitruvius proud.

SPAIN, GRANADA

Alhambra

THE ALHAMBRA IS, IN A UNIFYING SENSE, A HYPHENATED PLACE. THE PALACE-FORT IN SOUTHERN SPAIN IS AN ARAB-EUROPEAN, MUSLIM-CHRISTIAN MELTING POT. ITS SPRAWL OF SMALL INTERLOCKING SPACES REVEALS THAT PARADISE ON EARTH MAY NOT NECESSARILY BE A CONTRADICTION IN TERMS.

An architectural realization of an earth-paradise is what the fourteenth-century Nasrid craftsmen had in mind when they enclosed a complex of domestic buildings within a set of fortifications. Moorish towers looked out over Spain and in on an evolving maze of buildings clustered around quadrangles of varying sizes and joined into a whole with alleyways and subcourtyards. Everywhere trees and flowers rub up against formalized decorative foliage.

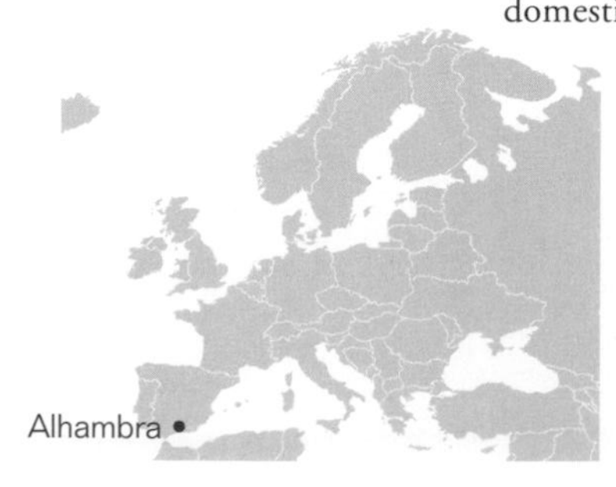

Divine geometry Stilt arches, columns, domes, and muqarna-stalactite ceilings give a distinctive non-European feel. Walls and floors are covered with painted tiles of intertwined flowing patterns that echo the architectural complexity and suggest infinity. At the root of the Alhambra's geometrical iconography is an Islamic conception of divine order. It follows the Mudéjar style, which saw Western ideas influencing Arabic craftsmen who worked in isolation from the rest of Islam.

Granada's cultural mix changed when eight centuries of Muslim rule ended in 1492. By 1527 Charles V had inserted a Renaissance palace, beginning a process of Italianate revisions that continued until Philip V's death in 1746. Spain's empire then dwindled and the Alhambra was neglected until the nineteenth century.

TIME LINE

9th century
First reference to Qal'at al-Hamra citadel.

1241–1492
Citadel commissioned and extended by sultans of the Nasrid dynasty.

January 2, 1492
City surrenders to forces of Ferdinand V, and Moors are driven out of Spain.

16th century
Charles V builds a European-style palace.

18th century
Philip V makes additions.

1870
Declared a national monument after years of damage and neglect.

1984
Declared a UNESCO World Heritage Site.

Above right: The dome of the Two Sisters Room, decorated in Moorish stalactite vaulting.

Right: Still waters reflect the arches and intricate stonework of the Partal.

Above: Described as "a pearl set in emeralds," the Alhambra is a kaleidoscope of color and light.

Right: A peek into the Court of the Lions reveals a tiny realm of delicate architecture and decoration.

Patio de los Leones A highlight of the complex is the Court of the Lions, a quadrangle where a central fountain plays into an alabaster basin resting on the backs of a dozen marble lions. Galleries and pavilions enclose a space that seems under the benign guard of 124 slender columns. Blue and yellow tiled walls are framed in enameled blue and gold.

Color and light defines the Alhambra. An unnamed Arab poet described the exterior walls and surrounding woodland as "a pearl set in emeralds," and there is a kaleidoscopic richness to its appearance. Its Arabic name means "red castle" and that's how most recall it.

Paradise Originally Al-Hamrā, the name dropped its hyphen long ago and the joined-up word has now gone global. There are many Alhambra theaters, hotels, and nightclubs. There is an Alhambra car, beer, and movie company. Alhambra is a Californian town, and there are countless suburban houses called Alhambra. All are united in striving for a touch of paradise.

PORTUGAL, LISBON

Belém Tower

EARLY SIXTEENTH-CENTURY PORTUGAL LOOKED OUTWARD. ELEGANT CARAVELS SET SAIL ON VOYAGES FROM A CAPITAL WHOSE CITIZENS ALSO EXPECTED VISITORS, SOME OF THEM HOSTILE. CUE FOR THE BELÉM TOWER, A CASTLE THAT DOUBLED AS AN ATTRACTIVE GATE AND ENDURES AS AN ARCHITECTURAL JEWEL.

The chunky little tower with its bastion/pier sticking out into the river marks the spot from where Vasco da Gama led the first European sailing expedition to India in 1497. Built on the orders of King Manuel I between 1515 and 1521, the tower is 4 miles/6 km west of Lisbon on the Tagus River's north bank, just before the river flows into the Atlantic. Belém Tower was thus always freighted with significance.

Decorative kaleidoscope With its dinky spires, ribbed cupolas, arched windows, and castellations, the design is a charming hotch-potch of the Gothic and the Moorish. The lioz limestone, however, is strictly local, and the sculptures that adorn it are Christian and European, and specifically Portuguese. The parapets display repeated representations of the cross of the Military Order of Christ. King Manuel I and Vasco da Gama were both members of a religious order that had eased from medieval crusading zealotry to voyages of discovery and early imperial acquisition.

Images of religion jostle with images of conquest. There are lions and a rhinoceros and there is a statue of the virgin of Belém, holding a bunch of grapes in one hand and a child in the other. Elsewhere, carved ropes and knots drew attention to Portugal's naval prowess.

TIME LINE

1515–21
Tower constructed on an island in the Tagus River.

1580
It fails to defend Lisbon from Spanish invasion.

1755
Lisbon earthquake silts up the Tagus, linking the tower to the riverbank.

1907
Having been a lighthouse, a customs house, a telegraph station, and a prison, Belém Tower is declared a national monument.

1983
Listed as a UNESCO World Heritage Site.

Opposite: While the structure of Belém Tower is predominantly European Gothic, the detail owes much to Moorish style.

Right: Melon domes topping the bastion's sentry posts are Moroccan; the parapet shields with the Order of Christ are Christian; the carved rope is specific to Portuguese seafaring.

Below: Belém depicts animals from an emerging empire. In 1513 a boat carrying a rhino sank nearby. The corpse was the model for this sculpture as well an Albrecht Dürer print.

Defensive role The tower might look like a fantasy castle but it had a serious military intent. Sited on a basalt island (now joined to the mainland due to a build-up of silt), it was the third part of the estuary's defense system, together with the Cascais fortress on the right bank and St. Sebastião da Caparica on the left bank. The integral pier had 16 gun emplacements split over two levels. Inside the square tower there is a spiral staircase rising through four floors to give lookouts a view of approaching ships and to mount flares as warning beacons. Above are six watchtowers and below is a vaulted storage room, later used as a prison.

The business end of the fort was the Governor's room, which opens out to the bastion terrace and its guns. The remaining rooms had functions that were less military. The ornate King's room on the second floor has an elaborate seven-arched Renaissance balcony overlooking the river. An Audience room on the third floor gives all-round views, and there is a chapel on the fourth floor.

GIBRALTAR

Rock of Gibraltar

THE TRIANGULAR SHAPED LIMESTONE OUTCROP THAT IS THE ROCK OF GIBRALTAR LOOMS LARGE IN THE WORLD—FAR LARGER THAN ITS ACTUAL DIMENSIONS. THIS IS DUE TO ITS STRATEGIC POSITION AS A CITADEL OVERLOOKING THE ENTRANCE TO THE MEDITERRANEAN SEA, AND AS EUROPE'S CLOSEST POINT TO AFRICA.

Without the Strait of Gibraltar the landlocked Mediterranean would gradually evaporate, so it is a vital safety valve. But the great rock overlooking it once marked the end of the known world. Beyond, out in the wild Atlantic, lurked the monstrous terrors of the unknown and the western abode of the dead. To pass through, as the intrepid Phoenicians did, was to traverse a mythic portal.

Pillars of Hercules Classical writers tell of the labor of Hercules that required him to cross Mount Atlas at the far western end of the Mediterranean. A reluctant climber, our hero smashed through the peak instead, thereby opening the channel and forming the Pillars of Hercules. The northern pillar was known as Mons Calpe. It became Jabal al Tāriq (Rock of Tariq) in 711, when Tariq ibn-Ziyad launched the Moorish occupation of Spain, and from this the name "Gibraltar" was derived.

Strategic importance The Moors based their fleet at Gibraltar and built a fortress on the rock to guard it. Possession of Gibraltar gave them dominance over the Mediterranean until 1462, and its importance became obvious to all the European sea powers. In 1713, at the end of the War of the Spanish Succession, Spain was forced to cede Gibraltar to Britain. It still wants it back.

TIME LINE

950 BC
Phoenician rule.

AD 711
Moorish rule.

1462
Spanish rule.

1704
British rule (confirmed at Treaty of Utrecht in1713).

1779–83
Unsuccessful Great Siege of Gilbraltar by French and Spanish troops.

1969
Spain severs communications with Gibraltar; Britain reaffirms that it will not cede Gibraltar to Spain against the population's wishes.

2002
Referendum rejects shared sovereignty with Spain.

2006
First Iberia Airlines flight lands at Gibraltar.

2009
Gibraltar and Algeciras ferry, closed in 1969, reopens.

Opposite: Gibraltar is one of the world's most densely populated places, and its strait is among the world's busiest shipping lanes.

Right: Europa Point is the southernmost tip of the Rock. A lighthouse to guide shipping through the strait was built there in 1838.

The Rock has become a byword for invincibility, a physical symbol of the Gibraltarians' stout independence. It is riddled with tunnels dug during the Great Siege, which its garrison successfully withstood for four years.

Residents and travelers The territory's population of 30,000 is very diverse: 27 percent originated in Britain, 26 percent in Spain; others from all over. The Rock itself is home to Barbary macaques (Europe's only wild monkeys) and Barbary partridges; its subtropical climate supports a rich flora that includes some unique species. Migrating birds use it as a stopover point, exploiting the same advantages that have attracted humanity. Gibraltar has always been both central and peripheral to human geography, and the human traffic past this cornerstone of Europe is still as intense as ever.

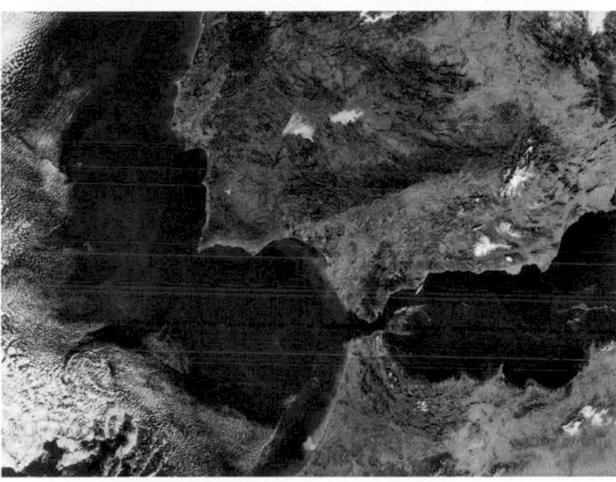

Right: The 8.9-mile/14.3-km Strait of Gibraltar is a strategic pinch point between Europe and Africa.

Below: Gibraltar's territory covers an area of 2.6 sq miles/6.85 sq km; the Rock rises to 1,398 ft/426 m.

ITALY, VENICE

St. Mark's Square

NAPOLEON IS SUPPOSED TO HAVE CALLED THIS LOVELY SQUARE "EUROPE'S DRAWING ROOM." IT IS VENICE'S PRINCIPAL OPEN SPACE, BUT INCREASINGLY OFTEN, AS THE RISING SEA THREATENS TO ENGULF THE FRAGILE CITY, IT MIGHT BE MORE ACCURATELY DESCRIBED AS EUROPE'S WADING POOL.

The Piazza San Marco has been the center of the city for a thousand years. Bordered by the great basilica and the Palace of the Doges, it lies at the heart of Venice's political, religious, commercial, and social life. It is known simply as the Piazza, because every other square in Venice is a *campo*. Not plagued by cars like other great urban spaces, the square is filled instead with people, pigeons, and the jostling music of rival café orchestras.

St. Mark's Basilica The church that dominates the eastern end was founded to house the relics of St. Mark—stolen from Alexandria by Venetian merchants—and to function as a private chapel for the Doge. The extraordinary Byzantine-style building dates from the eleventh century, but was much altered in the succeeding centuries. As every returning Venetian merchant ship brought some treasure to decorate it, some far older than the church itself, the brick facade gradually disappeared beneath marble, fine carvings, and glittering mosaics.

Ceremonial space The square was created because a power struggle between Holy Roman Emperor Frederick Barbarossa and Pope Alexander III—who excommunicated Frederick—ended in the pope's favor with the Peace of Venice in 1177. Frederick's submission was made with

TIME LINE

832
Foundation of St. Mark's.

1177
Peace of Venice.

12th century
Construction of Procuratie Vecchie, destroyed and rebuilt in sixteenth century.

1513
Campanile achieves final form.

1586
Foundation of Procuratie Nuove.

1720
Caffè Florian opens.

1807
Basilica consecrated as cathedral.

1810
Napoleonic wing at west end built to enclose square.

1902
Collapse of campanile, restored in 1912.

Right: The riches of Byzantium arrived in Europe on the glittering facade of St. Mark's, transformed by marble and mosaic in the thirteenth century.

Far right: Perched on the central arch, St. Mark watches over the square accompanied by his winged lion, which the republic adopted as its emblem.

Right: Delicate Gothic tracery around the Doge's Palace is echoed on the roofline of the basilica.

Left: Since 1723 the square has been paved with dark trachyte blocks, with a carpetlike design in contrasting white travertine.

Below right: Participants in Venice's annual carnival check their costumes in the gilded mirrors of Caffè Florian.

all possible pomp at St. Mark's, and its forecourt had to be enlarged for the occasion by filling in a canal and a dock beside the palace.

Social space The arcaded sixteenth-century buildings around the Piazza were the offices of the Procurators, the Republic's highest officials after the Doge. Now they house museums, stores, and the venerable coffee houses Florian, Lavena, and Quadri, with their competing rosters of celebrity patrons from Casanova to Woody Allen. If you sit at a table in the Piazza, your coffee may be the most expensive you've ever drunk, but the people-watching will be priceless. If you prefer a bird's-eye view, the campanile, Venice's tallest building, is open to the public.

Wet feet The Piazza is the lowest-lying part of the city, so is the first to flood when spring tides coincide with windy, rainy weather. Locals listen for the sirens warning of another *acqua alta* (high water), street traders load their stalls with plastic boots, and the tourists lining up to get into St. Mark's shuffle along raised walkways.

ITALY, VENICE

Bridge of Sighs

THE SIGHS WERE SAID TO BE THOSE OF CONDEMNED PRISONERS CATCHING THEIR LAST SIGHT OF VENICE ON THEIR WAY TO EXECUTION—A SENTIMENTAL AND BOGUS NOTION, BUT IT GAVE THIS PRETTY BRIDGE LASTING FAME AND A WHIFF OF ROMANCE, TURNING IT INTO A MAINSTAY OF THE TOURIST TRAIL.

In the Venetian Republic the Doge's Palace was a court of justice as well as a ducal residence, and prisoners languished in cells in the dank cellars or—for the classier inmates—up in the "leads" under the roof. When a new prison was built on the other side of the Rio de Palazzo, a footbridge was needed to provide access from the interrogation chamber in the palace.

Baroque design Venice's only covered bridge, made of white limestone, was the work of Antonio Contino, who had previously assisted his uncle with the design of the Rialto Bridge. The 36-ft/11-m span is elaborately decorated with scrolls and rusticated pilasters, with grotesque heads grimacing down at the canal; inside all is plain and severe, divided into two narrow corridors so that prisoners going in opposite directions would not be able to communicate with each other.

The Grand Tour By the time the bridge was built in 1602, Venice's most fearsome period of summary arrest and execution in the name of the Inquisition was over. The new cells held ordinary criminals instead of prisoners of conscience. In the era of the Grand Tour, however, the contrast between the beauty of the structure and its dismal purpose caught the Romantic imagination and resulted in its evocative name—Ponte dei Sospiri, or

TIME LINE

1589–1616
Building of New Prisons.

1602
Bridge of Sighs completed.

1757
Giacomo Casanova, arrested as a spy, claims to have escaped from the prison.

1797
End of Venetian Republic.

1818
Publication of Canto IV of Byron's *Childe Harold's Pilgrimage.*

2010
Bridge of Sighs shrouded in controversial advertising billboards during restoration of Doge's Palace.

Opposite: The bridge was built in Baroque style, even though the recent rebuilding of the palace had preserved its Gothic appearance.

Right: A gondolier floats his passengers under the bridge at the magic hour to test the theory that it guarantees eternal love.

Below: Prisoners would have glimpsed only restricted views through the pierced stonework of the low windows.

Bridge of Sighs. Lord Byron was the first to use its English name, in *Childe Harold's Pilgrimage*:

> I stood in Venice, on the Bridge of Sighs,
> A palace and a prison on each hand …

The poem, completed in 1818, made Byron phenomenally famous and created the figure of the Byronic hero: a cynical and world-weary yet deeply attractive outcast, and just the type to have fallen foul of the law and made that fateful walk over the bridge.

Bridge for lovers There's a good view of the world-famous bridge from the Ponte della Paglia farther down the canal, which is probably where Byron was really standing, since you can only stand "in" and not "on" the Bridge of Sighs. However, the full-blown tourist experience demands that you float under it in a gondola. Local lore maintains that a couple who kiss under the bridge at sunset will enjoy eternal love, thus ensuring a brisk trade for the gondoliers. It's all too romantic for words.

ITALY, FLORENCE

Florence Baptistery

MICHELANGELO IS SAID TO HAVE CALLED THE BAPTISTERY'S EAST DOORS THE GATES OF PARADISE, AND THE UNRIVALED DECORATION BESTOWED ON THIS ANCIENT BUILDING BETWEEN THE ELEVENTH AND FIFTEENTH CENTURIES REFLECTS THE CENTRAL IMPORTANCE OF THE CHRISTIAN SACRAMENT OF BAPTISM.

It's only a legend that the building was once a Roman temple, but an octagonal baptistery is known to have stood here by the early fifth century, making it the earliest Christian foundation in the city. The present, much larger Romanesque building dates from the eleventh century, a period when Florence was growing in wealth and power.

Romanesque No expense was spared in the beautification of the rebuilt Battistero di San Giovanni. The walls were opulently faced with white Carrara and dark green Prato marble. Inside, a great marble pavement was laid, and on the ceiling a glittering Byzantine-style mosaic depicted the Last Judgment. Dante Alighieri, who was baptised here around 1265, might have taken inspiration for his *Inferno* from the vivid scenes of the damned being fed to monstrous serpents or spit-roasted. By the time zebra-striped marble pilasters had been added to the outer corners at the end of the thirteenth century, the crumbling old cathedral opposite was looking crude and inadequate for the aspirational city, and in 1296 the foundations were laid for a new one that would match the baptistery in splendor.

The doors Embellishment of the baptistery was the responsibility of the Arte di Calimala, one of the greater guilds of Florence—the bodies that held the reins of

TIME LINE

Late 6th century
Octagonal building dedicated to John the Baptist by Theodolinda, Queen of the Lombards.

1059–1128
Baptistery rebuilt in Romanesque style.

12th–13th century
Marble floor and ceiling mosaics created.

1330–36
South doors by Andrea Pisano.

1403–24
North doors by Lorenzo Ghiberti.

1425–52
East doors by Ghiberti.

Opposite: Florence's Piazza del Duomo is a great ecclesiastical set-piece, crammed with outstanding buildings designed and decorated by masters of the early Renaissance.

Right: Ghiberti's bronze panels depict multiple episodes from Old Testament stories, including Adam and Eve in the Garden of Eden (above) and the story of Joseph (below).

civic power before the rise of the Medici. In 1330, on the recommendation of Giotto, they recruited Andrea Pisano to create a pair of gilded bronze doors, with 28 panels depicting scenes from the life of John the Baptist.

In 1401 the Calimala announced a competition to design a second set of doors. The finalists were Filippo Brunelleschi and Lorenzo Ghiberti. Ghiberti won, and while Brunelleschi abandoned metalwork in disgust and went on to design his masterpiece—the dome of the cathedral—Ghiberti embarked on what would become his life's work. After 21 years working on the 28 panels of scenes from the New Testament, he was famous; a shower of commissions included a second one for the baptistery, which he accepted.

Gates of Paradise For the east doors, on which he worked for the next 27 years, Ghiberti adopted a radically new, naturalistic style. The ten large panels of Old Testament scenes are full of action, drama, and depth, thanks to the newly discovered principles of perspective: for many they represent the birth of the Renaissance.

Below: Many Italian baptisteries adopted an octagonal shape, based on Rome's Lateran Baptistery.

Below right: Ghiberti's original east doors are now housed in the cathedral museum and have been replaced by replicas.

ITALY, PISA

Leaning Tower of Pisa

AN ARCHITECTURAL SLIPUP DEFINES PISA IN THE EYES OF THE WORLD, EVEN THOUGH THERE'S FAR MORE TO IT THAN ITS CAMPANILE. THE PIAZZA DEL DUOMO IS KNOWN AS THE "FIELD OF MIRACLES" FOR ITS OUTSTANDING ROMANESQUE TREASURES. IT'S ALSO A MIRACLE THAT THE TOWER IS STILL STANDING.

Medieval Pisa was a powerful and wealthy maritime republic, with trading posts all around the Mediterranean. All that changed in the thirteenth century when the River Arno silted up: Pisa lost its access to the sea, its power declined, and it was eventually conquered by Florence. But the magnificent ecclesiastical buildings clustered on the Campo dei Miracoli date from the period of its greatest glory.

Shaky foundations The ground, at the confluence of two rivers, was marshy and unstable, yet an early Christian cathedral had been built here on the site of even older Etruscan and Roman temples. The splendid *duomo* was founded in 1064, and building continued until the thirteenth century. Even this isn't quite vertical: the large bronze lamp that hangs over the main aisle like a plumb line clearly shows that it's a little off-center.

Eight centuries of leaning The taller, slimmer bell tower suffered far more. The design followed the Romanesque style of the cathedral, with six loggia tiers over a base of blind arches and a smaller belfry at the top. But the foundations, laid in 1173, were shallow, and when the structure was only three stories high it started to tilt. By this time Pisa was almost constantly at war, and work stopped for about a century. When it was

FACT FILE

Height
183 ft 3 in/55.86 m on low side, 186 ft/56.7 m on high side.

Angle
3.99 degrees since stabilization: top of tower displaced by 13 ft/3.9 m from vertical.

Stabilization
A drainage system installed in 2003 has solved the problem of a fluctuating water table and stabilized the tower.

Architects
Original plans now thought to be by Diotisalvi, who designed the Baptistery; later work by Nicola and Giovanni Pisano.

Opposite: The freestanding campanile is sited behind the cathedral, whose vertical walls provide a clear point of comparison.

Right: Matching the exterior of the cathedral, the white marble facing of the tower is ornamented with dark gray stone that emphasizes the architectural details.

Below: The tower was designed not just to hold bells but as a belvedere for the citizens of Pisa, who could view events in the square from its loggias.

resumed in 1272, the upper floors were adapted to try to correct the tilt, and the belfry was finally added in 1370. The two-century timespan had allowed the spongy ground to compact under the tower's weight, otherwise it would certainly have toppled.

In the nineteenth century the angle increased. Pisans said that only God was holding up the tower. Mussolini tried to straighten it up by having concrete poured into the foundations, but this made the problem even worse. By 1990 the masonry was cracking. The tower was closed indefinitely and tourism in Pisa fell by 45 percent.

Saving the tower Steel tendons, lead weights, and anchored cables were all deployed, and total collapse narrowly avoided. Eventually, careful extraction of soil from under the higher side allowed the tower to settle back to its early nineteenth-century angle: enough to be safe while preserving the distinctive lean. It's now said to be more stable than ever before, and since 2001 visitors have again been able to clamber up its 294 narrow steps.

ITALY, ROME

The Colosseum

THE COLOSSEUM IS A WORLD-FAMOUS SYMBOL OF ROME—INDEED, OF THE WHOLE OF ITALY—AND CAN SOMETIMES SEEM AS FULL OF VISITORS NOW AS IT WAS IN ITS ANCIENT HEYDAY, WHEN CAPACITY CROWDS OF MORE THAN 50,000 CHEERED ON THEIR FAVORITE GLADIATORS AND WATCHED CRIMINALS COME TO GRISLY ENDS.

Rome's top new entertainment venue in AD 80, the vast Flavian Amphitheater acquired its better-known name from a nearby statue. In an astute and popular move, the stadium was built in the grounds of the detested Emperor Nero's extravagant palace by his successors, Vespasian and his son Titus. While Nero's Golden House was obliterated, his 100-ft/30-m statue remained, remodeled as the sun god. Centuries later, its nickname was applied to the building.

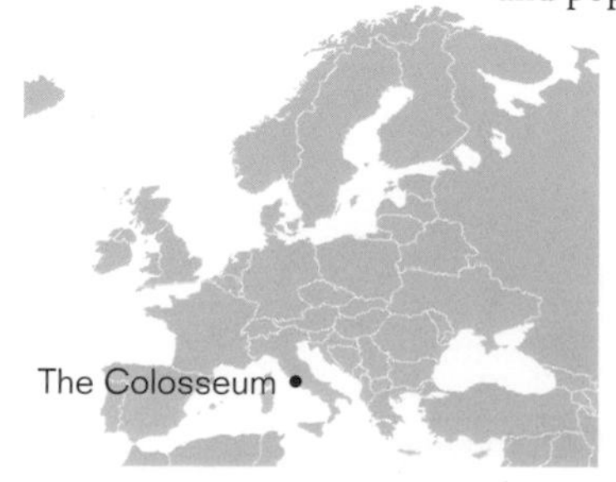

Stadium design The design was a massive ellipse, with three arcaded levels, each with 80 arches, and a top story with small windows. All the ground floor arches were entrances, numbered to help spectators find their way to their seats, and covered walkways ran behind the tiers. The emperor sat in his box at the north end, while another box to the south was reserved for the Vestal Virgins. Between them, members of the Senate occupied the best seats, raised just far enough above the sand-strewn arena to avoid getting splashed with blood. Although all the sightlines were good, the lowest-ranking spectators at the top (workers, the poor, women) would have been at least 330 ft/100 m from the arena.

Spectacle For the inaugural games, which lasted 100 days, plumbing was installed so that the arena could

FACT FILE

Construction
Begun AD 72 by Emperor Vespasian, completed AD 80 by his son Titus.

Size
615 ft/189 m long; 510 ft/156 m wide. Outer wall 157 ft/48 m high. Arena 287 ft/87 m long and 180 ft/55 m wide.

Capacity
Seating for 50,000 people (5 percent of first-century Rome's population).

Opposite: Half of the outer wall was destroyed by an earthquake; the remains were reinforced with brickwork wedges in the nineteenth century.

Right: As part of a campaign to end capital punishment, the Colosseum is symbolically floodlit in gold when a death sentence is commuted in the world.

be flooded for a mock sea battle, but the novelty wore off; the crowd preferred gladiatorial contests and dangerous wild animals—sometimes thousands were killed in one day. Emperor Domitian had a basement built under the arena, where animals and gladiators awaited their entrances. Teams of stagehands used winches to hoist lions and tigers through trapdoors so that they could leap dramatically into the heart of the action.

Decline and dismantling After the games petered out in the sixth century, a church was built in the amphitheater, the arena became a cemetery, and people lived and worked in the arcades. An earthquake in 1349 destroyed the south outer wall, creating a useful supply of building stone, and the rest was gradually stripped of its fine travertine facings and bronze fittings until 1749, when Pope Benedict XIV declared the arena a sacred site of early Christian martyrdom. Although there was little evidence to support his assertion, it saved the Colosseum for posterity, and it is now revered in a different way: as the paramount icon of the Roman Empire.

Right: Gladiators, criminals, and caged animals were confined in the narrow passages under the arena.

Below: The brick and concrete remains convey the immense scale and engineering of the building, still a pattern for stadiums of the modern era.

ITALY, ROME

St. Peter's Basilica

THE GREATEST CHURCH IN CHRISTENDOM HAD TO BE CROWNED WITH THE GREATEST DOME, AND FROM ITS CONCEPTION ST. PETER'S DOME WAS INTENDED TO BE THE HIGHEST EVER SEEN. FOUR HUNDRED YEARS LATER IT IS STILL ROME'S TALLEST BUILDING, AND THE FOCAL POINT OF CITY VIEWS FROM THE SURROUNDING HILLS.

St. Peter's has the largest interior of any Christian church—marks on the floor of the nave proudly demonstrate how other great cathedrals of the world would fit easily inside it—and this is no accident. When Pope Julius II decided to rebuild the church that had stood on this site since the fourth century, it was his intention to make it the grandest church in Christendom. Achieving such a feat took 120 years, and some of the greatest artists of the day applied their skills to the task.

Old St. Peter's The old basilica was itself a splendid affair of marble and mosaic, built on the orders of Rome's first Christian emperor, Constantine, on the site of the Circus of Nero, where it was said St. Peter had been martyred and buried. Charlemagne was crowned Holy Roman Emperor there in 800, followed by 22 of his successors, and it was filled with the tombs of saints and popes. It had been a major pilgrimage destination for a thousand years, and people believed that the golden cockerel on its bell tower would crow to signal the end of the world. But it was crumbling, and the masters of the Renaissance were conveniently on hand to design its replacement.

Michelangelo's dome Donato Bramante was the first to be commissioned, and he planned a Greek cross

TIME LINE

AD 64
Martyrdom of St. Peter.

AD 330
First basilica built during reign of Constantine.

1505–06
Old basilica partly demolished and new foundations laid.

1547
Michelangelo is named architect of St. Peter's and redesigns dome.

1590
Completion of dome.

1624–33
Lorenzo Bernini creates baldachin.

1626
Consecration of new basilica.

1656–67
Bernini designs piazza.

Right: The dome rises directly over the traditional site of St. Peter's tomb, over which Bernini's great bronze baldachin, or canopy, frames the Papal Altar. The mosaic letters of the inscription around the base of the dome are 6 ft 6 in/2 m high.

Right: Up to 300,000 people can crowd into Bernini's vast piazza.

Left: Early pilgrims used the Ponte Sant' Angelo, built during the reign of Hadrian, to cross the Tiber to St. Peter's. The basilica's iconic dome dominates the Roman skyline.

Below right: A surprise on the Aventine Hill: a peep through the keyhole of the Priory of the Knights of Malta gives a distant view of St. Peter's dome, perfectly framed by clipped hedges.

with a dome inspired by Rome's Pantheon. Raphael and Antonio da Sangallo contributed different designs, but it was the elderly and reluctant Michelangelo who created a unified whole from their various ideas. He also designed the great parabolic dome, which was constructed in just a couple of years by a team of 800 builders. It is still the largest brick dome in the world. Like the pioneering structure designed by Brunelleschi in Florence, to which Michelangelo referred, it has a double shell, and stairs between the inner and outer dome lead up to the cupola at the very top, 400 ft/120 m above the altar.

Change of plan The Renaissance vision of Bramante and Michelangelo was ultimately compromised by Pope Paul V's decision to extend the nave eastward to match the ground plan of the old basilica. By 1607, a Greek cross carried the taint of paganism, and the Latin cross plan was seen as more purely Christian. Carlo Maderno's nave and massive Baroque facade consequently blocks the view of Michelangelo's dome from St. Peter's Square.

ITALY, ROME

Trevi Fountain

SO MANY COINS ARE THROWN INTO THE WATER THAT ABOUT €3,000 (AROUND $4,200) IS COLLECTED DAILY: EVERY VISITOR TO THE CITY WANTS TO BE SURE OF THEIR CHANCE OF RETURNING. TREVI IS ROME'S LARGEST BAROQUE FOUNTAIN, AND THIS TRADITION NEATLY GUARANTEES THAT IT WILL ALWAYS BE THE MOST VISITED.

The ancient Romans constructed sophisticated aqueducts to supply their cities with fresh water, and Rome itself had 11 of them, built over about 500 years, which terminated in various parts of the city. One of the most important was the Aqua Virgo, which brought water from a spring discovered in 19 BC (apparently with the help of a virgin, hence its name).

All of Rome's aqueducts were broken by besieging Goths in the sixth century, but during the Renaissance eight were restored, each terminating in an elegant fountain (a *mostra*, or showpiece) as had been the custom in the ancient city. The first to be repaired was the Aqua Virgo (now the Acqua Vergine) in 1453. Pope Nicholas V commissioned Leon Battista Alberti to carry out the project, and his *mostra* was a simple basin.

Later popes demanded something much more theatrical. The fountain was resited to face the Quirinal Palace, then a papal residence, and the new design, by Niccolò Salvi, was eventually completed in 1762.

Baroque drama Before a triumphal arch set against the classical facade of the Palazzo Poli, nature and architecture are strikingly juxtaposed. The sculpture depicts the god Oceanus and two Tritons taming unruly winged sea horses among tumbling rocks. The virgin of the

TIME LINE

1st century
Aqua Virgo built to supply Baths of Agrippa.

1453
Aqueduct restored by Pope Nicholas V.

1629
Pope Urban VIII commissions large basin designed by Bernini.

1730–62
Fountain built by order of Pope Clement XII, designed by Niccolò Salvi and completed by Giuseppe Pannini.

1996
Fountain turned off and draped in black on death of Marcello Mastroianni, star of *La Dolce Vita*.

Opposite: The whole ensemble, with its classical columns, niches filled with allegorical figures, and expansive elliptical pool, almost fills the small square in which it stands.

Right: The mythical hippocamps, or winged sea horses, in the scene represent the power of water, in this case being subdued by the even greater power of the gods.

aqueduct can be seen in a relief above them. Over to the right, a large vase standing on the balustrade was Salvi's way of disguising an intrusive shop sign, which a curmudgeonly barber refused to take down.

Big fountain, small square Unlike other Roman fountains, Trevi is not the centerpiece of a busy piazza but tucked away in a small square at a junction of narrow lanes—its name comes from *tre vie* (three streets)—so that you are aware of its sound before you see it. And over the water's roar you hear the raised voices of the crowds around the pool, jostling to reach the rail so they can throw in a coin, which must always be flung with the right hand over the left shoulder.

When Anita Ekberg played mermaid in the most celebrated scene of Fellini's iconic *La Dolce Vita,* the little square was deserted; no paddling is allowed now, but at night when the underwater lights create dancing reflections, or at dawn before the hordes of tourists and souvenir sellers arrive, it's still possible to recapture something of the seductive atmosphere of Rome's iconic fountain.

Right: The money raked out each day goes to a charity that supports the poor.

Below: The drama increases when the fountain is lit from below at night.

GREECE, ATHENS

The Parthenon

TAKEN TOGETHER, THE PARTHENON AND ITS SCULPTURES ARE A TOUCHSTONE OF EUROPEAN ARCHITECTURE AND AESTHETICS. THEY ARE THE BEST PHYSICAL SPECIMENS OF IDEAS OF CLASSICAL BALANCE AND HARMONY THAT HAVE FLOWED FROM THE ANCIENT GREEKS INTO CONTEMPORARY CULTURE.

Without the Parthenon, the West's most admired buildings would not exist in their current proportions. It's that important. While it is obvious that not all Western landmark architecture derives directly from it, both Gothic and Modernist approaches were reactions to Greek Classicism. The Parthenon was first on the block, as were its sculptures, which astonished people in their day and have set standards of beauty and vitality ever since.

The Parthenon •

Classicism In general, "classic" is what is good and made to last; specifically, it refers to Greek or Roman antiquity. The Parthenon checks both boxes. It was built in the fifth century BC as a treasury and temple to the goddess Athena and sits on a limestone outcrop 500 ft/150 m above Athens. This rocky promontory had its summit leveled to form the Acropolis—literally the "highest city," or citadel. Today its architectural remains are the Parthenon itself, the Propylaia, or monumental gateway, plus the Erechtheion and Athena Nike temples. All were intended as classics, demonstrating how thought and art could contrive monuments in perfect balance with the natural landscape.

Greek influences Why are the roofless Parthenon and its chipped statuary so important? The broad answer is that they are the prime remaining physical expression

Left: As well as being an enduring symbol of ancient Greece and its rich legacy of art and thought, the 2,500-year-old Parthenon stands as an icon for the whole of Western civilization.

Right: The geometric symmetry of the 46 outer columns is counterpointed at the top by bas-relief panels (metopes), depicting epic battles between humans, gods, giants, and mythical creatures.

Below: The marble reliefs of the Parthenon frieze originally decorated the temple's inner chamber. They are generally thought to depict a religious procession in a narrative that begins with the preparations of participants and horses.

of the Greek philosophy and mathematics that informed Renaissance ideas, which evolved into Enlightenment science and modern technology. Plato and Aristotle are still relevant to the modern condition. The narrower architectural explanation of the Parthenon's significance is that eighteenth-century Neoclassicism made detailed reference to this above all other classical structures.

Straight lines The Parthenon is the supreme example of the Doric architecture that found fresh forms in Enlightenment estates and cities. Doric columns stand directly on a pavement, and the Parthenon originally had 46 such columns, fluted and surmounted by capitals supporting the entablature, which in turn supported roof beams some 43 ft/13 m above the pavement.

Despite the disciplined appearance, there are few right angles or straight lines. The pavement curves slightly upward in the center (primarily to facilitate drainage), while the columns lean imperceptibly inward. Each also bulges minutely, in yet another part of a

Left: A key display in the ultra-modern Acropolis Museum is the Panathenaic Procession, a recreation of the Parthenon's frieze from original blocks and casts of those held in the British Museum and elsewhere.

Below left: Access to the Acropolis is via a monumental gateway, the Propylaia. To its right, on a raised bastion, can be seen the recently restored and classically elegant Temple of Athena Nike.

symphony of subtle curves that defies perspective to give an optical illusion of straight lines.

Curves Up on the entablature and in the pediments at either end were the reliefs and statues that are a separate part of the Parthenon's renown. They give another version of perfection. Instead of straightness, the curves of accurately modeled figures were wrapped in the asymmetries of violent events. The fluid beauty of the body, especially when in Athenian clothing, is shown in repose and in conflicts with outside forces from myth and history. There is harmony both in the architectural geometry and in statuary that gives as full an artistic account of the human body as the world has seen.

Politics This creativity marked the peak of Athenian power and, like every expensive showpiece, the Parthenon denoted political clout. That soon dwindled and the Parthenon's history has been a tumultuous one of occupation and plunder. Its 39-ft/12-m high gold and ivory cult statue of Athena went to Constantinople in the fourth century AD and was destroyed during the Fourth Crusade in 1204. The Parthenon was a church from the

TIME LINE

447–432 BC
Construction of Parthenon.

1460s
Ottoman Turks use it as a mosque and add a minaret.

1687
Venetian bombardment.

1806
Earl of Elgin removes sculptures and sells them to the British Museum.

1822
Acropolis is handed over to the Greeks and minaret is demolished above roofline.

1983
Greek government begins campaign to have Parthenon Marbles returned to the new Acropolis Museum.

1987
Inscribed on UNESCO World Heritage List.

Right: The Porch of the Caryatids—female figures taking the place of supporting columns—is on the Erechtheion, another temple dedicated to Athena, which stands to the north of the Parthenon.

sixth century to the fifteenth, then a mosque under the Ottoman Turks, who unfortunately also hid their ammunition there when Venetian troops attacked Athens in 1687. The Venetians bombarded the building and the resulting explosion blew off the roof, took down the southern columns, and destroyed many statues.

In 1806 the British ambassador to the Ottomans took 40 percent of the remaining statues and frieze fragments and sold them to the British Museum. Ownership of these Elgin/Parthenon Marbles divides opinion. The Greek government demands their return, while the museum believes they belong in London as an integral part of a collection telling the story of world cultures.

Back in the Parthenon, the cult statue of Athena is as long gone as the religious fervor she invoked. She was goddess of war, civilization, wisdom, strength, strategy, crafts, justice, and skill and we still inhabit realms where these things must be held in some kind of a balance. A definition of humanity is the capacity to conceive of a harmony that might exist in a brighter future and that definitely exists in the remains of what went before.

Below: The Acropolis dominates Athens. The Propylaia is visible on the skyline to the left, below the Parthenon's western pediment.

GREECE, EPIDAVROS

Epidaurus Theater

THE CLICHÉD THING TO DO WHEN VISITING THIS THEATER IS TO SIT IN ITS UPPER TIERS AND LISTEN TO SOMEONE DROPPING A COIN IN THE "GAZING AREA" BELOW. THE SOUND TRAVELS UP FLAWLESSLY CLEAR, FOR THIS OLDEST OF THEATERS HAS THE MOST PERFECT ACOUSTIC.

Is this luck or judgment? Recent consensus holds that the classical Greeks knew exactly what they were doing when they built the bowl-shaped auditorium and fashioned 34 tiers of seating out of corrugated limestone blocks. Polykleitos the Younger engineered a theater where the irregular surfaces diffuse low-frequency audience noise and amplify high-frequency tones from the actors. With its *skênê* (scene) backdrop and proscenium, Epidaurus set the stage for a theatrical tradition that still survives.

Sound judgment The Greeks judged drama and music with the utmost seriousness, and Aristotle linked the performance arts to healing. Indeed, a healing center predated the theater at this site. As the birthplace of Asclepius, god of healing and son of Apollo, by 600 BC Epidaurus was the foremost Grecian health sanctuary. A good performance was all part of the treatment, and it was quite logical that medical profits should fund a theater. The natural hillside setting goes beyond logic and back into aesthetics, for this theater is quite simply one of the most beautiful and harmonious structures in the world.

Good luck That it has remained intact as the best-preserved classical Greek monument is more luck than judgment. Roman soldiers plundered the sanctuary in

TIME LINE

6th century BC
Healing site established around Temple of Asclepius at Epidaurus.

5th century BC
Theater designed by Polykleitos the Younger.

87–67 BC
Epidaurus attacked by Roman soldiers then Cilician pirates; theater unharmed.

AD 50
Roman restoration adds 21 tiers.

AD 150
Theater praised by Pausanias.

1881
Excavations begin.

1954
Euripides' *Hippolytos* performed as prelude to annual festival inaugurated in 1955, now held during July and August.

1988
Inscribed as a UNESCO World Heritage Site.

Opposite and below: Views down onto the stage of the world's oldest surviving theater. If the play become too dull or too tragic to bear, the audience can always gaze out to the Peloponnese Mountains.

Right and below right: Thanks to the contours of the stones, the acoustic of the bowl-shaped theater is so remarkable that the breathing of someone standing on the central stone is fully audible.

87 BC but left the theater alone. Once Greece was assimilated into the Roman Empire, the theater came back into use and, in another piece of unexplained good fortune, the Romans didn't follow their standard practice of truncating old circular theaters. Instead they augmented Polykleitos' building with another 21 tiers, upping the audience capacity to 15,000 and retaining the miracle acoustic. After the Romans left, the theater got buried and was excavated only in the late nineteenth century.

Old traditions Since the 1950s Epidaurus has again been pulling in the crowds as a living theater, mounting performances of plays by Sophocles, Euripides, and Aeschylus with never a microphone in sight. It is on the cultural tourist itinerary, and once people have listened to the clatter of a dropped coin they can visit a museum to see ancient surgical equipment, carved reliefs showing snake cures, and stone inscriptions of potions and pills. While medical practice has changed beyond recognition, the Epidaurus Theater proves our dramatic heritage comes straight from classical Greece.

GREECE, DELOS

Terrace of the Lions

THE TERRACE OF THE LIONS ON THE GREEK ISLAND OF DELOS FORMS A GHOSTLY GUARD OF HONOR TO ANTIQUE BELIEFS THAT HAUNT THE ROCKY LANDSCAPE. FIVE TAUT BODIES AND FIVE EYELESS WEATHERBEATEN SNARLS STAND WATCH OVER THE ROAD TO THE SANCTUARY OF APOLLO. BEWARE.

While it is hard to even guess at the precise fears the Delos lions once summoned, there are some constants to explain why these battered white marble statues are still impressive. Lions have long stood for power and kingship, and throughout human history they have symbolized bravery and strength. The lions at Delos date back 2,600 years to the time when the 1-sq mile/3.4-sq km island was a holy landscape dotted with temples dedicated to Apollo, Artemis, and Dionysus. The Terrace of the Lions defended Apollo, the god who oversaw music, poetry, the sun, medicine, light, and knowledge. The god has lost all sway, but everybody still values at least some of the qualities minded by the guardian lions.

Time of the lions Delos was and is a strange place. It is now uninhabited, except for archaeologists and official tourist guides, and was much the same in the second century AD according to Pausanius, who wrote that the temple guards were the sole residents. It was equally set aside from normal life in the time of the lions.

The Delphic Oracle, under the patronage of Apollo, ordered the island to be purged of dead bodies and decreed that nobody should be allowed to either die or give birth there. Those about to do either were ferried to

FACT FILE

600 BC
Terrace of Lions erected as guardians at the gate of the Sanctuary of Apollo.

88 BC
King Mithridates slaughters Delos population and island falls prey to pirates.

2nd century AD
Pausanius notes a derelict island.

17th century
One Delos lion is taken to Venice Arsenal.

1886–1906
Remaining lions excavated by École Française d'Athènes.

1990
Inscribed as a UNESCO World Heritage Site.

1999
The lions are moved into the local museum and facsimile statues put in their place.

Opposite: The surviving lions stand on a terrace overlooking the site of the sacred lake, but it is likely that they and their lost fellows would originally have flanked a processional way.

Right: Sculpted with snarling mouths and poised ready to spring, the lions appear to have been designed to inspire fear in worshippers passing beneath them.

the adjacent island of Rinia, and the fate of transgressors in this life or the next can only be imagined. The all-seeing lions controlling the birthplace of Apollo and Artemis would not have been pleased with them.

Rediscovery There were originally 16 lions here, arranged similarly to an avenue of Egyptian sphinxes. As classical Greece declined, the statues eroded or were vandalized or stolen—only five are left. After the king of Pontus killed or enslaved its population in 88 BC, Delos fell into ruins. The lions were buried in earth and undergrowth until one, headless, was discovered and taken to Venice in the seventeenth century.

Shadows of the past The remaining lions were unearthed as part of excavations initiated by the École Française d'Athènes in 1872. Their work continues, and in 1999 the lions were moved into the Archaeological Museum of Delos and replicas put in their place. The sleek copies keep shadows of the past alive in statuary that appears strangely modern, with semiabstract forms evoking ancient memory and enduring archetype.

Below: Delos's sacred territory was protected by the three Cycladic islands surrounding it.

TURKEY, ISTANBUL

Hagia Sophia

EAST MEETS WEST IN BYZANTIUM, ALSO KNOWN AS CONSTANTINOPLE AND (SINCE 1930) ISTANBUL. PERHAPS THE MAIN MEETING POINT IS THE HAGIA SOPHIA, WHICH HAS VARIOUSLY BEEN AN EASTERN ORTHODOX CATHEDRAL, A ROMAN CATHOLIC CATHEDRAL, AN IMPERIAL MOSQUE, AND (SINCE 1935) A SECULAR MUSEUM.

The clutter of names around a building also known as Sancta Sapienti, Aya Sofya, and Magna Ecclesia results from a cultural and architectural clutter sometimes willed by existing incumbents, sometimes introduced by new ones. Its instigator, Emperor Justinian, plundered building materials from throughout the Byzantine Empire. Hellenistic columns came from the nearby Temple of Artemis, and Corinthian columns were shipped from the Lebanon along with green marble from Macedonia, black stone from Bulgaria, yellow stone from Syria, and porphyry from Egypt.

Outdoing Solomon Walls and ceilings were covered in gold mosaics revealing God's holy fire surrounded by lords and ladies, young lovers, shoals of leaping fish, ecstatic musicians and choirs, solemn saints, and soaring angels. Justinian declared: "Solomon, I have outdone you," and the Hagia Sophia remained the largest temple in the world until Seville Cathedral was completed in 1520. By then, the building was a mosque and many of its mosaics had been plastered over, in accordance with the Islamic ban on figurative images.

At ground level, most of what now confronts the visitor is still Islamic. Higher up, Orthodox Christian iconography is being uncovered. Maintaining a balance of

Opposite: The domes and minarets of Hagia Sophia, high above the Bosphorus, have been Istanbul's principal landmark for nearly 1,500 years.

TIME LINE

AD 562
Building completed.

1204–61
Made a Catholic cathedral by Western Crusaders.

1261–1453
Reverts to Eastern Orthodoxy.

1453–1923
Mosque for the duration of the Ottoman Empire.

1935
Becomes secular museum.

1985
Inscribed on UNESCO World Heritage list as part of Historic Area of Istanbul.

Above: The apse mosaic of the Virgin and Child, dating back to the ninth century, is the oldest of the surviving mosaics.

Right: Sunlight flooding into the Hagia Sophia makes the main dome appear still more elevated than its actual height of 182 ft/55.6 m.

religious, restorative, and conservation interests is most difficult in the dome, where Islamic calligraphy overlays an Orthodox picture of Christ as Master of the World.

Art of levitation The 100-ft/30-m diameter dome is uncluttered in form, and what was without precedent when Hagia Sophia was built in the sixth century remains utterly extraordinary. It is a monument of unaging intellect, designed by a physicist (Isidore of Miletus) and a mathematician (Anthemius of Tralles), who between them realized the world's first pendentive dome. The elegance is augmented by an arcade of 40 windows around the dome's base from which, in a way that invokes a spiritual response regardless of creed, light diffuses through the whole building and makes the dome seem to hover above the nave.

Hagia Sophia now hovers above religious divides. A museum administered by a secular state, this monument to wisdom has somehow overarched the vicissitudes of time, volcanic eruptions, and violent regime change.

TURKEY, ISTANBUL

Maiden's Tower

ON EITHER SIDE OF THE BOSPHORUS STRAIT LIE EUROPE AND ASIA. MIDSTREAM IS THE MAIDEN'S TOWER, AN ARCHITECTURAL HYBRID THAT IS FIXED IN THE IMAGINATION AS A SYMBOL OF TURKEY. ITS DUMPY, CHURCHLIKE SHAPE FILLS OUT A TINY ISLAND ON A BOUNDARY BETWEEN TWO CONTINENTS.

Visible from land and sea and brightly lit at night, the tower and its pitched-roof precincts stand alone 220 yd/200 m off the coast of Üsküdar, the Asian quarter of Istanbul. A square stone tower supports a domed cupola, which is topped with a hefty pole bearing the flag of the Turkish Republic. Nearby, a triangular structure holds a lighthouse beacon that supplements the tower's main modern function as a national identifier.

Guarding the strait The first known building on the island, between what were then the cities of Byzantium and Chrysopolis, dates back to 408 BC. An Athenian general, Alcibiades, exploited the potential for a near complete surveillance of the Black Sea entrance and built a fort that guarded the narrow strait. In 341 BC Charis, another Greek general, adapted the fort into a mausoleum for his wife Damalys. In AD 1110 Emperor Alexius Comnenus constructed a new Byzantine fort.

The first record of a Maiden's Tower lighthouse is from 1509, the year that a wooden structure was built there following an earthquake. The present island tower results from late-Ottoman reconstructions during the reigns of Ahmet III in 1719, Mustafa III in 1763, and Mahmud II in 1832.

Above: The Maiden's Tower occupies a strategic point in the Istanbul sea lane, from where it overlooks a sweep of intercontinental geography and history.

Right: The Turkish landmark, which has variously served as a fortress and a prison, has now been recruited into civilian life as a restaurant and museum.

TIME LINE

Mythological time
Death occurs of a maiden, either a sultan's daughter or Hero, a figure from Greek mythology.

408 BC
Fort built by General Alcibiades to monitor shipping in the strait.

341 BC
Becomes a mausoleum for General Charis's wife.

1110
Greek remnants replaced by Byzantine fort.

1719
Erection of present tower.

2000
Refurbished and opened to the public.

Who was the maiden? While the tower is distinctive, the identity of its maiden is unclear. Local mythology locates her origins in either Asia or Europe in a pair of unhappy tales of female incarceration that have much in common with the Lady of Shalott. The Eastern version is of a sultan's daughter embowered in the tower to keep her safe following a prophecy of death before her 18th birthday. Come the day, a basket of fruit arrives and in it is a venomous snake. The European story also ends with an imprisoned young woman's death: in the Greek myth of Hero and Leander, the grieving Hero flings herself off her water-bound tower after her lover Leander drowns during one of his nightly swims to visit her.

New identity In 1995 the Turkish authorities leased the tower to a private company that restored the building and opened it up to visitors. Restoration was completed in 2000 when the Maiden's Tower started a new life as a museum, restaurant, and viewing point back into the many-domed Istanbul.

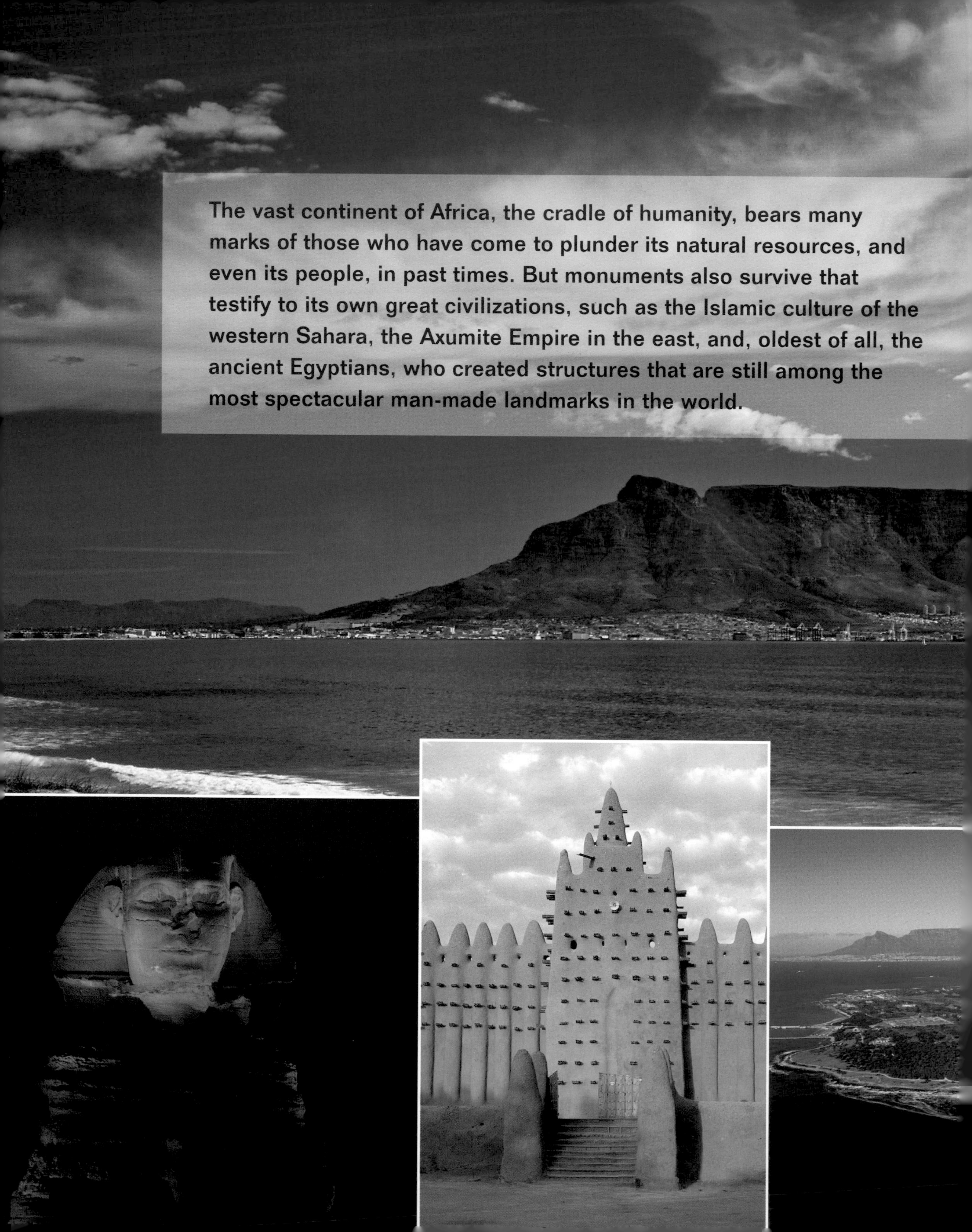

The vast continent of Africa, the cradle of humanity, bears many marks of those who have come to plunder its natural resources, and even its people, in past times. But monuments also survive that testify to its own great civilizations, such as the Islamic culture of the western Sahara, the Axumite Empire in the east, and, oldest of all, the ancient Egyptians, who created structures that are still among the most spectacular man-made landmarks in the world.

AFRICA

EGYPT

Great Sphinx of Giza

THIS VAST, REGAL CREATURE HAS PATIENTLY WATCHED OVER THE GIZA NECROPOLIS FOR THOUSANDS OF YEARS: IT IS THE WORLD'S OLDEST KNOWN MONUMENTAL SCULPTURE, AND SOME BELIEVE IT PREDATES THE PYRAMIDS AND MORTUARY TEMPLES IT GUARDS. NO ONE REALLY KNOWS ITS AGE, OR WHO CARVED IT, OR WHY.

The civilization of ancient Egypt was amazingly strong and stable, surviving for almost three millennia, but its most enduring symbols—the pyramids—were constructed during a relatively short period, beginning around 2650 BC and culminating in the great pyramids of the Fourth-Dynasty pharoahs Khufu, Khafre, and Menkaure, which dominate the Giza Necropolis on the west bank of the Nile. Each was part of a larger funerary complex that included a mortuary temple and a causeway running up to it from a lower temple at the riverside.

Great Sphinx of Giza •

The Great Sphinx, which appears to preside over the tombs of Giza, sits to the east of the site, gazing toward the river. Unusually in Egyptian iconography—in which many deities are depicted with human figures and animal heads—the Sphinx has the body of a lion (a guardian figure) and the head of a king, identifiable by its royal headcloth. Its face is thought to be a portrait of Khafre, and it is in almost exact alignment with Khafre's mortuary temple. But it bears no inscriptions, and its age and origin are still the subject of debate.

The Sphinx is a monolith, 240 ft/73 m long and 66 ft/20 m high, carved in situ from a rocky knoll. The figure lies in a dip on the plateau because its lower body

Left: The sphinx is a mythical creature with the body of a lion and a human head, but unlike the vicious female Greek version, the Egyptian sphinx was considered a benevolent guardian figure.

Right: The Great Sphinx of Glza sits like an outsize guard dog in front of the Pyramid of Khafre, the pharoah with whom it is most closely associated. He was a son of Khufu, and reigned from 2558–32 BC.

Below: Between the creature's giant forepaws the so-called Dream Stele was set up around 1401 BC by Thutmose IV. It gives an account of the king's dream about restoring the Sphinx and shows him making offerings to it. In front of the stele is a granite altar, placed there in the Roman period.

was formed by quarrying stone out of the base rock around it. The blocks obtained in this way were used in the construction of the surrounding temples. At the level of the body the limestone is yellow and rather crumbly, so the statue was faced with blocks of granite similar to that used for Khafre's pyramid. Above this level, the stratum from which the head was carved is a harder, grayer stone. Surviving particles of pigment on the surface of the stone show that the Sphinx was once painted.

The riddle of the Sphinx Despite its identification with Khafre, some archaeological and geological evidence has been interpreted to suggest that the Sphinx is much older, and was merely restored during the Old Kingdom. The so-called "Inventory Stele" discovered in the nineteenth century says that Khufu ordered a temple to be built alongside the (already existing) Sphinx, and local legends date it to long before the building of the pyramids. The American geologist Robert M. Schoch believes that the erosion on the body could only have

Left: Nightly *son et lumière* presentations provide a kitsch but engaging introduction to the pyramids. They are narrated, in half a dozen languages, by the "voice of the Sphinx."

been caused by water, implying that it existed when Egypt was subject to severe rainfall, which would have to be before 5000 BC, and that the dynastic head—which is certainly small in relation to the body—is a later re-carving. However, this controversial theory presupposes a "lost" ancient civilization for which Egyptologists have found no other evidence.

Restoration After the necropolis was abandoned the Sphinx's body was engulfed in sand—people were said to walk up to its head and press their ears to its mouth in the hope of gaining wisdom. A granite stele mounted between the creature's front paws relates the dream of Thutmose IV (reigned 1400–1390 BC), who fell asleep in its shade while hunting. He dreamed that the Sphinx complained to him about its ruinous state and promised him the throne if he would restore it. When he did indeed become king he cleared away the sand and repaired the facing.

By the time of Napoleon's Egyptian campaign at the end of the eighteenth century, the Sphinx was again buried up to its neck in the sand. Napoleonic troops are

FACT FILE

2650–2575 BC Third Dynasty (Old Kingdom) Pyramid building begins with Djoser's Step Pyramid at Saqqara.

2575–2467 BC Fourth Dynasty (Old Kingdom) Building of Great Pyramids and Giza temple complexes.

ca. 2150 BC Collapse of monarchy at end of Old Kingdom; Giza tombs plundered.

1419–1386 BC 18th Dynasty (New Kingdom) Reign of Thutmose IV, whose dream is recorded on the stele between the Sphinx's paws.

500 BC Herodotus visits Giza, but fails to mention the Sphinx in his account, perhaps because it is buried in sand.

AD 1798 Beginning of French occupation of Egypt and European exploration of ancient sites.

1979 Giza Necropolis listed as UNESCO World Heritage site.

Right: Most of the polished casing stones that originally covered the pyramids of Giza have fallen away, revealing the huge scale of the limestone blocks used in their basic construction.

often said to have used its face for target practice and destroyed the nose, but this is a myth, since earlier sketches made by Frederic Louis Norden in 1737 show that the nose was already missing.

There were several nineteenth-century attempts to clear the sand, but all were abandoned, though Giovanni Battista Caviglia found a piece of the royal beard that had fallen from its chin. (It is now in two pieces, in the British and Cairo museums respectively.) Emile Baraize eventually revealed the whole figure in 1925–36.

At present the stone is vulnerable to chemical damage from the Cairo smog. Over a period of six years in the 1980s there was a further attempt at restoration, but the new blocks that were added flaked away and the left shoulder crumbled in 1988. The focus now is on finding a way to prevent further erosion.

Below: The ensemble of pyramids on the Giza Plateau has been the preeminent emblem of ancient Egypt since the classical period, when the Great Pyramid was named as one of the Seven Wonders of the World.

EGYPT, LUXOR

Karnak

THE BEWILDERING TEMPLE COMPLEX AT KARNAK, BORDERING THE RIVER NILE, COULD BE SAID TO BE THE LONGEST-EVER CONSTRUCTION PROJECT—30 SUCCESSIVE PHAROAHS ATTEMPTED TO OUTBUILD THEIR PREDECESSORS AND IN DOING SO CREATED THE BIGGEST RELIGIOUS THEME PARK IN THE WORLD.

Over 1,300 years this swathe of ancient Egypt was covered with some 30 temples, connected by spooky avenues lined with statues of inscrutable deities, cats, birds, deer, sphinxes, and other fantasy animals. There are even shrines for the boats that transported the raw materials used to build this sandstone phantasmagoria. And everywhere the hieroglyphics and relief carvings make for signage systems more dense than on a Formula One racing car.

Precinct of Amun-Re Access to most of the site is restricted to archaeologists, who are excavating the Precinct of Mut, the Precinct of Montu, and the Temple of Amenhotep IV. Only the largest of the precincts is open to visitors and this is the Precinct of Amun-Re. One of the chief Egyptian gods, Amun-Re is a figure of mutating weirdness depicted variously as a cackling goose, a ram, a frog-headed man, a crocodile, an ape, and a bearded man with a beetle's body and a hawk's wings.

Though Amun's name means "hidden god," there is nothing hidden about his large-scale tributes: the precinct dedicated to him contains several huge statues, such as the 35-ft/10.5-m standing figure of his high priest Pinedjem I, plus a collection of obelisks including the 72-ft/22-m high Obelisk of Thutmose I. Isolated by

FACT FILE

Location
Near Luxor, 500 miles/800 km south of Cairo.

Area
247 acres/100 ha.

Dates
Constructed 1600–300 BC.
First European mention of monuments in Upper Egypt and Nubia in 1589.
First European drawings of Karnak published in 1704.

Pop culture
Agatha Christie's *Death on the Nile* is set onboard the SS *Karnak*.
Lara Croft visits Karnak in *Tomb Raider: The Last Revelation*.

Right: The Great Hypostyle Hall has 134 columns, which, in common with other surfaces throughout Karnak, are decorated with reliefs and hieroglyphics.

Left: Modern lighting adds drama to the ancient Great Hypostyle Hall, the most spectacular structure in the Karnak temple complex.

Right: Nearly every surface is covered with delicate reliefs, such as this one showing flora and fauna.

Far right: The greatest of the pharoahs, Ramesses II, decorated part of the Great Hypostyle Hall in the thirteenth century BC.

time and geography, Karnak's range of imagery and identities is too broad for a clear picture of the complex as a whole to have formed in most people's minds.

Great Hypostyle Hall One monument, however, imprints itself indelibly. The Great Hypostyle Hall is a regularly spaced forest of 134 columns elaborately sculpted in the form of papyrus plants. Of these, 122 are 40 ft high/12 m, and the 12 in the central rows are 70 ft/21 m high with a diameter of over 10 ft/3 m. The architraving supported by these huge columns weighs around 70 tons, and the method used to lift it into place is an unresolved engineering mystery, wrapped in the larger mystery of the people who labored on the Temple of Karnak and who sustained an outpouring of religious architecture across a span of 13 centuries.

Right: The Avenue of the Sphinxes, or Sacred Way, once stretched 2 miles/3 km through the Karnak complex and out to the Temple of Luxor.

ETHIOPIA

Obelisk of Axum

THE 1,700-YEAR-OLD OBELISK OF AXUM IS ONE OF ETHIOPIA'S MOST IMPORTANT NATIONAL SYMBOLS. HOWEVER, IN 1937 IT WAS LOOTED BY ITALIANS AND TRANSPORTED TO ROME, WHERE IT STOOD FOR NEARLY 70 YEARS. IT WAS FINALLY REERECTED ON ITS ORIGINAL SITE IN 2008, TO MUCH NATIONAL REJOICING.

Topping the pinnacle of the Obelisk of Axum is an elegantly formal half circle of stone. We don't know if the fourth-century Ethiopian masons had in mind an image of heaven or of sunrise. We do know they looked upward and speculated. It is what humankind has always done.

The 78-ft/24-m high obelisk—or stele, as it is more properly termed—is oriented to the sun and faces south, as do 120 other monuments in Ethiopia's Northern Stelae Park. Far more ancient obelisks have long collapsed into a maze of underground chambers that reveal this as an ancient burial site. Some say it contains the remains of the Queen of Sheba, who is mentioned in the book of Genesis. In fact, the graves' occupants are as little known as the beliefs that drove the erection of the giant gravestones.

Inaccessible In pre- and post-Christian times, this part of what is now northern Ethiopia was a prosperous political center where the rich and powerful built monuments to somehow connect them to the heavens. From a distance, the multistory Obelisk of Axum appears to have windows, fine lintels, beam-ends, and a bolted door behind which there must be an interior that might unlock old beliefs. But the doors and windows are trompe l'oeil motifs on a solid structure of unyielding

TIME LINE

3000 BC
First stelae erected in the Kingdom of Axum.

AD 300
Obelisk of Axum erected.

1529–43
Many Axum stelae toppled during Ethiopian–Adal War.

1937
Obelisk of Axum taken to Rome.

1947
UN agrees that Italy should repatriate the obelisk.

May 28, 2002
Obelisk struck by lightning; it is dismantled and put into storage near Rome airport.

2008
Flown back to Ethiopia.

Opposite: Ethiopia's Northern Stelae Park has 120 standing obelisks, including King Ezana's Stele in the center and the repatriated Obelisk of Axum (far right).

Right: The Obelisk of Axum was erected about 1,700 years ago. It faces south and is a grave marker that probably also had a solar or astronomical measuring function.

Below: The 108-ft/33-m Great Stele, carved from a single block, is believed to have toppled and broken while being erected.

granite. The hardness of the stone has kept the 1,700-year-old illusion realistic.

Roaming stones The least to be said is that structures like this represent upward aspirations. They are also repositories of memory and identity, and the Obelisk of Axum is freighted with a recent post-colonial history. In 1937, following the Italian invasion of Ethiopia, occupying soldiers shipped it in pieces to Naples, from where it was transported to Rome and reassembled to celebrate the birth of Mussolini's new Roman empire. That particular empire soon fell, and in 1947 a democratic Italian government agreed to return what had been taken. It took 56 years and a bolt of lightning before the obelisk was removed from Rome's Porta Capena Square. Politics and logistics combined to delay repatriation further. Ethiopia's war with Eritrea meant the obelisk couldn't reenter by sea; the landing strip at Axum needed to be lengthened; American transport planes were tied up in Iraq. In the end it was a Russian-built Antonov An-124 plane that flew the 160-ton obelisk home in three trips.

Home from Rome Amidst scenes of jubilation, the monument was unveiled in its original home on September 4, 2008. Was the individual originally memorialized turning in their grave? Would they have believed that their carefully crafted heaven-pointing pinnacle could have flown so high on its journey back to them?

MALI

Great Mosque of Djenné

THE GREAT MOSQUE OF DJENNÉ IS A BUILDING OF THE PEOPLE THAT HAS SPRUNG FROM THE SOIL OF MALI. THE AESTHETIC IS ENTIRELY LOCAL, FOR IT IS CONSTRUCTED FROM LOCALLY SOURCED ADOBE BRICKS AND PALMWOOD IN A CENTURIES-OLD STYLE SUITED TO THE WEST AFRICAN CLIMATE AND CULTURE.

Every spring, the serious business of building maintenance is converted into fun for all the family. During the early months of the year, everybody joins in to prepare a plaster (*banco*) from earth and rice husks. Wading in muddy pits of the curing *banco*, children make a game of mixing it into a workable building material. The mosque finally gets plastered after a night of revelry that ends with a race to take the first load from the pits to the mosque.

Throughout the day, women and girls carry water and prepare food while the men climb up palmwood ladders and scramble over the projecting bundles of sticks that form built-in scaffolding. The old people sit in Djenné's town square, watching and no doubt complaining that the younger generation is making a mess of things.

Exterior The annually renewed plaster gives a smooth finish to the thick mud-brick walls, which insulate the interior from extremes of heat and cold and bear the weight of the high towers. Spires on top of the minarets are capped with ostrich eggs to symbolize purity and fertility. Ceramic guttering projects from the walls to throw off rainwater, and the palm stick bundles the plasterers climb on also act as minimal ornamentation. The Great Mosque's main eastern aspect is a miracle of subtle

TIME LINE

1240
Sultan Koi Kunboro converts to Islam and turns his palace into a mosque.

1830s
Sheikh Amadou builds a more modest adobe mosque.

1907
The current mosque is built using the old techniques.

1988
Old Towns of Djenné listed by UNESCO as a World Heritage Site.

2009
A section of the southern large tower of the *qibla* wall collapses after 3 in/75 mm of rain falls in one day.The Aga Khan Trust for Culture helps fund rebuilding plus other renovation work.

Above right: Over 3,000 worshippers can fit into the arcaded prayer hall.

Right: Mali has a hot, arid climate, but the annual rains wash a layer of adobe off the walls of the mosque.

Above: The symmetrical arrangement of the main towers is distinctly West African in style. However, in facing toward Mecca, this *qibla*, or prayer wall, follows Muslim orthodoxy.

Right: The whole community goes into action for the annual *crepissage* festival, when the walls are replastered to repair damage from rain and extremes of temperature.

proportion, and the regular sprinkling of softly molded pinnacles and protrusions brings a sense of uplift and lightness to the windowless facade.

Interior Windows and doors are to the north and south of the building. The structure's footprint is faintly trapezoid, but it sits on a 250-ft/75-m square plinth raised above the marketplace and accessed by six sets of stairs. Inside the prayer hall, nine walls pierced with high arches support the roof; views through the arcades are restricted in the dim light.

Demarcation Only the faithful can enter the earthen-floored prayer hall. Those who run this well-mannered, parochial building have banned non-Muslim visitors since 1996, when a fashion magazine exploited the mosque as the backdrop for a photo shoot—a disrespectful move. More than most buildings, the Great Mosque of Djenné is an intimate physical part of its society and a communal focal point where the care is literally hands-on. It demands respect.

SOUTH AFRICA

Table Mountain

TABLE MOUNTAIN IS A NATURAL LANDMARK WHOSE FLAT TOP WARNS SAILORS THEY ARE ABOUT TO PASS THE CAPE WHERE THE ATLANTIC AND INDIAN OCEANS CONVERGE. IT IS A LANDLUBBER'S REFERENCE POINT TOO, FOR CONSTANT SIGHTINGS OF ITS RECOGNIZABLE BULK ARE A FEATURE OF CAPE TOWN LIFE.

The mountain's obviously apt name establishes a domestic theme that extends to approach routes called the Back Table and the Nursery Ravine. The reference is also there in the "tablecloth" cloud cover that drapes the plateau when sea breezes meet colder air on the mountain. The puffy clouds are locally seen as a smoking competition in which the devil takes on a cheerily named pirate called Van Hunk.

African view The reward on getting to the top of the mountain, tablecloth permitting, is a wonderful panorama off the tip of Africa and out into the southern seas. The former prison colony of Robben Island is easily visible. In the middle distance, Cape Town and its vineyards nestle far below along the edge of Table Bay. Immediately below are the mountain's exposed southern crags, their sheer faces of hard sandstone barring most routes up.

Travel options The easy way to the flat summit is a five-minute sprint in a swish modern cable car, which rotates so that nonwalkers get all-round views without even having to turn their heads. The only viable hiking route from the Cape Town side is a tough scramble up the Platteklip Gorge, where hikers follow a gargantuan stairway of white sandstone leading through a scrubby cleft at the center of the giant geological table.

Above: A classic view from Blouberg beach, showing Table Mountain's profile to perfection. Flanking it are Devil's Peak (left) and Lion's Head and Signal Hill (right).

Above right: Nestled under the eastern slopes of the mountain is Kirstenbosch Botanical Garden, founded in 1913 to preserve the Cape's unique flora.

Right: A Cape sugarbird, a specialist nectar feeder, perches on protea flowers at Kirstenbosch. Proteas are also known as sugarbushes.

FACT FILE

Altitude
3,563 ft/1,086 m.

First European ascent
António de Saldanha, 1503.

Flying ascent
Table Mountain Cableway opened in 1929, upgraded 1997. Cars whisk sightseers 2,311 ft/704 m from lower to upper station.

Flora
Nearly 2,300 plant species grow on Table Mountain and the Cape Peninsula.

Fauna
Dassies (rock hyraxes), porcupines, mongooses, snakes, tortoises, klipspringers, rooikats, and baboons.

African plant life There are longer and gentler hikes from other directions, and on these the terrain is less harsh and windblown and the plant life varied. Over 1,500 plant species are found on the mountain, including several proteas. The main vegetation here is the Cape *fynbos*, the species-rich heathland that forms part of the Cape Floral Region.

African wildlife This is now an urban mountain, and the big cats that once roamed here are long gone; the last lion was shot in the early nineteenth century and the last leopard was seen in the 1920s. Most easily spotted today are the rock hyraxes, which look like small brown cushions on legs and scamper about fearlessly scrounging food from tourists. Less cuddly are the tortoises, porcupines, and mongooses.

Right: Getting to the top from Cape Town involves a two-to-three-hour walk, or a short trip by revolving cable car, with spectacular views out to Robben Island.

SOUTH AFRICA

Robben Island

LYING OFF SOUTH AFRICA'S CAPE IN TABLE BAY, ROBBEN ISLAND IS A FLAT, SURF-LASHED OUTCROP SO MISERABLE AND DRAB THAT IT WOULD SEEM TO DESERVE ZERO RECOGNITION AS A LANDMARK. YET IT IS UNIVERSALLY KNOWN, MADE NOTEWORTHY BY A MAN WHOSE IMPRISONMENT THERE PUT IT ON THE WORLD MAP.

Nelson Mandela was incarcerated in Robben Island prison, along with many other black leaders, including South Africa's current president Jacob Zuma, for opposing the country's apartheid regime. From his arrest in 1962, Mandela refused to renounce the use of arms against a racist government. He was released in 1990, elected South African president in 1994, and remained in office until 1999.

Inhumane Mandela was on the island for 18 of his 27 years in captivity. He lived in a square cell barely wide enough for a sleeping mat and with nowhere to hide a toilet bucket. The tourists who now visit the jail after a wind-blown, 45-minute ferry ride from Cape Town fall silent as they peer into a tiny domain through a barred door nearly the width of the room.

Inescapable Political prisoners were allowed one letter and one visitor every six months and, when not in solitary confinement, labored in a limestone quarry. In the distance they would have seen Cape Town's Table Mountain, but escape from the island was impossible. They knew of previous inmates, such as the Xhosa leader Makanda Nxele, whom the British colonial government sentenced to life imprisonment in 1819. Having escaped the prison island, he drowned on the shores of Table Bay.

TIME LINE

1498
One of Vasco da Gama's ships makes first recorded landing; island becomes a prison and leper colony.

1939
Military training ground.

1960
Designated a maximum security prison.

1962
Nelson Mandela imprisoned on island.

1990–96
After Mandela's release, last political prisoners leave in 1991; last criminal prisoners are removed in 1996.

1997
Prison becomes a museum and island is listed as a World Heritage Site in 1999.

Opposite: Mandela on his release from incarceration on February 11, 1990.

Below: The austere maximum security prison was built in 1961.

Opposite: A formidable stretch of turbulent water separates the former prison island from Cape Town, South Africa's legislative capital.

Right: Nelson Mandela's tiny prison cell is preserved as a memorial to the long years of imprisonment that a leader-in-waiting had to endure.

Indomitable Robben Island is a relic of apartheid that has come to symbolize a hope that justice will prevail. It is now a tourist destination visited not for architecture or antiquity or charm but to celebrate an idea that was tested there and did not break. On the day of his release on February 11, 1990, Nelson Mandela made a speech in Cape Town that ended thus: "In conclusion I wish to quote my own words during my trial in 1964. They are true today as they were then: 'I have fought against white domination and I have fought against black domination. I have cherished the ideal of a democratic and free society in which all persons live together in harmony and with equal opportunities. It is an ideal which I hope to live for and to achieve. But if needs be, it is an ideal for which I am prepared to die.' "

The power of language has rendered Robben Island into a landmark every bit as potent as Table Mountain, that "beacon of hope" that, according to Mandela, "represented the mainland to which we knew we would one day return."

Many of Asia's key landmarks measure their histories in millennia. Their spiritual resonances reflect the evolution and juxtaposition of different faiths and cultures, whether they have succeeded in coexisting peacefully or are still engaged in painful struggles for dominance. Newer monuments are symbols of political power, or bold statements by nations that are establishing themselves as wealthy and confident players on the world stage.

ASIA

JAPAN

Mount Fuji

THE SNOW-CAPPED, CLOUD-WREATHED, CONICAL SYMMETRY OF JAPAN'S HIGHEST MOUNTAIN HAS FORMED A CULTURAL CLASSIC OUT OF A WORK OF NATURE. MOUNT FUJI, WHICH IS VISIBLE ON CLEAR DAYS FROM TOKYO, HAS PROVIDED A DEFINING IMAGE FOR JAPANESE MYTHOLOGY, HISTORY, AND IDENTITY.

Fuji's distinctive lines were imprinted on the global consciousness in the mid-nineteenth century, with the publication of *Thirty-six Views of Mount Fuji*, Katsushika Hokusai's best-selling series of woodblock prints. But long before that, volcanic Fuji-san was central to Japanese culture, and the many routes up it are dotted with ancient Buddhist temples and Shinto shrines.

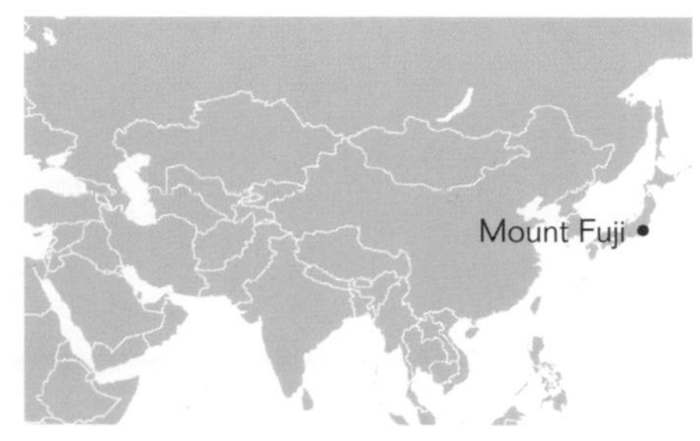

Mountain mythology The Fujiko sect believes Mount Fuji is not merely holy but has a soul. It was sacred to the Ainu, Japan's aboriginal inhabitants whose gods included Fuchi, the guardian of the domestic hearth, and it has been suggested that she gave her name to the national mountain. Buddhists revere it as a gateway to another world; in their tradition, it emerged from the earth in 286 BC after an earthquake. (Geologists date its creation to the Pleistocene era, 600,000 years earlier.)

The Shinto goddess of the mountain is Sengen-Sama, the blossom princess who symbolizes delicate earthly life and who has a shrine at the summit. Adherents believe that she prevents the volcano from erupting, which last happened in 1707.

Getting to the top The sacred mountain is also a cracking good climb, and the spirits of pilgrimage and tourism now have to coexist on Fuji's steep slopes. What

FACT FILE

Height
Japan's highest mountain at 12,388 ft/3,776 m.

Diameter
31 miles/50 km at base.

Volcanic activity
Three tectonic plates meet at Mount Fuji. The last eruption began in November 1707; seismic activity has increased since 2000.

Temperature
Average monthly temperature at summit is below freezing except in summer; lowest recorded temperature is -36°F/-38°C; highest 64°F/17.8°C.

Opposite: Nature and nurture meet in a classic view of old Japan: an orderly tea plantation before the elegant natural iconography of Mount Fuji.

Right: Dense forests and deep lakes surround Mount Fuji, seen here from the Yamanashi Prefecture.

Below: *The Great Wave Off Kanagawa* is Hokusai's most celebrated image of the mountain that he made famous all around the world.

appears serene in distant views, made familiar by countless paintings, etchings, and photographs, close up is steep, lava-strewn, prone to rock falls, and something of a free-for-all. Ancient meets modern during the brief officially sanctioned climbing season, from July 1 to August 26, when the snow has melted enough to make climbing safe. Buses deliver walkers to the fifth station, (about halfway up), tractors haul supplies up to cafés along the route and, to the fury of the authorities, a few mountain bikers speed down from the top.

Every year some 300,000 people make the stiff eight-hour ascent, about a third of them foreigners. Many Japanese climb at night in order to witness the sunrise from the summit, and a few still wear traditional white robes. All those who have made the trek, for whatever reason, will hear the contemporary Japanese cliché, which holds that those who never climb Mount Fuji are fools, while those who climb it more than once are twice the fool.

JAPAN, HIROSHIMA

Hiroshima Peace Memorial

THE GENBAKU DOME IS SIGNIFICANT FOR ITS NEAR DESTRUCTION AND SUBSEQUENT PRESERVATION RATHER THAN FOR ITS ORIGINAL CREATION OR BEAUTY. IN THIS IT IS UNIQUE. THE BUILDING IS ALSO UNIQUE FOR HAVING SURVIVED AT THE EPICENTER OF THE WORLD'S FIRST NUCLEAR ATTACK.

At breakfast time on August 6, 1945, an air-burst atomic bomb released shockwaves and heat rays that killed 70,000 people in an instant, with another 70,000 suffering fatal radiation. This mega-death is commemorated at the Genbaku Dome in Hiroshima's Peace Memorial Park.

The grimly named "Little Boy" bomb exploded some 2,000 ft/600 m above the Hiroshima Prefectural Industrial Promotion Hall. Despite the phenomenal force of the blast, the building's core remained intact. As the dust settled on that August day, the dome's iron-framed skeleton emerged from a cityscape of flattened rubble. It still stands, a brick and iron remnant of unconventional and unexpected beauty, a vivid reminder of the utterly abnormal.

Trade center into shrine The dome was originally covered in copper and crowned a plaster and stone-clad five-story tower. It was the centerpiece of an exhibition complex commissioned in 1910 from a Czech architect, Jan Letzel. Japan was beginning to open up to the world.

Less than half a century later, Hiroshima had to be rebuilt around the dome, and in 1966, amid some controversy, the city council declared an intention to preserve the ruined building in perpetuity. What started as a piece of banal and expendable commercial architecture

TIME LINE

1915
Hiroshima Commercial Exhibition Hall opened.

1933
Renamed Hiroshima Prefectural Industrial Promotion Hall.

8:15 a.m., August 6, 1945
Building becomes Genbaku ("Atomic Bomb") Dome.

1950–64
Peace Memorial Park laid out.

1966
Hiroshima City Council resolves to preserve dome forever.

1996
Inscribed by UNESCO as a World Heritage site.

Opposite: The ruined Genbaku Dome stands as a witness to the destructive force of nuclear attack and as a symbol of hope for world peace.

Right: Every year on August 6, memorial paper lanterns are illuminated and set afloat in the Motoyasu River next to Hiroshima's Peace Memorial Park.

has been transformed into an enduring memorial to the dead and a global symbol.

Preservation of the ruins Conservation of the dome follows the leave-as-is approach and is a delicate operation. The floor is strewn with bricks and the overall structure remains as it was immediately after the bomb detonated. Steel girders support the fragile structure, whose walls are now capped at the top. It is vulnerable because century-old internal building materials have been exposed to the elements and the old bricks are held together with mortar degraded in a nuclear furnace.

In 1996 the dome was registered on the UNESCO World Heritage List. The United States dissociated itself from the decision on the grounds that listing a memorial to a "war site" would omit necessary historical context. However, in August 2010 a representative of the U.S. government attended the Memorial Park anniversary for the first time. The ambassador, John Roos, said: "For the sake of future generations, we must continue to work together to realize a world without nuclear weapons."

Below: The cenotaph in the Hiroshima Peace Memorial Park, commemorating all those who died in the nuclear attack, frames the view of the Genbaku Dome.

JAPAN, KYOTO

Zen Garden, Ryoan-ji Temple

AMONG THE WOODLAND AND PONDS IN THE EXQUISITE GROUNDS OF THE RYOAN-JI TEMPLE IS A MAN-MADE LANDSCAPE IN MINIATURE. RYOAN-JI, THE TEMPLE OF THE PEACEFUL DRAGON, IS HOME TO A ROCK GARDEN THAT IS POSSIBLY JAPAN'S ARTISTIC MASTERPIECE AND IS THE HIGHEST EXPRESSION OF ZEN CREATIVITY.

The garden is an austere artifact, comprising a 33 x 98-ft/10 x 30-m rectangle of white gravel interspersed with 15 rough and mossy boulders arranged in five groups, the whole surrounded by a low wall. At ground level, at least one boulder is always obscured from view. Monks rake the gravel around the rocks into precise rippling patterns that vary slightly from day to day. Generally, the gravel runs in lines parallel to the long side of the rectangle, with concentric circles framing the rock groups. When the straight lines touch the circles, they terminate without a single misplaced stone.

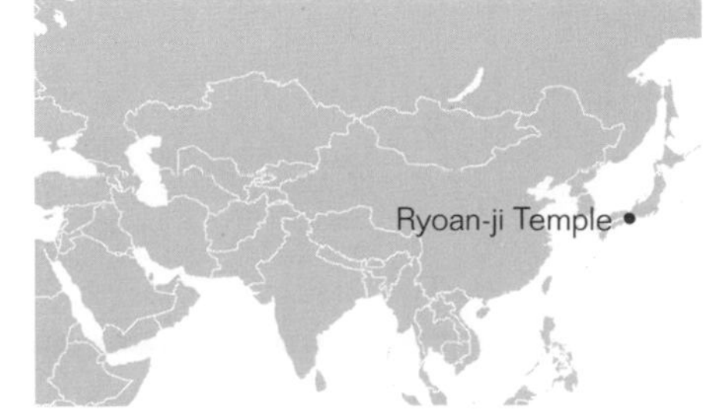

Minimal landmark The Zen garden demands context if it is to be appreciated as more than pretentious outdoor decoration. The Ryoan-ji Temple in Kyoto belongs to the Rinzai branch of Zen Buddhism, in which much is made of paradoxical puzzles and questions. *Zen* is Japanese for "meditative state," and the garden to the south of the temple building invites a meditation on life's contradictions.

This most minimal of landmarks is full of emptiness. Here is a place where even the fiercest dragon might be peaceful; the garden hints at mystery within order, irregularity within symmetry, complexity within simplicity, and stillness within the changing of the seasons. Cherry

TIME LINE

11th century
Fujiwara estate includes original Ryoan-ji Buddhist temple.

Late 15th century
Hosokawa Katsumoto occupies residence until it is destroyed in Onin Wars, and wills estate to become a Zen temple.

1488–99
Hosokawa's son Masomoto builds temple and lays out garden, possibly with trees.

Mid-17th century
First written record of the dry garden, with only nine rocks.

Late 18th century
Garden created in its current form.

1994
Temple and garden inscribed on UNESCO World Heritage List.

Opposite: The calm sweep of the rock garden is suggestive of timelessness and infinity. The cherry tree in the background is a reminder of mutability.

Right: Across the lily pond in the grounds of Ryoan-ji, a Zen master and a number of monks live simply, study, and meditate in the small sub-temple of Daishu-in.

trees beyond the wall of the garden blossom in the spring, and their leaves color in the fall. Snow clings to the moss in the winter.

Zen meditation Wherever the garden is viewed from, all 15 rocks are never in sight, for Buddhist numerology holds that the number 15 signifies completeness. Only deep Zen meditation can attain enlightenment sufficient to earn a view of every stone at once. There are other precise interpretations of the garden's abstractions: the gravel symbolizes the sea and the rocks are islands; or the garden represents a tigress leading her cubs across a river; or it depicts a branching tree. A less literal view is that *karesansui*—dry landscape gardens, of which this is the archetype—are what Zen masters call "direct pointing to reality" in calm surroundings that encourage viewers to turn inward.

Behind a simple temple overlooking the garden is a *tsukubai*, a stone basin for visitors to purify themselves with a ritual of hand-washing and mouth-rinsing. An inscription carved into the top of the basin reinforces the minimalist teachings of Buddhism, reading: "What one has is all one needs."

"What's so special about the garden at Ryoan-ji?" a traveler once asked a Buddhist monk.

"The spaces between the rocks," the monk replied.

Below: One of the daily monastic duties at Ryoan-ji is raking the gravel—the monk here is finishing the job by inscribing curving furrows around one of the rocks.

CHINA

Great Wall of China

THE GREAT WALL OF CHINA RESIDES IN THE POPULAR IMAGINATION AS A LIVING ENTITY. LIKE THE TAIL OF A DRAGON IN A NEVER-ENDING CHINESE FESTIVAL, IT UNDULATES FROM THE SEAS IN THE EAST ALONG THE VAST PLAINS AND MOUNTAIN RANGES THAT DEFINE THE SOUTHERN RIM OF INNER MONGOLIA.

Measured in both time and distance, northern China's Great Wall is the world's longest-ever building project. Construction began over 2,500 years ago with a series of independent walls built from lumber and compacted mud. As the Chinese states began to unify, separate walls were consolidated and fortified with watch-towers that communicated via smoke signals during the day and fires at night.

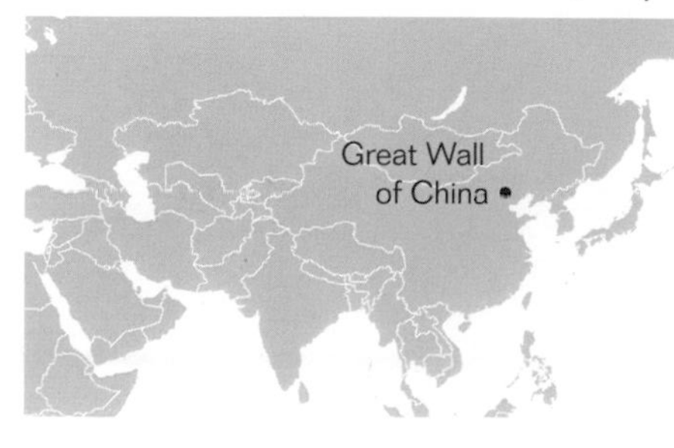

Ming consolidation Constant extensions and repairs led to a concerted period of building during the Ming dynasty (1368–1644) when the wall's length grew to nearly 4,000 miles/6,500 km. This is what is commonly referred to as the Great Wall of China, although, when all the fortified defenses of the different dynasties are included, the total length exceeds 30,000 miles/48,000 km.

Sections near the Ming capital of Beijing are especially solid, although they didn't repel the Manchu invasions that culminated in the formation of the Qing dynasty. The wall near the Chinese capital is 25 ft/8 m high and 16 ft/5 m wide; its stone-and-brick ramparts, with battlements lining the uppermost sections, dominate the wild landscape. The magnificent tower-dotted structure seems to stretch into eternity and, as with all the boldest projects, myths have attached themselves.

FACT FILE

Length
Approximately
4,000 miles/6,500 km.

Typical dimensions
25 ft/8 m high,
16 ft/5 m wide.

Construction period
About 2,000 years, from Warring States period (476–221 BC) to Ming dynasty (1368–1644).

UNESCO listing
Inscribed on World Heritage List in 1987.

The Wall is not ...
... visible from outer space, nor is it a continuous structure.

Opposite: The spectacular Jinshanling section of the Great Wall snakes along the crest of a mountain range, each peak crowned with a watchtower.

Right: Seen here from a watchtower window, the restored Badaling section near Beijing is the most visited part of the wall.

Below: Jiayuguan Fortress was built in the fourteenth century to protect the pass at the wall's western end.

The moon myth First, the wall is not a single structure, but rather a series of disparate fortifications, some running in parallel, with some of the westerly reaches now eroded by sandstorms. Second, the Great Wall cannot be seen from outer space. In an early reference to this myth, the English antiquarian William Stukeley wrote in 1754: "The Chinese Wall ... makes a considerable figure upon the terrestrial globe, and may be discerned at the moon." Not so, for the width of the wall if seen from the moon would be equivalent to that of a human hair viewed from a distance of 2 miles/3 km. Alan Bean, who actually walked on the moon in 1969, provides clinching evidence: "The only thing you can see from the moon is a beautiful sphere, mostly white (clouds), some blue (ocean), patches of yellow (deserts), and every once in a while some green vegetation. In fact, when first leaving Earth's orbit and only a few thousand miles away, no man-made object is visible."

Nevertheless, the Great Wall will continue to coil through the collective memory, a monument to brute endeavor and to an ancient human propensity to spare no expense in the guarding of borderlands. It has recently become an international tourist destination. Most visitors arrive from Beijing—the best time to be there is in the fall, when the leaves are turning and the weather is least likely to be too hot, too cold, or too rainy.

CHINA, BEIJING

Tiananmen Square

A CITYSCAPE OF SUPERLATIVE SCOPE AND DIMENSION, IT IS THE LARGEST CITY SQUARE IN THE WORLD AND A TESTIMONY TO CHINA'S GEOGRAPHICAL, DEMOGRAPHIC, AND POLITICAL IMMENSITY. THIS EXTRAORDINARY SPACE CAN ACCOMMODATE OVER HALF A MILLION OF THE NATION'S 1.3 BILLION CITIZENS.

Tiananmen Square was immense in conception. Built in 1417, Tiananmen, the huge "Gate of Heavenly Peace," was a statement of dynastic might, and its impact was bolstered as a grand imperial square developed before it in later centuries. But in the 1950s everything changed. In a gargantuan assertion of state socialism, the square was enlarged fourfold. Down came the 400-year-old Gate of China and up went the monuments that now predominate.

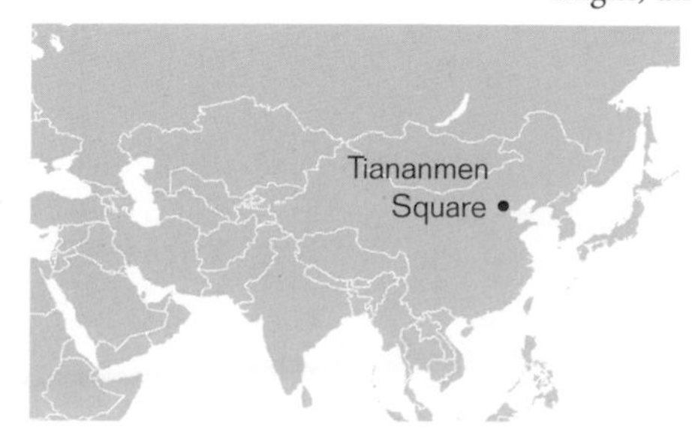

Monuments to history The square (in fact, a rectangle 960 x 550 yd/880 x 500 m), is bounded with monumental buildings that tell of China's recent and more distant past. To the north, Tiananmen is the entrance to the Forbidden City, barred to all except a feudal elite. Medieval Chinese craftsmanship is evident in the gate's delicately carved marble and imperial yellow tiles. To the south are two twentieth-century structures that illustrate another China. First is the Monument to the People's Heroes, a 10-story obelisk erected in 1959 to celebrate a decade of communist rule. Behind it is a Memorial Hall, dated 1976 but fronted in Neoclassical style with a dozen marble pillars. Chairman Mao's crystal coffin lies somewhere beyond.

Active state power occupies the west of the square in the Great Hall of the People, another 1950s building,

TIME LINE

1417
Construction of Tiananmen, gate to the Forbidden City.

1651
Tiananmen Square designed and built.

1860
British and French invaders set up camp in square.

October 1, 1949
Mao Zedong proclaims People's Republic of China.

1954
Demolition of Gate of China to allow for enlargement of square in late 1950s.

1976
Mao's Mausoleum founded on site of Gate of China.

1989
Tiananmen Square protests; troops fire on demonstrators, killing 400–800 people.

1990s
Construction of National Grand Theater.

Opposite: Beyond the rooftops of the Forbidden City, the fifteenth-century Tiananmen faces memorials to twentieth-century political revolution across the square.

Right: Red flags fly in the sun, with the National People's Congress in the distance; Tiananmen Square is at the emotional and geographical heart of Beijing and thus of China.

which holds the National People's Congress, a 5,000 seat banqueting hall, and myriad government offices. Facing it across the square is the National Museum of China, opened in 2003 and home to a million artifacts that portray 10,000 years of Chinese history.

Protests of 1989 This adamantine place of paving stones, granite, and marble has mutated into a flower-strewn vastness offering a welcome to outsiders. But the defining recent event followed the collapse of Iron Curtain regimes in Europe, when demonstrators gathered here in the hope that their own government might become more yielding. The image of a lone man facing down a column of tanks in Tiananmen Square is as resonant of the place as any triumphalist panorama.

Below: Entertainers perform a traditional lion dance on Tiananmen Square, during the cultural festival mounted as part of the 2008 Olympics in Beijing.

Right: A soldier stands guard in front of Chairman Mao's portrait on the Gate of Heavenly Peace, the fifteenth-century entrance to the Forbidden City.

CHINA, BEIJING

Beijing National Stadium

THE BIRD'S NEST: IS IT SCULPTURE OR ARCHITECTURE, STRUCTURE OR FACADE, ORGANIC OR INORGANIC, EASTERN OR WESTERN, COMMUNIST OR CAPITALIST, COLLECTIVE OR INDIVIDUALISTIC, FRAGILE OR SOLID, YIN OR YANG? DOES IT SOAR OR SQUAT? IS IT A CERAMIC BOWL OR A TWIGGY NEST?

"There should be many ways of perceiving a building," says Li Xinggang, the head of the China Architectural Design and Research Group, which assisted the stadium's lead architects Herzog & de Meuron. Li is explaining that he approves of the stadium's nickname, for, as he says: "In China, a bird's nest is very expensive, something you eat on special occasions."

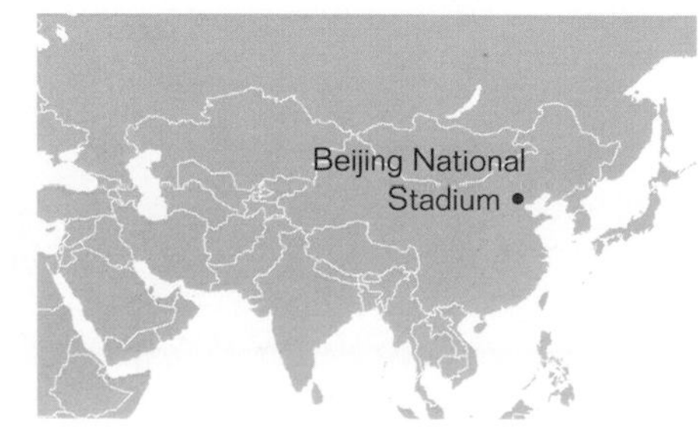

Well, the Bird's Nest was the focal point for the special occasion of the 2008 Olympic feast and cost $423 million. The shape of the twiglike steel grid that now graces the Beijing skyline really does invite comparison with a nest. As in a nest, the gaps in the woven superstructure are filled to regulate wind, rain, and sunlight—in the stadium's case with inflatable cushions. The comparison runs deeper. Chinese culture elides the idea of a nest with a ceramic bowl, and the enormous stadium deliberately echoes the lines and symmetries of the nation's most enduring and delicate art form.

Bowl in a nest The design intention wasn't purely iconographic. The steel lattice was initially intended to support a retractable roof, an idea abandoned at the beginning of fabrication when a similar roof collapsed at Paris's Charles de Gaulle Airport in May 2004. By then, the stadium was assuming its recognizable form as some

FACT FILE

Architects
Herzog & de Meuron, China Architectural Design and Research Group.

Structural engineers
Ove Arup & Partners.

Cost
$423 million.

Form and materials
42,000-ton steel skeleton surrounding independent concrete bowl.

Construction
Building began December 8, 2003, opened June 28, 2008; the Bird's Nest is designed to last for 100 years and to withstand a force 8 earthquake.

Grass arena
9,342 sq yd/7,811 sq m.

Below: The closing ceremony of the Beijing Olympics on August 24, 2008: the spectacular architectural and ceremonial display, augmented by cheery and disciplined crowds, imprinted a new view of China on the world.

Opposite: From a distance, China's new national monument seems as fragile as a bird's nest.

Right: Seen close up, the steel latticework takes on the dimensions of branches rather than twigs.

7,000 building workers erected a miracle in concrete and steel. They built two separate structures: an outer steel skeleton based around 24 trussed columns (each weighing 1,000 tons) encases a concrete bowl seating 91,000 spectators. The stadium also contains an 80-room hotel, a restaurant, and an underground shopping center. It has green credentials too, with geothermal heating and rainwater collection for irrigation and sanitation.

Chinese puzzle The Bird's Nest offers complex, even contradictory messages, exemplifying current ambitions and multiculturalism. Jacques Herzog, the Swiss architect who had a clear brief that it should display the material progress of Chinese society, paid tribute to his paymasters: "They are so fresh in their mind. They have the most radical things in their tradition, the most amazing faience and perforated jades and scholars' rocks. Everyone is encouraged to do extravagant designs. They don't have as much of a barrier between good taste and bad taste, between the minimal and expressive. The Beijing stadium tells me that nothing will shock them."

CHINA, LESHAN

Giant Buddha of Leshan

IN THE SOUTHEAST CHINESE HEARTLANDS OF SICHUAN, THE LESHAN BUDDHA SITS IN A DEEPLY CARVED RECESS IN A SHEER CLIFF AT THE SWIRLING CONFLUENCE OF THREE RIVERS. THE STATUE PRESENTS A DRAMA IN FIXITY: THE BUDDHA, KNOWN AS MAITREYA OR DAFO, HAS BEEN THERE FOR 1,200 YEARS.

Viewed from a distance on the river, Maitreya is a serene deity, a still point around which hundreds of tiny figures are ascending and descending stairways. From a religious perspective, Maitreya is the future Buddha who will one day arrive and preach a code suited to a more enlightened world than this one. Meanwhile humanity scurries around in search of gods, or just another riverside attraction. An inscrutable Maitreya has time to sit and wait.

Up close and personal Viewed from the side of the cliff recess, where the head peeps out of the trees, Maitreya's face takes on a human aspect. Dafo seems an apt name for the droll individual who gazes over the wide plain to the mountains beyond. The face has a touch of the comical in the sleepy eyes and the faint suggestion of a smile, and there is a worldliness in the jowls and creased neck.

Legend has it that he brought the water spirits under control and calmed the rivers; common humanity says that, given a good enough joke, one of those big hands might rise and slap the big knee. The statue's expectancy and promise is not confined to future lives.

Looking up Viewed from below on the river's edge, Dafo is a very big boy. The neatly manicured toenails are the size of bulky armchairs, and the head, 233 ft/71 m

FACT FILE

Construction
713–803.

Height
233 ft/71 m.

Shoulders
92 ft/28 m wide.

Fingers
11 ft/3.5 m long.

Ears
22 ft/7 m long.

Eyebrows
18 ft/5.5 m long.

Hair
1,021 coiled buns.

Opposite: Tourists snake down the cliff stairways as they gaze up at Maitreya, who gazes out to infinity.

Right: The Leshan Buddha is set so far back into the rock face that his enormous toes don't go beyond the bottom of the cliff.

Below: There is a suggestion of divine comedy in Dafo's sleepy eyes and faint smile.

above, is alarmingly foreshortened. The scale of the long-ago 90-year sculpting program is apparent, and there seems good sense to the story that it was the huge quantity of rock spoil dumped into the turbulent waters that made the river navigable. And there is architectural sense in the guttering hidden in the head and arms, behind the ears and in the clothes, to provide discreet drainage and inner protection.

Threats Not all is benign though. The work was initiated in AD 713 by a monk named Hai Tong, who spent 20 years begging alms for it. When officialdom tried to steal the funds, Hai Tong said that they should sooner have his eyeball than the money for the Buddha. As good as his word, Hai Tong gouged out his own eye, and the alarmed officials ran away.

Twelve centuries later, modern officialdom is alarmed by the pressures of tourism and the effects of pollution. Both will have to be controlled if the Leshan Buddha is to endure into another millennium.

CHINA/TIBET, LHASA

Potala Palace

POTALA PALACE WAS TIBET'S SECULAR AND SPIRITUAL HUB UNTIL THE CHINESE TAKEOVER IN 1959. SINCE THEN, THE 14TH DALAI LAMA HAS LIVED IN EXILE AND NOW HIS PALACE AND ITS TEMPLES ARE OFFICIALLY DESIGNATED A MUSEUM. MODERN-DAY BUDDHIST PILGRIMS CLAIM SOMETHING DIFFERENT.

The scale of the palace matches its mountain setting. Rows of windows line the upper reaches of massive sloping ramparts, 16 ft/5 m thick at the base. Some more breathtaking numbers tell the story. Built at an altitude of 12,140 ft/3,700 m, with a maximum height of 394 ft/120 m, the palace has 13 stories and contains 1,000 rooms; they are filled with 10,000 shrines and 200,000 statues.

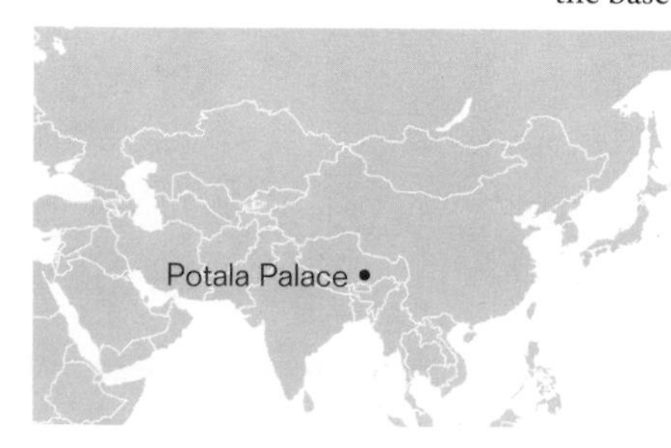

It is in fact two adjacent palaces with ancillary buildings, and the list of their many subdivisions reads like the imagined spaces of a computer game: White Palace, Red Palace, West and East Main Halls, North, South, East, and West Chapels, First, Second, and Third Galleries, with tombs, caves, and holy pillars thrown in. Potala's totality has grown willy-nilly down the centuries.

White Palace In AD 637 the Tibetan king Songtsen Gampo built a mountain palace for his Chinese wife, Queen Wen Cheng. It stood until the mid-seventeenth century, when the fifth Dalai Lama subsumed it into the White Palace. For the next three centuries this building was Tibet's political center, with rituals of state carried out in its East Main Hall. It is approached on a winding road leading to an open square. Inside is where successive Dalai Lamas once lived, their throne to the north

TIME LINE

637
Founded by King Songtsen Gampo.

1645
Construction of Red Palace begun by fifth Dalai Lama.

1694
Construction of White Palace begun.

1922
13th Dalai Lama renovates chapels and assembly halls in White Palace and adds two stories to Red Palace.

1959
Palace shelled by Chinese troops, who later loot 100,000 books and documents. The 14th Dalai Lama has been exiled ever since.

1989–94, 2002
Palace renovated.

1994
Inscribed on UNESCO World Heritage List.

Right: A Tibetan monk ascends to a higher state within the confines of the Potala Palace.

Far right: In nearby Lhasa, the world's highest capital city, a Tibetan woman sits on her front steps and spins a prayer wheel. Despite the discouragement of the Chinese government, Tibetan Buddhism remains a force in the land.

Right: Although it has been labeled a museum, Tibetan pilgrims, like this man spinning prayer wheels, treat the palace as a shrine.

Left: In an image of immensity, the Potala Palace sits high up in the Himalayan foothills.

Below right: In an image of harmony, natural calm runs in counterpoint to palatial grandeur.

and their living quarters on the upper floors. A yellow building at the side of the courtyard holds embroidered banners, which are draped over the outer southern walls during New Year festivals.

Red Palace The Red Palace to the west was intended for religious study and prayer. It was built in the 1690s to house the stupas holding the remains of the Dalai Lamas and is a multilevel maze with winding passageways leading to halls, chapels, libraries, and galleries. Its Great West Hall has four chapels where fine murals proclaim the glory and power of the fifth Dalai Lama, who started the whole extravaganza.

The northern chapel of the Great West Hall encloses the miniature intimacy of Potala's holiest shrine, a tiny vortex spiraling off into deep time and arcane religiosity. This is a chapel dating back nearly 1,400 years to King Songtsen Gampo. Over its entrance, in a blue and gold inscription, a nineteenth-century Chinese emperor proclaimed Buddhism as a "Blessed Field of Wonderful Fruit." Inside the chapel is a jewel-encrusted statue of Avalokiteshvara, an embodiment of the compassion of all Buddhas. A gloomy passageway in the floor leads down into the Dharma Cave, where Songtsen Gampo once studied Buddhism and a scholar named Sambhota developed Tibetan writing in the company of the Tibetan king, his Chinese wife, and, no doubt, many divinities.

INDIA, AGRA

Taj Mahal

THEY SAY THAT EVERY TIME YOU SEE THE TAJ MAHAL IT LOOKS DIFFERENT. THROUGH THE LENGTH OF DAYS AND SEASONS, ITS MARBLE TRANSLATES THE COLORS OF THE CHANGING UTTAR PRADESH SKY INTO SNOW WHITES AND PINKS, WAXEN YELLOWS, AND, AT FULL MOON, PASTEL SHADES OF TAN AND GRAY.

The Taj Mahal's curves and symmetry seem to render stone into flesh. It is an exuberant mausoleum that has won global recognition as the greatest single monument to love: "One teardrop upon the cheek of time," according to the Bengali poet Rabindranath Tagore.

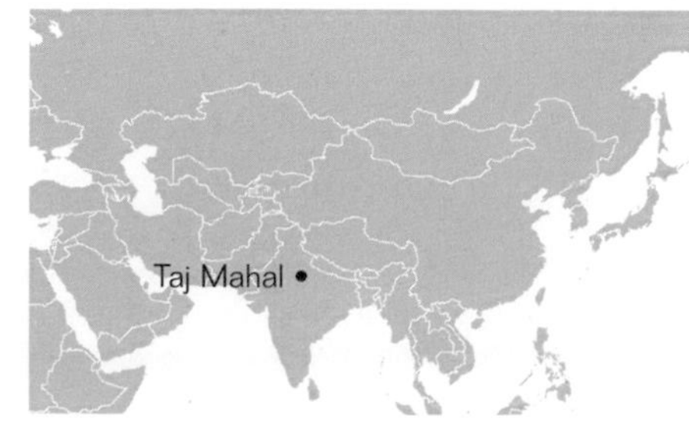

Multicultural The Mughal emperor Shah Jahan commissioned the Taj Mahal in 1632 in memory of his wife. Some say he was a Muslim, some claim him as a Hindu, but his building almost transcends cultural differences, for it is as eclectic as it is beautiful. The architecture is a blend of Persian, Islamic, and Indian. Some say a Turk named Ustad Isa was the main architect; others say it was a Persian engineer called Ahmad. A Persian calligrapher cut reams of Arabic lettering into the marble, and his signature is at the base of the dome: "Written by the insignificant being, Amanat Khan Shirazi."

Multisourced White marble was hauled from Makrana, 250 miles/400 km away. Jade and crystal were imported from China, lapis lazuli from Afghanistan, coral and mother-of-pearl from the Indian Ocean. Even the British can lay claim to an influence, if only in lawns laid during an early twentieth-century renovation. A more significant example of cultural integration is the

TIME LINE

1632–53
Construction.

1857
During Indian rebellion, British soldiers hack gems and lapis lazuli from walls.

1908
Completion of restoration ordered by Lord Curzon.

1942
Scaffolding put up in case of wartime bombing.

1965 and 1971
During India–Pakistan wars, scaffolding is again erected to mislead bomber pilots.

1983
Inscribed by UNESCO as a World Heritage Site.

Opposite: Erected in the period when the Mughal Empire was at the height of its wealth and power, no expense needed to be spared on the Taj Mahal.

Right: At sunset the Taj Mahal is suffused with warm pink, while its perfect symmetry is mirrored in the formal canal flanked by dark green cypresses.

Below: Inside the building, the sumptuous *parchin kari* (pietra dura) decoration can include as many as 35 different semiprecious stones in a single motif.

gilded bronze finial on the dome. The crescent moon with horns pointing skyward is an unequivocally Islamic motif, but the way its placement forms a trident shape strongly suggests Shiva, the Hindu supreme god.

Rule of four The curvaceous feminine shape of the dome makes engineering sense, for its bulge works to transfer the heavy load directly downward. Four replica onion domes surround it, with columned bases open through the roof to provide light inside. Four minarets broaden the symmetry outward. A rule of four continues throughout, using Arabesque ideas where each component is separate and yet integrates with the whole. The main structure is on a square platform facing four reflecting pools, which have further fourfold subdivisions.

What is written large in architectural and landscaped form appears in miniature counterpoint in the geometrical abstractions adorning the plinth, minarets, and walls. Some inscriptions spell out precise messages; others are vaguer and various ways of saying "love."

INDIA, AMRITSAR

Golden Temple of Amritsar

PUNJAB'S AMRITSAR TEMPLE IS THE CENTER OF SIKHISM. ITS NAME ONCE DESCRIBED A LAKE, THEN A TEMPLE BUILT IN THE MIDDLE OF THAT LAKE, AND THEN THE CITY THAT GREW AROUND IT. AMRITSAR MEANS "POOL OF AMBROSIAL NECTAR"—THE DRINK OF THE GODS AND A BALM TO BRING PEACE.

Strife and attacks on Sikhism's holiest site have caused the temple's name to mutate. In the 1760s, after Afghan Muslims had largely destroyed the original Amritsar, it was rebuilt and became known as the Golden Temple when 220 lb/100 kg of gold leaf gave the famous shrine its finishing sheen. Its most recent name change came in 2005, two decades after the Indian army attacked the Sikh separatists who had sought sanctuary in the temple. In an assertion of Sikh identity, the building is now Harmandir Sahib, "Abode of God." Perhaps the gurus wanted to shift the emphasis from goldenness to godlinesss.

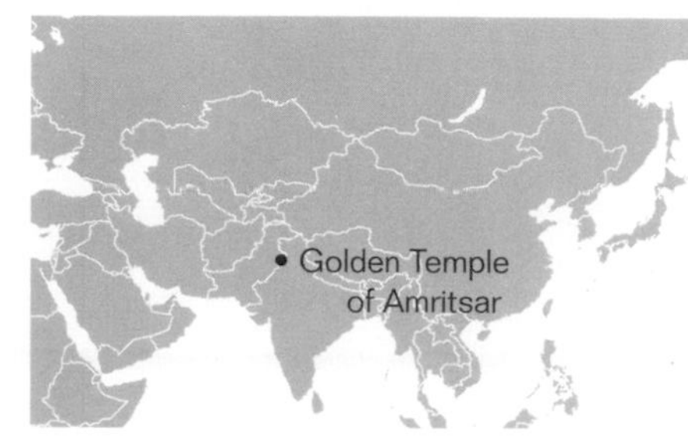

Harmandir Sahib was certainly never intended as a fortress. As the center of Sikhism—an inclusive creed founded in the fifteenth century—the *gurdwara*, or Sikh temple, reflects Sikh tenets of openness and a belief in human equality. Its four entrances symbolize a general welcome, indicating that it is open to travelers from all four directions. The architecture is a fusion of Hindu and Muslim references.

Journey to the temple The center of the complex should be approached clockwise on the Parikrama pathway around the lake. The path leads to the silver-gated Darshani Deorhi arch and out on to a marble causeway. Ahead are copper cupolas setting off the lotus-shaped,

Above: Harmandir Sahib, informally known as the Golden Temple, sits in the middle of the Amrit Sarovar, a "pool of nectar" fed by an underground spring.

Right: Devotees line up to pay their respects on the eve of the birthday of Sri Guru Nanak Dev (1469–1539), the founder of the religion of Sikhism.

Below right: Priests sit behind the Guru Granth Sahib, the Sikh holy book, during the Jalau ceremony to mark its first installation at Amritsar in 1604.

TIME LINE

1585–1601
Building of first temple.

1760s
Rebuilt after being sacked by Afghan troops.

1984
At least 500 die when troops attack the temple to defeat Sikh separatists. Four months later, Indira Gandhi, who ordered the attack, is assassinated by her Sikh bodyguards.

1998
Sonia Gandhi, daughter-in-law of Indira, apologizes for the 1984 attack.

2005
Temple officially renamed Harmandir Sahib.

golden dome. The bridge is a reminder to pilgrims of the soul's journey after death. All who walk it are on a living journey that culminates in the middle of the lake at the magnificent Harmandir Sahib temple.

Inside the temple Visitors to the temple, which is open to all, must remove their shoes, wash their feet, and cover their head. Once inside, the decoration is richer still. Islamic-style florally patterned and jewel-encrusted white marble walls are interspersed with gem-studded canopies. Every available surface is finely inscribed with verses from the Guru Granth Sahib, the Sikh holy book. There are numerous lavish memorials to Sikh gurus and martyrs and to the Sikh soldiers who died fighting in World Wars I and II.

Most visits end at the Guru-ka-Langar dining hall, where food is served to around 35,000 people a day. All are invited; nobody is compelled to pay. All sit on the floor regardless of caste, status, wealth, or creed and, for a while, all can taste equality's ambrosial nectar.

INDIA, DELHI

Red Fort

LAL QILA, OR THE RED FORT, IS A MUST-SEE PLACE IN THE INDIAN CAPITAL OF DELHI. BUILT IN THE MID-SIXTEENTH CENTURY AS A FORTIFIED IMPERIAL RESIDENCE FOR THE MUGHAL EMPEROR SHAH JAHAN, IT BECAME BARRACKS FOR THE BRITISH ARMY FROM 1857 TO 1947 AND THEN FOR THE INDIAN ARMY UNTIL 2003.

Today, the Red Fort is principally a tourist attraction devoted to commerce and display. Part of what's on display is pre- and post-colonial Indian autonomy: every evening, the richly carved walls shine brightly as the backdrop to a *son et lumière* account of Mughal history; every year, on August 15, the Indian prime minister celebrates independence from British rule in 1947 with a solemn ceremony of flag raising above the fort's sandstone ramparts.

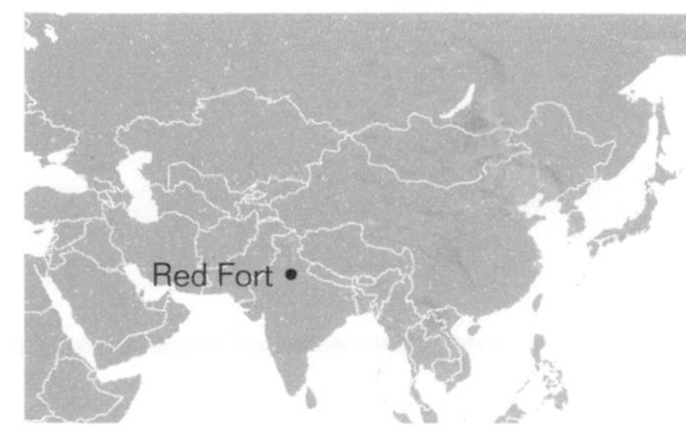

Fortification The tricolor Indian flag waves above a moated perimeter wall almost 1½ miles/2.5 km long and never lower than 60 ft/18 m high. The semioctagonal towers guarding the fort's two main entrances rear up to an intimidating height of 110 ft/33.5 m. And yet these pinnacles of high-testosterone castle architecture are finely decorated, hinting at the hidden glories defended inside.

Display The gardens and palaces, though much plundered during military occupations, are rich. They follow the highly decorative and colorful Shahjahani style, which drew on Persian, Timurid, and Hindu traditions. The main Lahore Gate (the site of Independence Day flag waving) leads into the Chatta Chowk, where the walls are lined with market stalls. This covered bazaar eventually opens out into an area of marble-clad

TIME LINE

1546
Salimgarh Fort, now ruined, is built to north of site.

1648
Red Fort, originally known as Qila-i-Mubarak ("blessed fort"), is completed and becomes main palace of Mughal emperors.

1783
Sikhs briefly occupy fort.

1857
Occupation by British forces, who destroy some residential palaces.

1913
Designated a monument of national importance.

1947
Indian army takes control of fort after Independence.

2000
Fort is attacked by Lashkar-e-Toiba in an attempt to upset India–Pakistan peace talks.

2003
Army cedes control of fort to tourist authorities.

2007
Designated a UNESCO World Heritage Site.

Opposite: The Red Fort's main entrance is the Lahore Gate, a symbolic gateway to India itself. It is the site of Independence Day ceremonies celebrating the end of British rule in 1947.

Right: Shah Jahan would emerge from his private apartments inside the fort on to this elaborate canopied *jarokha*, or elevated throne, to address his subjects.

pavilions, the pillars decorated with floral carvings inlaid with semiprecious stones. The Diwan-i-Aam (Hall of Public Audience) contains an ornately carved throne-cum-balcony, once protected by gold and silver railings, on which the emperor sat to speak or hear petitions. Nearby is the three-domed Pearl Mosque, its prayer hall inlaid with black marble outlines of prayer carpets.

Duality Bisecting the plaza is a wide road that once divided the fort's military functions to the west from the palaces to its east. The southern end of this avenue is the Delhi Gate, leading back into the city.

The Red Fort is now a place that symbolizes both division and unification. It is the most gorgeous of forts and was always intended to be good on the eye as well as being difficult to attack. The architectural message is: "Come hither, but don't dare get too close."

Below: Pavilioned in splendor, modern-day visitors can wander through astonishing architectural perspectives intended for the glorification of sixteenth-century emperors.

INDIA, NEW DELHI

India Gate

ALL ROADS IN NEW DELHI LEAD TO A MONUMENTAL ARCHWAY DESIGNED IN A GRAND EUROPEAN IMPERIAL STYLE. THIS GRANITE AND RED SANDSTONE STRUCTURE SITS IN A FORMAL LANDSCAPE OF LAWNS AND LAKES AND DOMINATES A PUBLIC SPACE AT THE FOCAL POINT OF THE NEW CAPITAL CITY.

One of the British Empire's last bold and presumptuous projects was shifting India's capital from Calcutta to Delhi. A new city was required and Sir Edwin Lutyens, an English architect whose name was synonymous with Edwardian country houses, took charge in 1912. By 1920, he was also a principal architect to the Imperial War Graves Commission and had designed the Cenotaph in London's Whitehall. His Indian arch was a late addition to what became known as his Delhi order of classical architecture, erected because Indian sacrifice in foreign wars was demanding recognition.

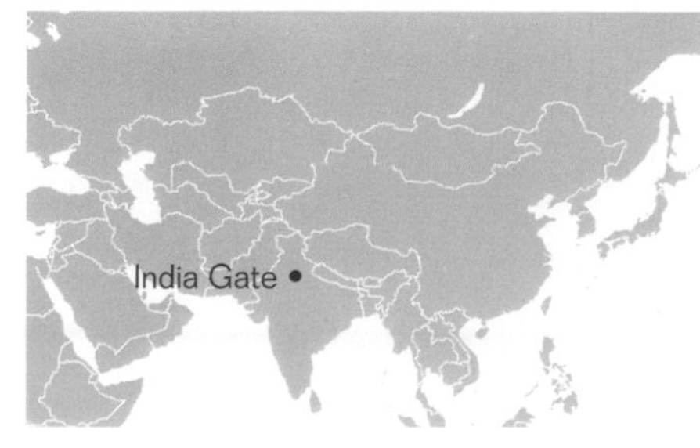

Memorial The walls of Lutyens' arch are engraved with the names of the 90,000 Indian soldiers who died fighting for Britain in World War I and the third Anglo-Afghan war in 1919. Immediately under the arch, flames burn on the four corners of the cenotaph, and a shallow dome at the arch's apex, 138 ft/42 m above, supports a bowl for burning oil in memory of the dead.

Pavilions and statues "INDIA" is written large on this twentieth-century version of a triumphal arch. A nearby canopy, another Lutyens design, has a more authentically Indian look, reflecting the shapes of pavilions built in pre-Raj times. It once covered a statue of King George V, which was removed after India gained

FACT FILE

Architect
Sir Edwin Lutyens, as part of his city plan for New Delhi.

Construction
Designed 1920, foundation laid 1921, inaugurated 1931.

Height
Overall height 138 ft/42 m; height of arch 88 ft/27 m.

Name
Originally known as All India War Memorial, since 1947 as India Gate.

Opposite: The ceremonial Rajpath (King's Way) leads up to India Gate, where the British Empire paid tribute to Indian soldiers who died fighting its wars.

Right: Behind the gate is a canopy, also designed by Lutyens but in a more Indian vernacular style.

Below: Mounted Indian troops converge on India Gate for Republic Day on January 26 and then head a parade of military might and cultural diversity down the Rajpath.

independence in 1947. Plans to put a statue of Gandhi in the English king's place never came to fruition.

Changes In 1931 the British Viceroy, Lord Irwin, unveiled the polyglot structure as the All India War Memorial. After 1947 it became the Indian national monument and was renamed India Gate. In the 1970s the Amar Jawan Jyoti ("flame of the immortal soldier") was lit in a new black marble cenotaph under the arch to commemorate a fresh generation of soldiers who had died in the Indo-Pakistan War.

Consumer choice India Gate is now a thoroughly contemporary sacred site. Each year on Republic Day (January 26) the country's politicians and military brass go there to pay homage to the Indian dead from many wars. Usually, though, the gate's environs have a carnival atmosphere, with vendors peddling their goods and cheerful crowds snacking on all the spicy, tangy, street foods North Indians call *chaat*—plus chips, ice cream, cotton candy, and soda pop.

CAMBODIA, SIEM REAP

Angkor Wat

IN A CORNER OF THE MINDS OF THOSE LIVING FAR FROM ANY JUNGLE SHIMMERS THE IMAGE OF A CAPACIOUS HIDDEN TEMPLE WITHIN A LOST DOMAIN HIDDEN DEEP IN A GREEN SHADE. ITS NAME IS ANGKOR WAT AND IT IS A TWELFTH-CENTURY CAMBODIAN CITY TEMPLE OF TOWERS, DECORATIONS, AND REFINEMENTS.

The temple's three-tiered structure steps up to five lotus-bud towers. There is mystery here. The polished sandstone pinnacles probably represent the five peaks of Mount Meru, mythical home of the Hindu gods. The building faces west, either because it was intended as a funerary temple for King Suryavarman II or because it was dedicated to Vishnu, god of the west.

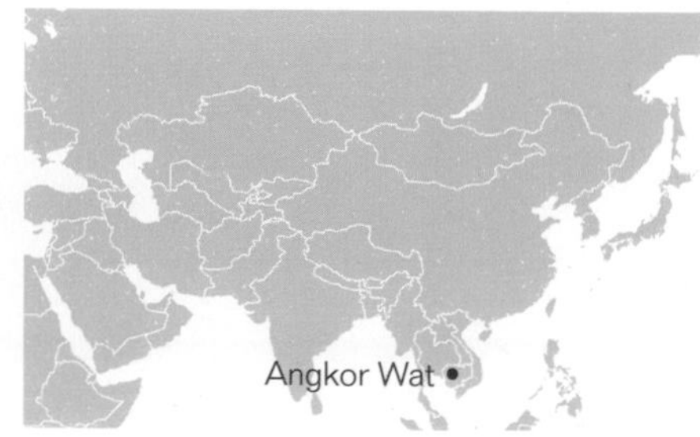

World's largest temple An estimated five million tons of sandstone (equal to that used to build Khafre's pyramid in Egypt) was brought down river from a quarry 25 miles/40 km away. The central tower, once a holy of holies accessible only to the priesthood and now a tourists' viewpoint over the lost city, is 213 ft/65 m high. An outer wall 15 ft/4.5 m high encloses a rectangle 1,120 x 875 yd/1,025 x 800 m, with a moat 207 yd/190 m wide beyond it surrounding the whole. The moat proved a strong defense, for Angkor Wat is just a fraction of a far larger metropolis that was reclaimed by nature after it was abandoned in the early sixteenth century. It is the only Angkor temple to have survived as a significant religious center, first for Hindus and then for Buddhists.

Stories in stone The workmanship is awesome. Instead of mortaring, the stone blocks are seamlessly interlinked with carved mortise-and-tenon or dovetail

TIME LINE

1113–50
Built as part of Hindu temple city during reign of Khmer King Suryavarman II.

1177
Sacked by the Chams, rivals of the Khmer.

1490s
Temple converted to Buddhism.

1580s
First account of temple by a European visitor.

1863
Angkor Wat's image is included on Cambodian flag.

1986 and 1992
Archaeological Survey of India carries out restoration work, after which Angkor Wat is declared a UNESCO World Heritage site.

Above right: Lucky children have probably been jumping into this Angkor Wat pool for 1,000 years.

Right: Detailed bas-reliefs, such as this depiction of a leper king, cover almost every available surface.

Above: Angkor Wat, a vast and delicate miracle in sandstone, is reflected in the wide moat that has protected it from the encroaching rain forest.

Right: In the twelfth century, the towers of Angkor Wat looked out over a jungle metropolis. Only Hindu clergy were allowed a view from the high central tower.

joints, and then buffed to a marble sheen. The internal work is equally fine, and equally immense, with endless bas-relief carvings covering walls, columns, and roofs. One frieze shows the Hindu creation myth, the Churning of the Sea of Milk, with Vishnu in the center above his turtle avatar Kurma, and there are depictions of scenes from the *Ramayana* and *Mahabharata* epics. Sculpture becomes architecture in expanses of exuberant stone comic strips showing battles and chariots, unicorns and gryphons, dragons and elephants, garlands, dancing girls, and cheery guardian spirits.

All this high-quality exoticism filtered into the western imagination only in the mid-nineteenth century, when Henri Mouhot, a French traveler, visited the hidden Cambodian realm. He wrote: "This temple—a rival to that of Solomon, and erected by some ancient Michelangelo—might take an honorable place beside our most beautiful buildings. It is grander than anything left to us by Greece or Rome."

ISRAEL, JERUSALEM

The Western Wall

THIS WALL IN JERUSALEM IS PROBABLY THE PLANET'S MOST CONTESTED SPOT, AND ITS NAME SHIFTS ACCORDING TO ALLEGIANCE. NINETEENTH-CENTURY EUROPEAN CHRISTIANS DUBBED IT THE WAILING WALL. FOR JUDAISM IT IS THE KOTEL; FOR ISLAM, AL-BURAQ. THE LEAST CONTENTIOUS LABEL IS PROBABLY THE WESTERN WALL.

Orthodox Jews claim the Kotel is the closest they can get to Judaism's holiest spot, which is the Foundation Stone on the Temple Mount (aka the Noble Sanctuary). Muslims claim that Al-Buraq guards the Noble Sanctuary (aka the Temple Mount), the place from which the Prophet Muhammad ascended to heaven. That, in brief, is the religious dispute coiling through the Arab–Israeli political conflict.

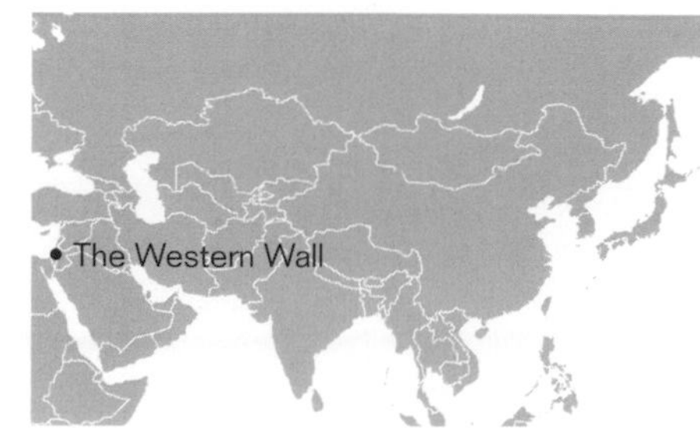

Original wall The Western Wall is a section of a longer rampart begun shortly before Christ's birth as a retaining structure for the platform now occupied by Temple Mount/Noble Sanctuary. The whole structure ran for 1,640 ft/500 m along the platform's base; the remaining visible sections are 262 ft/80 m in the south, the 26 ft/8 m of the Little Western Wall in the Muslim Quarter, and a length of 187 ft/57 m in the Jewish Quarter.

Recent history The Jewish Quarter section is the Western Wall. It is where Orthodox Jews are to be seen praying and chanting in a demonstration of their religious beliefs. (Hence the Wailing Wall, from the traditional Arabic name El-Mabka, "the place of weeping," reflecting Jewish lamentation over the destruction of the Temple.) The Wall was confined in an alleyway until 1967, when in the aftermath of the Six Day War, Israelis

TIME LINE

ca. 19 BC
Western Wall is constructed as a 24-course retaining wall near a temple built by Herod, a client king under Roman rule.

600–1500
Jerusalem comes under Arab control. Further courses added from 7th century.

1517–1917
Ottoman rule. Suleiman the Magnificent gives Jews the right to pray at the Wall.

1917–48
Jerusalem under British Mandate. Arab Mufti adds three courses.

1948–67
Under Jordanian control.

1967–present
Under Israeli control. Israelis create the Western Wall Plaza and excavate from street level to expose two courses of stones from Herod's time.

Opposite: The faithful pray at the 2,000-year-old Western Wall, while others gather in the 40-year-old plaza beside it. The golden Dome of the Rock beyond stands on the Temple Mount/Noble Sanctuary.

Right: Jews at the wall observe the Tisha B'Av fast commemorating the destruction of the Temple (above) and Sukkoth, a reminder of 40 years wandering in the desert after the Exodus (below).

demolished adjacent buildings to make the Western Wall Plaza, where thousands can now gather. They also dug down to expose two more courses of stone.

More stones in the wall The wall is 66 ft/20 m high, with the buried part and foundations going down about 33 ft/10 m. The first 24 courses of stone were laid in King Herod's time; today 7 of these are above ground, carved so precisely that they lock tight without mortar. The Umayyads added another 4 courses in the seventh century; 14 more were added in the nineteenth century and 3 during the British Mandate.

Deep history On the plaza's northern side is a doorway to the Western Wall Tunnel, a labyrinth where archaeological remains are identifiable from the first century BC to the Ottoman period. Some claim that deeper still will be found the foundations of Solomon's Temple, destroyed by the Babylonians in 587 BC.

Below: Their faces to old stones, Orthodox Jews flock to a bare limestone wall that represents the core of their beliefs.

SAUDI ARABIA, MECCA

The Kaaba

FIVE TIMES DAILY, DEVOUT MUSLIMS THROUGHOUT THE WORLD BOW DOWN IN PRAYER, ALL OF THEM FACING TOWARD THIS SPOT. THE KAABA IS AN ANCIENT STONE CUBE AND ISLAM'S MOST SACRED SITE, SITTING ISOLATED WITHIN THE WIDE COURTYARD OF THE VAST AL-HARAM MOSQUE IN MECCA.

The Kaaba is a simple, small building but it has a complex mythology that far predates the foundation of Islam in the seventh century. It is made of granite quarried from the hills near Mecca, and is a near cube nearly 40 ft/12 m in height, standing on a shallow marble plinth.

Kiswah The exterior stonework is normally almost completely shrouded by a black silk cloth, the Kiswah, which is embroidered in gold with verses from the Qur'an. This cloth is renewed annually and its predecessor cut into pieces and distributed to pilgrims. A more heavily gold-laden band encircles the Kaaba about 13 ft/4 m from the top, embroidered with the Shahada, the Islamic declaration of faith.

The Black Stone The Kaaba's eastern cornerstone is a smooth dark rock, in fact a collection of fragments held together in a massive silver frame. Polished and hollowed by the kisses of millions of pilgrims, this is the Black Stone, Islam's holiest object, held to be the only remnant of the original Kaaba built by Ibrahim (Abraham). In Islamic tradition it dates from the time of Adam, white when it fell from Paradise but blackened by human sin.

Inside the golden door The entrance is a solid gold door on the north side, 6½ ft/2 m above the plinth; a set of stairs is wheeled into place to reach it. The door

TIME LINE

AD 630
Prophet Muhammad reclaims the Kaaba, rebuilt by Ibrahim but taken over by pagan Arabs, for monotheism and installs the Black Stone.

683
The Kaaba is destroyed during siege of Mecca, then rebuilt, probably in its current shape.

930–52
The Black Stone is stolen and held for ransom, then returned to a freshly repaired Kaaba, which has not changed much since.

Opposite: The Kaaba is the austere structure at the focal point of Islam. Three million people swirl around the Kaaba during Hajj.

Right: Since 2010, pilgrims have told the time by the Mecca Royal Clock Hotel Tower. As clocks go, it's the world's highest (1,740 ft/530 m) with the largest face (141 ft/43 m square).

Below: At the end of every Hajj the Kaaba gets a brand new Kiswah, covered with Islamic calligraphy sewn with golden thread.

opens to reveal a bare limestone floor and walls clad in marble, their upper parts draped with a green cloth embroidered in gold with further verses from the Qur'an.

Few are allowed entry, however, for the heavy door swings open only twice a year for ceremonial cleaning—first before Ramadan and second before the annual Hajj pilgrimage. The surfaces are swept, washed in Persian rosewater, and perfumed with scented oil—the same oil used to anoint the Black Stone outside.

Hajj While few gain admission to the Kaaba, many come to walk around it. The structure is a unifying point for pilgrimage as well as prayer, because one of the five requirements of Islam is that, if at all possible, Muslims must journey to Mecca at least once in their life during Hajj, the annual pilgrimage. In a ritual called Tawaf, they must make their way through the Grand Mosque and walk seven times around the Kaaba in a counter-clockwise direction. At the climax of Hajj, three million people are converging on one small building.

UNITED ARAB EMIRATES, DUBAI

Burj Al Arab

SAMPLE THIS FROM THE HOTEL WEB SITE: "THE DELUXE TWO-BEDROOM SUITE HAS A LARGE DINING AREA ... KITCHEN ... TWO LOUNGES OFFERING MAGNIFICENT SEA VIEWS ... TWO BATHROOMS WITH JACUZZIS ... DRESSING ROOM ... YOUR PRIVATE BUTLER WILL ENSURE THAT EVERY LITTLE NEED IS MET."

And the price of meeting every little need? At the time of writing, $3,534.18 per night or (also quoted on the website) 2.55 ounces of gold, or 2.05 ounces of platinum, or a large chunk of change in any currency guests prefer. A stay in the Burj Al Arab ("Tower of the Arabs") promises a brush with celebrity. In the 1990s Dubai's Sheikh Mohammed bin Rashid Al Maktoum commissioned it as a celebrity culture magnet designed to define his country as more than an oil-rich trading post.

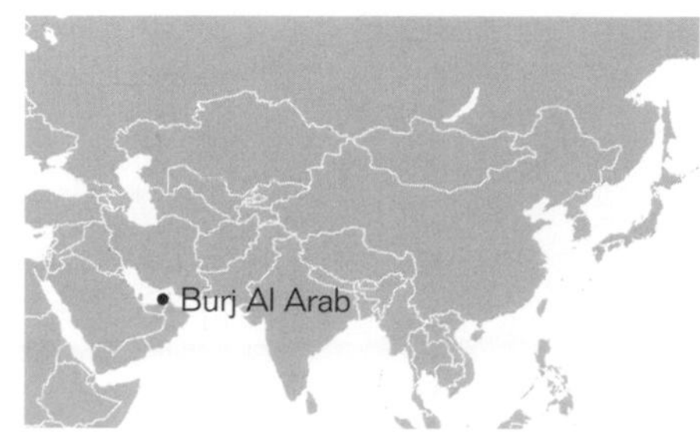

"Build me an icon" Atkins, a British architectural firm, won the contract. "All that was specified was a need to be iconic," says a spokesman. "We looked around Dubai for references, and saw dhows with nice curvy sails. But this was a city saying 'We're modern, we're going forward,' so we started thinking of something like a spinnaker." More luxury yacht than traditional trading vessel, the Burj Al Arab sailed straight into global recognition.

Supernatural The building is rooted in a man-made sand island on 230 concrete piles, each 131 ft/40 m long, supporting a structure shaped like a vast sail billowing from a mast. It comprises two main vertical sections linked with 279-ft/85-m steel trusses, which were winched 656 ft/200 m into the air before securing. This

TIME LINE

Architect
Tom Wright of Atkins.

Contractors
Murray & Roberts.

Construction
Building began in 1994 and the hotel opened in 1999; it took three years to reclaim the land from the sea.

Size
Height 1,053 ft/321 m; 60 floors, covering 1,200,000 sq ft/ 111,500 sq m.

Accommodation
202 duplex suites.

Web site
burj-al-arab.com

Opposite: Designed to resemble a sailing vessel, the hotel appears to float past more traditional architecture in the Dubai resort of Jumeirah.

Right: The building is literally at sea: it stands on a man-made island 306 yd/ 280 m off the beach.

Below: Inside the hotel, massive golden columns draw the eye up through the atrium toward the ceiling, 590 ft/180 m above.

engineering triumph forms a V enclosing a ground-level atrium and, suspended from the top of the mast, a restaurant. Seen from a distance across the Persian Gulf, especially when lit up at night, the hotel resembles a glittering waterborne vessel and seems unlikely to have an existence this side of the supernatural.

Superlatives The hotel has the world's only seven-star rating. Guests land on a helipad 60 floors up, or are whisked in limos over a private bridge. High-level diners take a high-speed panoramic elevator to the cantilevered Al Muntaha ("the Ultimate") restaurant for a meal with desert and ocean views; low-level eaters go to Al Mahara ("the Oyster Shell") via a simulated submarine voyage, and feast on seafood as they gaze into a vast aquarium.

Superb shape Flashy, elaborate, interior displays are a definite part of the building's fame. But in the end, conspicuous consumption is not what makes the Burj Al Arab memorable. People recall its unique profile, and that was the intention when British architects answered an Arab ruler's desire for something iconic.

AFGHANISTAN, GHOR

Minaret of Jam

THE MINARET OF JAM IS AN EXQUISITELY TAPERED STONE FINGER POINTING SKYWARD FROM ITS PLACE AT THE CORNER OF A DIRT ROAD DEEP IN CENTRAL AFGHANISTAN. THIS BEAUTIFUL BRICK TOWER HAS ENDURED NINE CENTURIES OF WARFARE, EARTHQUAKES, EROSION, PILLAGE, AND NEGLECT.

The minaret is 125 miles/200 km east of Herat, in a remote fastness where the Rivers Harirud and Jamrud meet amid the mountains. It could not be farther off the beaten track. Although near the old trade route that linked Constantinople with India, it was sufficiently well hidden to escape Genghis Khan's thirteenth-century rampages.

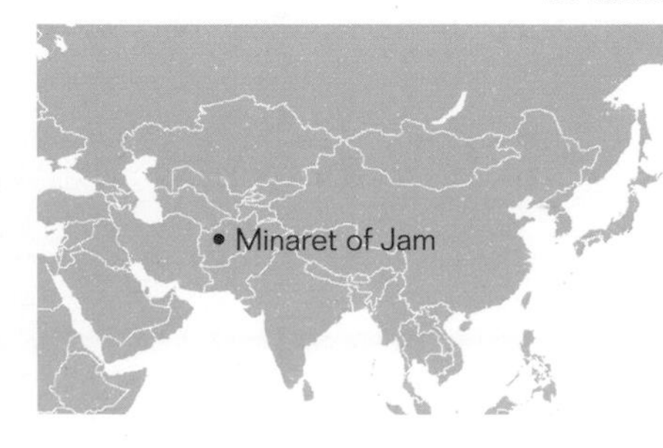

Memory Later colonists from the west also bypassed the Minaret of Jam. Several are credited with its so-called rediscovery, including an English geographer in 1886 and a French archaeologist in 1957. The fact is that it has stood in its valley, aging gracefully, since the 1190s, sole survivor of some 60 minarets that once beckoned the Central Asian Muslim faithful to prayer. It stands as a memorial to the short-lived Ghurid dynasty, which was swept away along with the palaces and mosques that probably first surrounded the tower.

Inside The original door is 13 ft/4 m below a layer of compacted earth that also obscures an octagonal base. Entry—for those foolhardy enough to go sightseeing in the middle of a modern battle zone—is now through a window and onto one of the two spiral stairways that ascend 131 ft/40 m of the minaret's full 213-ft/65-m height and together form a supporting skeleton for a building made up of four tapering brick shafts.

TIME LINE

1190s
Minaret constructed.

1215
End of Ghurid dynasty.

1886
Tower discovered by Sir Thomas Holdich, while working for Afghan Boundary Commission.

1957
Surveyed by French archaeologists André Maricq and Wiet Herberg.

1979
Soviet invasion of Afghanistan.

1996–2001
Taliban government, with Mujahidin and Taliban troops entrenched on either side of River Harirud.

2001–present
Afghan war continues to make access to minaret extremely difficult.

2002
Jam inscribed on UNESCO World Heritage list and added to list of World Heritage In Danger, on which it remains.

Opposite: The elegant, vulnerable minaret, now isolated in its high valley, was once part of the summer capital of the Ghurid empire.

Right: Two crumbling spiral staircases curl precariously around each other in a double helix that reaches about two-thirds of the way up the tower.

Outside The exterior surface is completely covered with intricate geometric relief work in brick and stucco. On the first section a broad pattern of eight vertical segments runs down to the octagonal base. Each vertical zone has a narrow band of inscriptions, in two forms of calligraphy, running in an unbroken line around each panel. Circular tracings suggest an organic floral design.

Geography and engineering The Minaret of Jam now stands in splendid isolation, cloaked in an inaccessibility that has kept it beyond the reach of both military campaigns and tourism. A marriage of geography and engineering has written survival into the building's genetic makeup and given longevity to a peculiarly human structure that combines refined decoration with mundane brickwork, fragility with strength, and the civilized with the wild.

Below: In the band of turquoise-glazed tiling that draws the eye to the top of the first section, kufic inscriptions refer to the "king of kings" and the minaret's completion in 1194.

From the most ancient sacred mountains to some of the most radical architecture of the modern age, Australia's landmarks are on a large scale. Its indigenous population has lived so lightly on the land that its man-made monuments date only from the relatively recent past: in the last few centuries incomers have imported their habits of imprinting themselves on the landscape. But Australia's natural landmarks are world beaters.

AUSTRALIA

AUSTRALIA, NORTHERN TERRITORY

Uluru

THIS SANDSTONE OUTCROP IN THE CENTRAL AUSTRALIAN DESERT IS A SHIFTING DEFINER OF MANY THINGS AUSTRALIAN: BY DAY, ITS TANNED FLANKS MAKE IT A DRAMATIC LANDMARK; AT SUNRISE AND SUNSET THE DRAMA INTENSIFIES INTO TRANSCENDENT REDS; AND ON RAINY DAYS IT IS A FORBIDDING GRAY EMINENCE.

The name of the great rock is as mutable as its colors. Uluru is its local Anangu (Aboriginal) identity and that's what it's mostly been called during 10,000 years of human habitation. From 1873, outsiders redefined land tenure and with it the language, so Uluru appeared on maps as Ayers Rock, in honor of Sir Henry Ayers, then Chief Secretary of South Australia, giving his name a lasting celebrity he might otherwise not have managed.

In 1993, in an official acknowledgment of its precolonial history, the rock was renamed Ayers Rock/Uluru and, from 2002, Uluru/Ayers Rock. Current Aussie shorthand for it is "the Rock," a swipe at sensitivities that attempts to sidestep indigenous and colonial roots.

Unshifting rock Uluru certainly has a singular shape, standing 1,142 ft/348 m high, with a circumference of 5.8 miles/9.4 km. Aeons ago, the surrounding landscape eroded to a plain, leaving an adamantine sandstone monolith with unchanging sheer sides that are bare of vegetation. The area below takes Uluru's runoff and is as lush and fertile as the outcrop is barren. It was thus a natural magnet for the desert's original inhabitants.

Shifting stories Traditional Anangu beliefs hold that ancestral beings, Tjukuritja or Waparitja, journeyed

TIME LINE

Dreamtime/500 million years ago
Uluru formed in Cambrian era.

10,000 years ago
First human habitation.

1873
Mapmaker William Gosse names it Ayers Rock.

1985
Australian government returns ownership of Uluru to local Anangu people, who then lease it back to the National Parks and Wildlife Agency.

1987
Listed by UNESCO as a World Heritage Site.

Opposite: Geologists call the huge rock an inselberg, or "island mountain," because it is an isolated remnant of an eroded upland range.

Right: The sandstone is renowned for its dramatic changes of color in different lights; it is particularly vivid at sunrise and sunset.

Below: Uluru's traditional caretakers politely ask visitors not to climb it; many still choose to do so, but the numbers are falling.

across a featureless void, creating life and landscape as they advanced. They left a living record of the Dreamtime in geology and cave paintings, and their spirits still inhabit the land. Other linked myths have accrued, concerning sleepy lizard women, or a woman python, or two fighting boys, or a great battle that caused the earth to well up in grief to become Uluru.

Recent white mythology connected with the area focused on nine-week old Azaria Chamberlain, who may or may not have been abducted by dingoes during a camping trip in 1980. The child was never found, but the mystery of her death has been told and retold in books, movies, music, drama, and opera.

Shifting identities Uluru is at the mythic core of a vast landscape. It is variously sacred as the center of a newly created world, or a newly discovered continent, or of a new sovereign state that must fairly accommodate its old and new peoples.

A carefully worded sign carries safety and cultural warnings: "We ask you to respect our Law by not climbing Uluru. What visitors call 'the climb' is the traditional route taken by ancestral man upon their arrival at Uluru in the creation time. It has great spiritual significance. 'The climb' is dangerous and too many people have died while attempting it. We feel great sadness when a person dies or is hurt on our land."

AUSTRALIA, NEW SOUTH WALES

Sydney Opera House

THE YOUNGEST BUILDING ON UNESCO'S WORLD HERITAGE LIST, SYDNEY OPERA HOUSE IS ONE OF THE WORLD'S MOST ACCLAIMED STRUCTURES AND HAS BECOME A SYMBOL OF MODERN AUSTRALIA AND THE VIBRANCY OF ITS LARGEST CITY. IT IS SURROUNDED ON THREE SIDES BY THE WATERS OF SYDNEY HARBOUR.

When the First Fleet arrived in Sydney Cove in 1788, the new settlers needed help communicating with the local people. Of the handful of Aborigines kidnapped for this purpose, one man, Bennelong, established cordial relations with the British governor, Arthur Phillip. Bennelong learned to speak English and Phillip had a hut built for him on a small tidal island in Sydney's beautiful natural harbor. Two centuries after his death, his name is globally famous, because in 1955 Bennelong Point was chosen as the location for the city's new arts center.

Eugene Goossens Sydney had had an Opera House before, but it was really more of a music hall and it survived for only about 20 years before the building was condemned. The number of theaters in the city dwindled in the twentieth century, and when the English composer Eugene Goossens arrived in 1947 as the new conductor of the Sydney Symphony Orchestra, the only concert venue was the town hall. Not only did Goossens lobby for a worthy center for live music, he also saw the potential of Bennelong Point. During the nineteenth century the point had been the site of Fort Macquarie, but this had been demolished in 1901 to make way for a tram depot. In 1955 Goossens got his way.

Left: The sublime curves of the Opera House fit neatly within the arc of Sydney Harbour Bridge to create the city's set-piece view.

Right: Bennelong Point juts out into the harbor just to the northeast of Sydney's high-rise central business district.

Below: For this building conceived as sculpture, the engineering challenges of constructing the curving roofs were unprecedented. The cost, originally estimated at Aus $7.5 million, eventually rose to over $100 million.

Peeling an orange The Danish architect Jørn Utzon won the international competition to design the building on the basis of a dozen preliminary drawings. Original and imaginative, his unconventional design with its sail-like roofs was immediately recognized as a potentially iconic building. Rising above a massive podium, the roofs were envisaged as a series of thin shells. But Utzon had originally drawn his shells as different parabolas, which would have entailed casting each section individually: a prohibitively expensive venture. It took five years and at least a dozen different approaches to find a workable solution, and the structural analysis by the engineers Ove Arup and Partners involved one of the earliest uses of computer-aided design.

In the final design each shell is a section of a sphere of the same 246-ft/75-m radius—an idea said to have been inspired by peeling an orange—which made it feasible to precast the 2,200 concrete ribs, as although their lengths differed they were all of identical shape. (Both

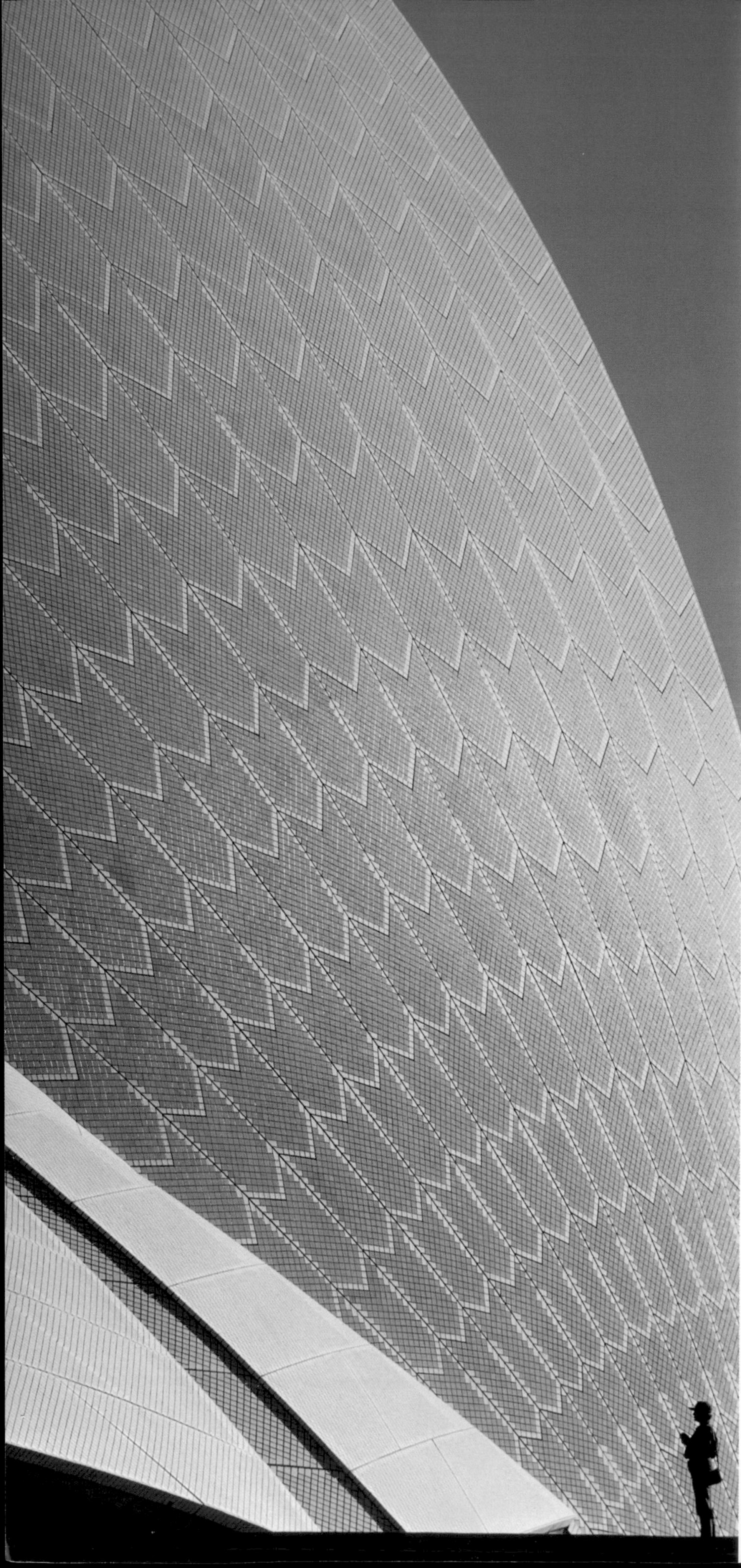

Left: The 1,056,006 Swedish-made tiles on the roofs have a subtle sheen inspired by Japanese ceramics. Utzon wanted the roofs to resemble sails.

Utzon and Arup later remembered being the one to come up with this ingenious solution.)

The roof panels were also prefabricated on the ground. They are covered in a herringbone pattern of glossy white and matte cream tiles, which appear uniformly white from a distance.

Inside the Opera House The arrangement of the shells reflects the interior space—low at the entrances, rising over the seating spaces and the high stage towers. Glass curtain walls light the foyers.

The building's name is misleading, because it is not just an opera house but a multivenue arts center giving over 1,500 performances a year, with four resident companies: Opera Australia, Australian Ballet, Sydney Theatre Company, and Sydney Symphony Orchestra. The Opera Theatre occupies the eastern shells and the Concert Hall is to the west. Smaller performance spaces—the Drama Theatre, Playhouse, and Studio—are under the Concert Hall, within the podium, and the paved forecourt and steps are also used as a performance area. A third, smaller group of shells houses the restaurant.

TIME LINE

1821
Fort Macquarie built on Bennelong Point.

1901
Fort demolished; site becomes tram terminus.

1955
Bennelong Point announced as site for new Opera House.

1957
Jørn Utzon wins architectural competition.

1966
Utzon withdraws and is replaced by a team of Australian architects.

1973
First public performance in Opera Theatre: Prokofiev's *War and Peace*, on September 28; Queen Elizabeth II opens Opera House on October 20.

1986
Forecourt plaza completed.

2003
Utzon wins Pritzker Architecture Prize.

2007
Opera House inscribed on UNESCO World Heritage List.

Right: Acoustic clouds are suspended over the heads of the Sydney Symphony Orchestra in the Concert Hall.

Below right: Jørn Utzon's vision for the interior of the Opera House demanded that the structural ribs of the roof should be exposed.

Architect vs. client Although it ended well, the story of the project wasn't a happy one. In 1965 Utzon's repeated requests for the next stage of funding were not met and, following a change of administration in New South Wales, relations became increasingly tense. The new Minister for Public Works demanded that costs be reined in, compromising the design. Utzon eventually resigned and returned to Denmark. When the Opera House was ceremonially opened in 1973, he was not invited, nor was his name mentioned.

Utzon's innovative plans for the interior spaces were not carried out, but in 1999 he drew up a set of design principles for future developments and worked on one area, now known as the Utzon Room, which was completed in 2004. He died at the age of 90 in 2008, without having returned to see his greatest building, whose visionary design helped to turn Sydney into a world city.

Below: Concertgoers in the foyers can look out over the harbor through glass walls in the open ends of the shells.

AUSTRALIA, NEW SOUTH WALES

Sydney Harbour Bridge

AN IRON LAW OF ARCHITECTURAL AESTHETICS IS THAT GOOD BRIDGES LOOK GOOD, AND ONE OF THE BEST-LOOKING BRIDGES IN THE WORLD IS THE SYDNEY HARBOUR BRIDGE. BIG AND CONFIDENT AND USEFUL, ITS FORM FOLLOWS ITS FUNCTION. IT'S A BEAUT.

The most obvious function of the Sydney Harbour Bridge is linking north Sydney to the central business district, converting a 12-mile/20-km trek into a short drive. Equally important is that the bridge is a visual reference point that has evoked a metropolitan image of Australia ever since it was opened in 1932. It is a span symbolic of optimism for, at a time when a third of Australians were unemployed during the Great Depression, 1,400 men worked on its construction. The bold new bridge breathed life into the city and its suburbs, and they called it "the Iron Lung."

Big A small modern workforce paints the steelwork and maintains the bridge's sleekness, though a clutch of statistics reveals the beef behind the elegance. The total weight of the bridge's steel is 52,800 tons, with the arch itself weighing in at 39,000 tons. The painters must cover 120 acres/485,000 sq m of surface, using some 7,900 gallons/30,000 liters of paint. It is the world's widest long-span bridge and the tallest steel arch bridge.

Confident Four towers, two at each end, appear to be anchoring this beast down in some way. Not so. Although abutments at the base of the towers support loads from the arch, the towers themselves have no structural purpose. They are for looks only, and were not even

Above: The arch-based design of the bridge has inspired its local nickname "the Coat Hanger." The extra-wide bridge carries rail as well as vehicular traffic and pedestrians.

Right: A mass "BridgeClimb" in 2008 celebrated ten years of this popular enterprise (above), but most tourists are content to admire the bridge from ground level (below).

FACT FILE

Number of rivets
6,000,000.

Length
3,770 ft/1,149 m, including approach spans.

Length of arch span
1,650 ft/503 m.

Height of top of arch
440 ft/134 m.

Height of towers
290 ft/89 m above mean sea level.

Steel
52,800 tons.

Concrete
335,000 cu ft/95,000 cu m.

Granite
600,000 cu ft/17,000 cu m.

Paint
72,000 gallons/ 272,000 liters for the initial three coats.

included on the original drawings. But the Sydneysiders demanded visual balance, and their concern with appearances extended to facing the towers with granite. The hard stone was quarried south of the city and transported on three specially built ships.

Useful Though the towers were initially form only, they have since become functional, for these days the southeast tower contains a museum and viewing point, the southwest tower holds traffic management technology, and the north shore towers store maintenance gear and have chimneys venting fumes from the Sydney Harbour Tunnel. That was opened in 1992, when the bridge's eight-lane highway was proving so useful that it was often overwhelmed with traffic.

It's strange to think that when the Sydney Harbour Bridge was built, it had a designated traveling stock route, so that sheep and cows could be herded across—but only at night and only with fair warning. Functions change but the form is now fixed as an Australian icon.

AUSTRALIA, NEW SOUTH WALES

Bondi Beach

BONDI, THE WORLD'S ÜBER BEACH, IS ONLY A BUS RIDE FROM THE COMMERCIAL HEART OF SYDNEY. IT IS A NATIONAL SYMBOL FOR A LARGELY ARID COUNTRY WHERE THE BULK OF THE POPULATION LIVES ON THE COAST AND WHERE THE ABIDING SELF-IMAGE IS ONE OF CHEER AND RELAXATION.

Bondi Beach is where the most easygoing of nationalities goes to relax after a day's work in Australia's largest city. Ten minutes' drive out of town is a 1,000-yd/1-km long arc of pale sand and blue sea. Behind this ideal sweep is a wide promenade, spacious green parkland, and any number of cafés and restaurants. A beer is always close at hand, but it is the sea and the surf that is the real draw.

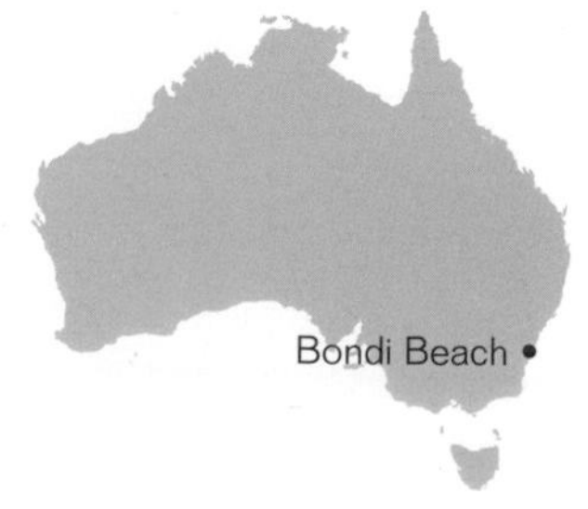

Surf *Bondi* is an Aboriginal word describing the noise of water breaking over rocks. The water breaks strong and loud all along Bondi Beach, and there is something in this playground for everybody. On a hazard scale of ten, the northern end of the beach has been rated a modest four, while the southern end is a more challenging seven due to a rip current running straight out to sea. The lifeguards call it the Backpacker's Express, because it's closest to the bus stop, where new arrivals eager to shake off the city immediately take a plunge.

Danger Inland Australian nature always carries the threat of a bite or a sting or some other peril. The coastal strip may be less hostile but the surf can be dangerous to the inexperienced, and locals know to look out for "bluebottles"—their name for Portuguese men-of-war. And only fools swim beyond the underwater shark net.

TIME LINE

1851
Francis O'Brien purchases 200 acres/80 ha of the Bondi Estate, renames it the O'Brien Estate, and turns the beach into a resort.

1882
Bondi Beach becomes a public beach.

1907
Bondi Surf Bathers' Life Saving Club becomes the first of its kind in the world; it invents the surf reel to haul swimmers back to the beach.

February 6, 1938
Black Sunday: 5 people drown and over 300 are rescued after three freak waves drag them out to sea.

1996
Completion of deep water ocean outfall means untreated sewage is no longer released near beach.

2007
1,010 women wearing bikinis set a Guinness World Record for the largest swimsuit photo shoot.

Opposite: The iconic sweep of pale sand right on the edge of Australia's largest city has played an important part in the world view of its people as sun-loving, laid-back beach bums.

Right: An Art Deco lifeguard station overlooks the beach (above): Christmas is Bondi's busiest time, when the lifeguards anticipate crowds of at least 30,000 tourists (below).

Beach life In the mid-nineteenth century, Australia was an early adopter of what has become a global beach culture. The beach is where normal inhibitions are thrown off and between 1935 and 1961 rules were imposed: Aussie officialdom armed with tape measures patrolled the sand checking on the decency of swimsuits. Decency didn't include teeny-weeny bikinis. Come the 1960s, the rule book was thrown out, and by the 1980s topless bathing was a Bondi Beach norm. The southern end is the place to go.

Paradise Primeval life forms crawled up beaches on to dry land, and it is to the beach that their highly evolved modern descendants have returned. Nature is benign on the archetypal beach—a place of sun, sand, sea, surf, and not so many clothes as usual. Bondi Beach is the closest thing to many people's idea of paradise.

Below: Bondi is one of the world's top surfing locations, replete with surf schools and live webcams. Waves vary seasonally, and beginners as well as experts surf here.

AUSTRALIA, QUEENSLAND

Great Barrier Reef

THE EARTH IS A WATERY PLANET AND WE END THIS BOOK WITH ITS LARGEST WATER FEATURE. BROAD ENOUGH IN SWEEP TO BE VISIBLE FROM ORBITING SATELLITES, THE GREAT BARRIER REEF IS THE WORLD'S BIGGEST STRUCTURE MADE BY LIVING ORGANISMS. ITS VIVID BEAUTY IS BEYOND COMPARE.

Ours is a fragile planet and the reef is being sullied. Here in the Coral Sea off the coast of northeastern Australia, human activity is smudging its color and variety. The Great Barrier Reef Marine Park Authority considers the greatest threat to be climate change. Ocean warming causes bleaching of coral and prompts fish to seek new habitats, thus disrupting food chains of seabirds, sea turtles, and dugongs. Other disruptions to a delicate equilibrium are fishing, tourism, and agricultural runoff. Nature finds new balances. Degraded and overfished waters suit the crown-of-thorns starfish, which thrives on coral polyps. Some 66 percent of one reef's live coral cover disappeared as a result of an outbreak of these creatures during 2000.

Microcosm Coral is a marine organism that secretes calcium carbonate to form a hard skeleton. The age of the Great Barrier Reef is about 8,000 years, and it is a product of long-term environmental change, for today's living reef has grown on a coral platform begun 20,000 years ago. Between then and about 6,000 years ago, sea levels rose 394 ft/120 m. As the sea rose it covered the coastal plain, and hills were submerged or transformed into continental islands. The corals gradually overgrew the hills to form the present cays and reefs.

Above: The reef has formed over a coastal plain that was submerged as sea levels rose, turning its hills into continental islands, such as the Whitsunday group.

Above right: Visible from space, the reef extends over 1,600 miles/2,600 km and comprises some 3,400 individual reefs and 900 islands.

Right: The green sea turtle, an endangered species with about 20 nesting sites around the reef, flaps over the coral accompanied by a typically varied group of fish.

FACT FILE

4,500 mollusk species.
2,195 plant species.
1,500 fish species.
500 marine algae and seaweed species.
400 coral species.
330 ascidian species.
242 bird species.
125 shark, stingray, skate, and chimaera species.
30 whale, dolphin, and porpoise species.
17 sea snake species.
15 seagrass species.
9 sea horse species.
6 sea turtle species.
1 human species.

Macrocosm In the 133,000 sq miles/344,400 sq km of this enormous structure there are three main types of reef: platform or patch reefs, resulting from radial growth; wall reefs, resulting from elongated growth, often in areas of strong water currents; and fringing reefs with growth on subtidal rock. The tiny corals provide an astonishingly varied backdrop for the thousands of marine species listed in the fact file.

New views That we are creatures of imagination has been evident throughout this book. Imagination and technology have enabled us to move from our natural habitat on land into the sea and air, to witness the beauty of the Great Barrier Reef from within and above. Yet its existence is now threatened by the very technological progress that has allowed us to be fascinated by it.

Right: The reef's biodiversity makes it a huge draw for divers, and tourism is now the biggest commercial activity in the region; about two million people visit each year.

PICTURE CREDITS

The publishers are grateful to the following organizations and individuals for permission to reproduce the photographs in this book. Key: l = left, r = right, c = centre, t = top, a = above, b = below.

© Bret Arnett, 87l
© Corbis/Frank Lukasseck, 205l; /Ocean, 111r; /Reuters/Michael Kooren, 99bl; /Jane Sweeney/JAI, 224, 225b; /Adam Woolfitt, 111l
© dese/Ingvar, 121a
© Alessandro Frenza, 107cr
© Getty Images/Peter Adams, 58–9, 142–3, 213b; /AFP, 29a, 135c, 164c, 207c; AFP/Mladen Antonov, 124t; /AFP/Torsten Blackwood, 228; /AFP/Cris Bouroncle, 177l; /AFP/Frederic J. Brown, 201t; /AFP/Timothy A. Clary, 25l; / AFP/Tiziana Fabi, 156; /AFP/Goh Chai Hin, 200; /AFP/Louisa Gouliamaki, 164t; /AFP/Alexander Joe, 189c; /AFP/Menahem Kahana, 219c; /AFP/ Wolfgang Kumm, 102c; /AFP/Liu Jin, 204; /AFP/Marco Longari, 219t; /AFP/ Juan Mabromata, 40–41b, 48, 49c, 49b; /AFP/Miguel Medina, 59bc, 87r; / AFP/Filippo Monteforte, 58–9b, 157t; /AFP/Narinder Nanu, 211c, 211b; / AFP/Johan Nilsson, 119l, 119r; /AFP/Mustafa Ozer, 220, 221l, 221r; /AFP/ Aizar Raldes, 50t, 51b; /AFP/Manpreet Romana, 215l; /AFP/Christophe Simon, 138l; /AFP/Toru Yamanaka, 195a; /Jerry Alexander, 217t; /Max Alexander, 181cl; /Steve Allen, 53c; /Theo Allofs, 226–7, 232–3b; /Altrendo, 16, 108, 127b, 128–9, 129t; /Noriyuki Araki/Sebun Photo, 195b; /Doug Armand, 110; /Samuel Aranda, 136; /AussieDingo – Lyndon M, 133a; /Scott Barbour, 65b, 191bc, 212, 223r/Graham Barclay, 163l; /David Barnes, 86b; / Emily Barnes, 19b; /Remi Benali, 185c; /Daryl Benson, 176; /Daniel Berehulak, 64t, 64c; /Souvik Bhattacharya, 190–91b, 216; /Walter Bibikow, 18r; / Bloomberg/Jock Fistick, 95t; /Christophe Boisvieux/hemis.fr, 170; /Mark Bolton, 150; /Shaun Botterill, 189t, 203b; /Charles Bowman, 117a, 149tl; / Fernando Bueno, 45r; /Shelouise Campbell, 118; /Martin Child, 137l, 153bl, 155r; /China Photos, 203a, 205r, 207tl; /Manuel Cohen, 166, 167t, 167c, 167b; /Ed Collacott, 232l; /Martial Colomb, 60–61a, 89b; /Wendy Connett, 17tr; /David Constantine, 155l; /Alan Copson, 139b; /Joe Cornish, 81br, 83b; / Adam Crowley, 38; /Ian Cumming, 93r, 177r; /Damian Davies, 39bl; /De Agostini Picture Library, 80, 175bc, 180, 181cr; /De Agostini/C. Sappa, 88; / De Agostini/G. Sioen, 229l; /De Agostini/S. Vannini, 181b; /Michael DeFreitas, 44, 55bl; /Danita Delimont, 39br, 61c, 215r, 217c; /Fred Derwal, 89c; /Werner Dieterich, 101a; /Marco Di Lauro, 161c; /Massimo Di Nonno, 149b; /Doruk Photography, 172–3; /Travis Drever, 233c; /Teun van den Dries, 101b; /Michael Dunning, 57br, 231l; /Antony Edwards, 78; /Eightfish, 62, 67bl, 197b; /Gerry Ellis, 187c; /James Emmerson, 79r; /Epics/RDImages, 76; / EyesWideOpen, 95b; /Grant Faint, 13l, 145r, 159t, 163r; /Axel Fassio, 149tr; / Feng Li, 117b, 207tr; /Chantal Ferraro, 238–9; /Ed Freeman, 191br, 209r; / Jason Friend, 82; /Bertrand Gardel, 93l; /Robert Giroux, 11l, 11ra; /Glow Images, 39a; /David Goddard, 61b; /Godong, 190bl, 207b; /John K. Goodman, 237t; /Tim Graham, 201c; /Jorg Greuel, 27a, 127t, 148; /Scott Gries, 50c; / Christopher Groenhout, 190bc, 194; /Guang Niu, 202; /Deborah Lynn Guber, 152; /Darrell Gulin, 154; /Robert Harding, 122; /Roger de la Harpe, 189b; / Jason Hawkes, 73br, 79l; /Tim Hawley, 8bc, 36; /Gavin Hellier, 41br, 55br, 56, 94, 99br, 105t; /Andrew Holt, 71l; /Andrew Hounslea, 199r; /Jim Howarth, 98; /John Humble, 33b; /Jeff Hunter, 239c, 239b; /Image Source, 214; / Imagno, 129c, 129b; /Fernand Ivaldi, 85; /Jumper, 141b, 144; /Keren Su, 217b, 219b; /Michael Kitromilides, 161b; /Christian Kober, 37a; /Isao Kuroda, 192; / Patrick Landmann, 139a; /Klaus Lang, 13r; /LatinContent/Keiny Andrade, 47r; /LatinContent/FotoArena, 42, 43t, 43c; /LatinContent/Pedro Kirilos, 41bc, 43b; /LatinContent/Alexandre Schneider, 45l; /Latitudestock, 116; /Siegfried Layda, 102b, 105b, 159c; /Le-Dung Ly, 113b; /Frans Lemmens, 59br, 96, 123r, 147b, 174–5, 174–5b, 186, 188; /Yoray Liberman, 173b; /David Livingston, 37b; /Harvey Lloyd, 226bc, 231r; /Jon Love, 237c; /Frank Lukasseck, 199l; / LWA, 226–7b, 229r; /John McCabe, 175br, 182, 183r; /Paul McConnell, 233t; /David Madison, 53b, 133b, 171r; /Ludovic Maisant, 71r; /Jacques Marais, 124c; /Maremagnum, 91br, 103; /Richard Maschmeyer, 54; /Ethan Miller, 32; / David Min, 8bl, 12; /Justin Minns, 181t; /Camille Moirenc, 91a; /Hiroyuki Nagaoka, 206; /Eric Nathan, 187t; /National Geographic/Thomas J. Abercrombie, 225a; /National Geographic/Martin Gray, 179a; /Donald Nausbaum, 185t; /Marvin E. Newman, 137r; /Richard Nowitz, 34–5, 174bl, 178l, 218; /Franco Origlia, 157c; /Richard Osbourne, 65a; /Sylvia Otte, 171l; Tracy Packer Photography, 55a; /Panoramic Images, 69c, 84–5, 124–5b, 140–41, 174bc, 184, 210–11; /Chris Parker, 153r; /Amit Pasricha, 209l; / Douglas Pearson, 90; /Carlos Sanchez Pereyra, 126; /Nicholas Pitt, 226bl, 236; /Leonid Plotkin, 185b; /Ingolf Pompe, 132; /Adrian Pope, 6–7, 26–7, 164–5b; /Chris Pritchard, 227bc, 234–5; /Ed Pritchard, 64b; /Geoff Renner, 69tr; / Andreas Rentz, 113a; /Anne Rippy, 138r; /Martin H. Rose, 222; /Martin Ruegner, 106; /Kalim Saliba, 66; /David Sanger, 35b; /Joel Sartore, 125a; / Science & Society Picture Library, 28r; /Neil Setchfield, 69tl; /Marco Simoni, 169a; /Sites and Photos/Samuel Magal, 143c, 165a; /Ulf Sjostedt, 143b; /Slow Images, 151r; /Jonathan Smith, 123l; /Joseph Sohm/Visions of America, 15bl, 40bc, 46–7; /Chip Somodevilla, 21c; /Cameron Spencer, 235c, 237b; / Stocktrek Images, 147c; /Oliver Strewe, 235b; /Stephen Studd, 178–9b; /David Sutherland, 143t; /Jane Sweeney, 183l; /Adam Tail, 190–91, 198; /Murat Taner, 161t; /Jami Tarris, 40bl, 50; /Taxi, 8–9b, 35c; /Mark R. Thomas, 67a, 67br; / Ron and Patty Thomas, 15br; /Paul Thompson, 77b; /Time & Life Pictures/ Buyenlarge, 29b; /Time & Life Pictures/Katsushika Hokusai/Buyenlarge, 193l; / Time & Life Pictures/Chris Niedenthal, 105c; /David C. Tomlinson, 58bc, 63; /Tomonari Tsuji/A.collection, 193r; /Travel Ink, 28l, 147t, 208; /Travelpix Ltd, 19a, 92, 160; /Uyen Le, 4, 9bc, 20; /Guy Vandereist, 58bl, 100, 112, 149c, 158, 162; /Luis Veiga, 104; /Marc Volk, p86c; /The Washington Post, 17c, 18l; /Ken Welsh, 146; /Wide Group, 40–41a, 52; /Andrew Wong, 201b
© Gregorius Mundus, 109c
© Guggenheim Bilbao, 134, 135t, 135b
© Hobby-Photograph, 107t, 107cl, 107b
© iStockphoto/John Archer, 25r; /Frank van den Bergh, 97t, 168; /bigworld, 11rb; /Lya Cattel, 15a; /drbueller, 14; /Jeremy Edwards, 9r, 24; /Grafissimo, 57a; /ginevre, 10; /Cheryl Graham, 73bl; /Joanne Green, p89t; /Ian Hamilton, 77c; /Juneisy Hawkins, 72; /Peter Ingvorsen, 81a; /jfc215, 33t; /Steven Jones, 17tl; /Mableen, 21t; /Joe McDaniel, 23a; /Andrew Morris, 77t; /S. Greg Panosian, 21b; /Gareth Patrick, 86t; /Ogen Perry, 81bl; /rest, 73a; /Jan Rihak, 57bl; /RiverNorthPhotography, 22, 23b; /Lucie Rouche, 17b; /Silent Wolf, 130; /Alexander Wishkoski, 83a; /Ziutograf, 127c
© Gary Jacobson, 114, 115a, 115bl, 115br
© Beverley Jollands, 75c, 75b, 97cl, 97cr
© Moi of Ra, 121br
© NASA, 30–31 (all), 227br, 239t
© Netherlands Board of Tourism & Conventions, 97b
© Nienke's Travels, 145l
© Jaime Pérez, 196
© Pirate Alice, 151l
© George Reader, 153t, 153c
© Sailornappo, 109t
© Schimonski, 102t
© sfPhotocraft (Jim Schnobrich), 157b
© Shutterstock/Paolo Gianti, 197a; /godrick, 74–5a; /Jane A Hagelstein, 33c; /Aija Lehtonen, 95c; /newphotoservice, 169b; /Morozova Oxana, 223l; /Bill Perry, 213a; /Jose Alberto Tejo, 49t; /Vacclav, 27b
© sipazigaltumu (Klaus Wagensonner), 159b
© Statue of Liberty/P. Banks, 24a
© Sydney Opera House, 5, 230
© Table Mountain Aerial Cableway © 2011, 187b
© visitlondonimages/britainonview, 68, 69b, 70
© Richard Walker, 91bl
© Astrid Westvang, 121bl
© David Wilmot, 120
© Wiener Riesenrad, 131c; Wiener Riesenrad/Kernmayer Photography 131t, 131b